THE *fires* OF EXCELLENCE

SPANISH AND PORTUGUESE ORIENTAL ARCHITECTURE

'*Since*
the fires of excellence
shine at your door,
generosity itself smiles.'

Inscription in the Court of the Myrtles,
Alhambra Palace, Granada, in praise of Ibn Nasr
who ordered its construction

THE *fires* OF EXCELLENCE

SPANISH AND PORTUGUESE ORIENTAL ARCHITECTURE

MILES DANBY

Photography by
MATTHEW WEINREB

Garnet
PUBLISHING

The Fires of Excellence
Spanish and Portuguese Oriental Architecture

Published by
Garnet Publishing Ltd
8 Southern Court, South Street
Reading, RG1 4QS, UK.

First Edition 1997

ISBN 1 85964 087 7

British Library Cataloguing-in-Publication Data
A catalogue record for this book is available from
the British Library.

House Editor **Anna Watson**
Design by **David Rose**
Production Control **Nick Holroyd**
Picture Research **Emma Hawker**
Colour reproduction by **Advance Laser, Hong Kong**
Printing in **Hong Kong,** *through* **Bookbuilders Limited**

FACING TITLE PAGE
*The Patio de los Leones (Court of the Lions) at
the Alhambra Palace, Granada.*

PAGE 6
*The Patio de los Arrayanes (Myrtle Court) at
the Alhambra Palace, Granada, by Girault de
Prangey. (See also p. 139.)*

CONTENTS

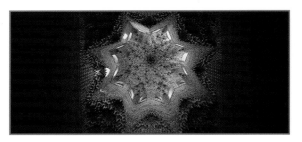

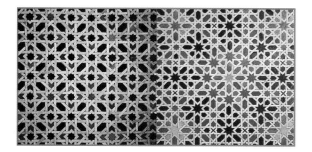

SPAIN *and* PORTUGAL
with key places and stages of
MUSLIM-CHRISTIAN RULE

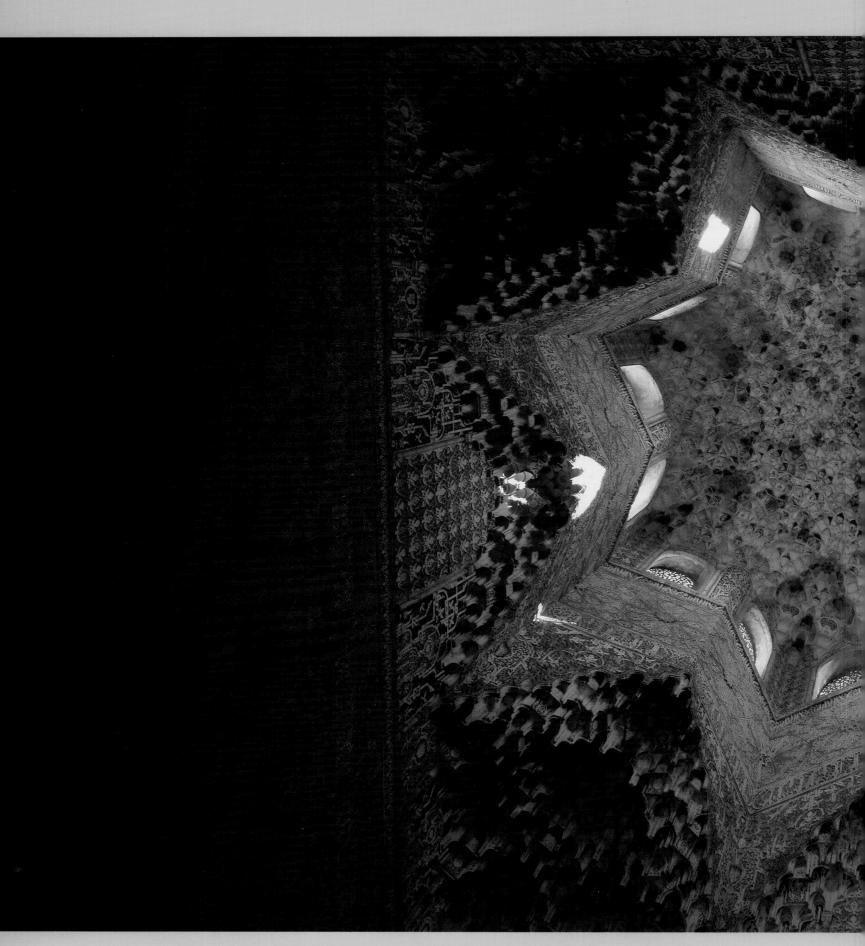

The magnificently decorated domed ceiling of the Sala de los Abencerrajes in the Alhambra palace. It is supported on a sixteen-sided structure of elaborate muqarnas *or stalactites.*

PROLOGUE

The Patio de los Arrayanes seen from the Sala de la Barca at the Alhambra. The elegant arcade is reflected in the rectangular pool which is flanked by two neat myrtle hedges.

One of the entrance doors to the prayer hall of the Great Mosque at Córdoba. It is known as the Puerta de al-Hakam II because it was built during his reign, 961–976. The horseshoe arch over the door is flanked at high level by two stone window-grilles and surmounted by an arcade of five interlacing pointed horseshoe arches.

This work is an attempt to trace the development of a unique mode of architectural expression that occurred in the Iberian Peninsula over many centuries. The title, *The Fires of Excellence,* is taken from a quotation: 'Since the fires of excellence shine at your door, generosity itself smiles'. It is part of an Arabic inscription in the Patio de los Arrayanes in the palace of the Alhambra at Granada and was written in praise of Ibn Nasr who in the fourteenth century ordered the construction of this wonderful building, which typifies the oriental character of much of the medieval culture of the Peninsula. There are countless inscriptions throughout the palace buildings. They are of three types: verses from the Quran, traditional religious sayings and many poems praising the Nasrid builders of the Alhambra. The poems are attributed to Ibn Zamrak, a contemporary statesman.

The rediscovery of the romantic beauty and sophisticated charm of this architectural masterpiece by scholars, poets and artists from the late eighteenth century onwards revived the appreciation of a civilisation whose architecture, poetry and music had absorbed influences from Roman, Christian and Islamic sources. This fusion of cultures began after the collapse of the Roman Empire, when the Visigoths brought fresh ideas of architectural form from the eastern Mediterranean to blend with the existing tradition that was mainly of Roman origin. The Arab Muslim invaders of 711 slowly introduced yet more design features and brought the skills to express them with conviction. The Peninsula was to remain almost wholly and later partly under Muslim rule until 1492.

By the tenth century, Córdoba, the capital of al-Andalus, the new state under Arab leadership, had become the centre of a culture of outstanding brilliance, far in advance of the rest of Europe. Later, the expansion of the Christian kingdoms of the north led to the decline of Muslim political power. Oriental characteristics were, nevertheless, adopted in the architectural expression of the Christians. Alfonso the Wise, king of Castile, maintained his magnificent court at Toledo in a spirit of toleration so that Christian, Muslim and Jew were able to contribute to its rich cultural heritage.

The supreme flowering of the oriental style took place in the midfourteenth century when, simultaneously, Pedro the Cruel of Castile and Ibn Nasr (Mohammed V), the Muslim emir of Granada, extended and rebuilt their palaces, the Alcázar at Seville and the Alhambra in Granada, employing many of the same skilled craftsmen. But rivalry and confrontation between the religions of Islam and Christianity was later exacerbated by the intolerant activities of the Inquisition. Both the Muslims and the Jews were eventually expelled from the Peninsula. In spite of this, the surviving buildings in the oriental style continued to fascinate many, including the royal houses of Spain and Portugal, although senior churchmen did their best to demolish them or convert them into an obviously recognisable Christian form. Oriental characteristics continued to appear in the architecture for at least another century. In some crafts, such as joinery and pottery, the geometrical basis of pattern-making has survived to the present day.

The ground floor arcades of the Patio de Doncellas at the Alcázar palace at Seville, which was built for King Pedro I of Castile, demonstrate the incredible skills of the craftsmen working in an oriental style.

These skills were also exported to Spanish and Portuguese colonies in America.

A rediscovery of the beauty of the oriental style occurred during the nineteenth century, in the age of eclecticism. It was then employed by architects and designers whenever their affluent clients wished to display a personal and romantic nostalgia for a past age of sophisticated luxury and culture. It was also considered ideal for public buildings, when a sense of occasion was required, or sometimes to represent a symbol of local or national identity. This continued well into the twentieth century. Theatres, cinemas, exhibition buildings and railway stations were often designed in an oriental manner. It was not always employed in an imitative way. Some designers, Gaudí is perhaps the most famous, created buildings that expressed a new approach, known as *Modernismo* in Spanish. In many cases they displayed a recognisable debt to the past architecture of oriental origin. His Casa Vicens in Barcelona is a remarkable and creative reworking of oriental themes to produce an original work of art.

In the subtitle of this book, the adjective 'oriental' has been used to indicate that the tradition or mode of expression under examination was created by influences from cultures that border the Mediterranean to the east of the Peninsula. It is necessary to stress that its use here does not refer directly to those Asian countries east of Arabia, from Persia to Japan, although there may have been some indirect influence from them, particularly in craft techniques and mathematics. Nor does it refer to the stylistic revival of Greek and Roman architecture usually referred to under the titles of Romanesque, Classical or Renaissance. This influence usually reached the Peninsula from Italy or from countries to the north, like France and the Netherlands.

To put this process of development in context, it is essential to examine the geographical position of the Iberian Peninsula, its physical features and those that lie to the east. To the northeast is the mountain barrier of the Pyrenees running east–west. Farther west is the coastline facing north on the Bay of Biscay, which continues due west until it turns directly south at Cape Finisterre along the Galician coast, past the Spanish-Portuguese frontier. From there it continues due south by the promontory of the mouth of the river Tagus, skirting Lisbon, and south to Cape St Vincent where, in an abrupt turn of 90° east, it passes Huelva. It proceeds to the Spanish-Portuguese frontier, where it starts to veer southwards past Cádiz to the southernmost point of the Peninsula at Tarifa, which is the point nearest to the continent of Africa at the straits of Gibraltar. Here the Atlantic Ocean and the Mediterranean Sea join. The tongue of Africa, with Tangier at the west and Ceuta at the east, forms the southern land boundary of the Straits. From Gibraltar the southern coast of Spain veers northeast to Málaga and then due east to Almería and the Cape de Gata. From this point the coast meanders in a general northeasterly direction by two promontories, at Valencia and the mouth of the river Ebro, up to Barcelona to another promontory, where it turns due north to join the Franco-Spanish frontier at the eastern end of the Pyrenees.

The greatest part of the margins of this vast land mass of 542,046 square kilometres is coastal, although a short section of coast opposite and very close to North Africa between Tangier and Ceuta has functioned in almost the same way as a land frontier. The Iberian Peninsula is both the westernmost and southernmost part of the continent of Europe. This position on the earth's surface has significance in the shaping of the climatic as well as the political, human, religious and cultural characteristics of the Peninsula.

Its position at the junction of the Atlantic and the western extremity of the Mediterranean is symbolic in many ways. For centuries it became the point of contact or conflict between two powerful systems of belief. The northern land frontier of the Pyrenees provided the opportunity for contact and infiltration of ideas as well as for offensive or defensive military activity. It also formed a climatic frontier in that, generally, it is both warmer and drier to the south of the mountain range. There is, therefore, a change in the appearance of the landscape which coincides with the change in language, except at the west, where the hills and mountains are lower and less of a physical barrier. This is where the Basque-speaking people have settled on both sides of the Franco-Spanish frontier.

The greater length of coastline on the Atlantic, with the remainder on the Mediterranean, has a climatic significance in that the Atlantic, colder than the Mediterranean, tends to produce cooler, rain-bearing winds. There is in addition the effect of latitude. The average air temperature is higher in the south but this can be modified by height above sea level. These variations are further complicated by the fact that a large area in the centre of the

Peninsula consists of a high plateau, which is also distant from the sea, creating an extreme or continental climate. This area experiences cold winters, with snow on the high ground, as well as extremely hot, dry summers. The climatic variation in the Peninsula is great, from very hot and dry, warm and humid in western and northern coastal areas to very cold with snow and ice. The need for winter heating exists in most parts and the skilled use of building materials, shade, window openings and planting to produce cool and comfortable conditions in summer was universally understood, until recently. A number of mountain ranges mostly run approximately east–west. There are five major rivers, again running approximately east–west through fertile valleys. The Ebro in the northeast flows into the Mediterranean, while from north to south, the Douro, the Tagus, the Guadiana and the Guadalquivir flow into the Atlantic.

During the historical period, when the cultural influences that shaped the oriental architecture of the Peninsula were most active, there was considerable freedom of communication. The main channel for this was the Mediterranean, because the most efficient means of travel was by sea. In common parlance it was usually called 'the sea'. A fascinating stock of letters and business documents dating from the period 969 to 1250 was discovered at the end of the nineteenth century in a store room in an old and abandoned synagogue in Fustat (Old Cairo). This collection of documents was known as a *geniza* and survived because of an ancient Jewish belief that Hebrew is God's own language and so the Hebrew script also was holy. Any document written in the script was not destroyed even if it had an unimportant day-to-day purpose or was in a language other than Hebrew. From this vast collection of papers a picture of the commercial life of the time was pieced together.

It would seem that regular commuting between Egypt and the Iberian Peninsula was not unusual. 'The sea' was regarded as friendly, compared with the Indian Ocean, and was divided, in terms of perception rather than politics, into three regions. The east consisted of Egypt and the Muslim countries of southwest Asia. The west comprised all North Africa west of Egypt, including Sicily, with al-Andalus (the Muslim part of the Iberian Peninsula) as an important sub-section. The third was called 'the land of the Romans', originally Byzantium but used later in a vague manner to mean Christian Europe. Even at a time of great tension between Muslims and Christians, 1183–5, Ibn Jubayr, a Muslim scholar, travelled from Palestine to al-Andalus on board Christian ships. The Mediterranean operated much as a free-trade area and for a period the Almoravid dinar, a gold coin from the dynasty ruling al-Andalus and Morocco, was used as an international currency. Collections were made in the Peninsula for the Jewish Academy in Jerusalem and sent there without problems.

Ibn Battuta (1304–68), perhaps the most famous medieval traveller, left Tangier, his birthplace, at the age of 21 in 1325 with the intention of making the pilgrimage to Mecca, a journey of 4,800 kilometres. But he

A distant view of the Alhambra palace at Granada, set amongst orchards and trees, as it must have appeared to Ibn Battuta when he visited Granada about 1350.

travelled by land, taking ten months, joining caravans whenever he was able and enjoying the hospitality of holy men *en route*. In the next 29 years he travelled by land and sea over the entire Muslim world and beyond, as far south as Mali and as far east as China, where he was very impressed by the local artistic skills. He visited Mecca four times. He had an introduction to the Byzantine emperor Andronicus, whom he met in Constantinople and pleased with his descriptions of Bethlehem and Jerusalem. During his official tour of the city he saw the great church of Haghia Sophia but was unable to enter because he was unwilling to prostrate himself before the golden cross. In all, he covered 120,000 kilometres, three times the distance travelled by his predecessor, Marco Polo. About 1350, towards the end of his travels, he visited Granada, which was then at the height of its splendour. He considered it to be the metropolis of al-Andalus and the 'bride of its cities'. The sultan was ill so he was unable to visit the Alhambra but the mother of the sultan sent him a gift of gold dinars. He visited the principal sheikh, who lived on the outskirts of the city. He later recorded that the surroundings were very beautiful and did not have their equal in any country in the world. They extended for at least 64 kilometres and were crossed by the river Shannil and other streams. On every side were orchards, gardens, flowery meadows, noble buildings and vineyards. He died in or near Fez where he was serving as a judge, having completed his amazing book of travels.

Religion was more powerful in the shaping of the motives for travel than local politics. The duty of pilgrimage applied in all three religions. In the case of Islam, one visit to the holy city of Mecca was obligatory once in a lifetime, while for the Christian and the Jew a trip to the holy city of Jerusalem was a meritorious deed. Pilgrimage was often combined with, and financed by, business visits. Wandering scholars were welcomed and encouraged. They were not deterred by barriers of language, as Arabic, Latin and Hebrew were understood by traders and scholars throughout the region.

The Roman Empire at its greatest extent stretched the full length of the Mediterranean. The Iberian Peninsula was occupied by the Romans, as was the whole of France and most of Britain to the north, while to the south the North African coastlands were also conquered by Romans. Their influence was pervasive in many ways. In architecture, town planning and engineering their skills and discipline were to survive after the decline of the Empire. To the north the Irish, the Picts, the Franks and the Goths managed to resist occupation. Similarly, to the east of the Mediterranean, the Armenians, the Persians and the Arabs remained free of their domination, while the Berbers to the south in North Africa also continued to be independent. By the end of the fourth century AD the Roman Empire had divided into two parts, Eastern and Western.

As a result of the Goths' attempt to expand eastwards, the Huns reacted strongly and invaded, driving out the Visigoths who were settled in present-day Romania and who, with Roman support, then settled in northwest Greece. Later they moved in a northwesterly direction through Serbia and Croatia to northern Italy and then on to Rome itself in 410. Still seeking to maintain the values of Roman civilisation, they moved farther west through southern France. They reached Spain in 414, attacking the states that had been founded in the meantime by the Alans, Vandals and Suevi. Eventually they established a kingdom in southwestern France in 417, while the Suevi later founded a kingdom in Galicia and northern Portugal. The rest of the Peninsula remained part of the Western Roman Empire. By 470 this Empire had disintegrated and the Visigoths invaded from their base in France and conquered the Iberian Peninsula except for the kingdom of the Suevi and the Basque area. The Vandals had invaded part of present-day Tunisia, Algeria and Libya and became a maritime power occupying the Balearics, Corsica, Sardinia and Sicily. The Franks increased their power in the north and drove the Visigoths south to the strip of France on the Mediterranean.

By this time, at the beginning of the first quarter of the sixth century, the Christian religion had become supreme in the Mediterranean region but disputes had arisen concerning the nature of the Trinity. The Arian sect believed that God the Son was separate from God the Father, and it was thus declared heretical. The Franks adopted Catholicism, whereas the Visigoths were adherents of the Arian faith. Justinian became Eastern Roman Emperor in 528 and dedicated himself to the reconquest of the West. He destroyed the Vandal kingdom, and a Visigothic civil war gave him the opportunity to occupy the southern part of Spain. By 584 the Suevic kingdom had been annexed by the strengthened Visigothic kingdom, which established its capital at Toledo and reduced the Roman possessions in the Peninsula to a narrow southern coastal strip. In 589 Arianism was abandoned by the Visigoths and, at the Third Council of Toledo, Catholicism became the officially enforced religion of the kingdom.

In 616 the Persians occupied Egypt and Syria but in 622 a new religious faith, Islam, was founded at Medina in Arabia by the Prophet

15

Mohammed (570–632) after he and his followers had migrated there from Mecca. Whilst living in Mecca, the angel Gabriel had revealed to Mohammed on Mount Hira that he was the Prophet of God. Soon afterwards the Visigoths extended their mastery over the whole of the Iberian Peninsula, and the Arabs were politically and spiritually united by Mohammed. The successors of Mohammed, the Caliphs, after a power struggle, formed the orthodox dynasty. The third Caliph, Othman, was murdered and was succeeded by the Caliph Ali, the son-in-law of Mohammed, who reigned until his death in 661, when the Umayyads gained the succession.

This caused a schism in the followers of Islam that has lasted until the present day. Those who believed that Ali and his descendants were the rightful heirs of the Prophet became known as Shi'ites, while those who believed in the orthodox succession of the Umayyads were called Sunnites. From 636 the Arabs expanded their empire at a phenomenal speed. They conquered Syria, Egypt, Mesopotamia and then Tripolitania. In the meantime the remains of the Eastern Roman Empire had become the Byzantine Empire which managed temporarily to check the Arab advance westwards at Tunisia in 650. The Berbers, however, were converted to Islam and by 696 the whole of North Africa was overrun by the Arabs. With Berber support, they invaded the Iberian Peninsula in 711, defeating the Visigoths, and eventually conquered it all except for a narrow strip in the north, the land of the Basques, and the small kingdom of Asturias. They also took over the southwest corner of France for a time, but in 732 Charles Martel defeated the Muslim army at Poitiers and they retreated to the southern border of the Pyrenees, later making the occasional raid into France.

The joint invasion of the Peninsula by the Arabs and Berbers was achieved swiftly. Toledo, the Visigothic capital, was captured in 712, because the Visigothic hierarchy was not popular with the mass of the population and the Arabs were, on the whole, welcomed. The Jewish minority, in particular, had been very poorly treated and they were happy to use their talents under the encouragement of the newcomers. The majority of the Christian inhabitants submitted to the Arabs. They were allowed to practise their faith and were known as Mozarabs. They and the Jews were, however, expected to pay a capitation tax. Many Christians became Muslims and thus avoided the tax. They were known as Muladis. So began a long era, which lasted nearly eight centuries, during which the three religions of Christianity, Islam and Judaism were practised simultaneously in at least some part of the Peninsula. It was not until the beginning of the sixteenth century, after the Christian Reconquest had been completed, that Catholicism became the only officially recognised religion.

Islam, the newest of the three religions, is tolerant of the other two, in the fact that they all stipulate a belief in the same single deity. Together those following these beliefs are known as 'the people of the Book'. Sura (chapter) 4.171 of the Quran, left, reads:

O People of the Book!
Commit no excesses
In your religion: nor say
Of God aught but the truth.
Christ Jesus the son of Mary
Was (no more than)
An apostle of God,
And His Word,
Which He bestowed on Mary,
And a Spirit proceeding
From Him: so believe
In God and His apostles.
Say not 'Trinity': desist:
It will be better for you:
For God is One God:
Far Exalted is He above
Having a son. To Him
Belong all things in the heavens
And on earth. And enough
Is God as a Disposer of affairs.

16

The Christian concept of the Trinity is rejected in the sense that God is independent of all needs including a son to manage His affairs. In other sections of the Quran, although Judaism is monotheistic, it is criticised for formalism, exclusiveness and the rejection of Christ. For these differences alone, there are enough grounds for intolerance by Muslims of non-Muslims and there are in addition many other reasons for their disapproval of Christian and Jewish attitudes. Not least is their hatred of graven images, an attitude they share with the Jews. They also disapprove of a separate clergy and monasticism. The difference between the three is symbolised by the call to prayer: by word of mouth from an elevated platform in the case of the Muslims, by the tolling of bells from a raised position at the time of Christian worship and by the sounding of the *shofar* (horn) to initiate the prayers of the Jews. The design, form and arrangement of their places of worship also illustrate variations in their religious practices. Nevertheless, the opportunities for hatred, conflict and intrigue between the three groups were often countered by mutual dependence and respect. There were long periods of tolerance or *convivencia*, as it is called in Spanish and Portuguese, as well as occasions of war, slaughter and mutual destruction.

Change came mostly from the east along the Mediterranean either by sea or land along the coastal areas to the north or the south. First the Romans invaded, then the Goths moved across the lands to the north of the Mediterranean followed by the Arabs spreading along the north coast of Africa. To the west was the vast and then unknown Atlantic Ocean. Directly to the north is the Bay of Biscay and the Pyrenees frontier, and from here came Christian invasions and influence from Northern Europe. The cultural interaction which occurred in the Peninsula between those trends and ideas absorbed from the east with those from the north of Europe made it a unique part of the continent. This interaction also resulted in important changes in the history of Europe.

The oriental influences on architectural form began with the Romans who, apart from roads and military camps, built villas with rectangular courtyard plans often embellished with elaborate mosaic floors. The remains of two such examples survive at Conimbriga, a former Roman settlement just south of Coimbra in Portugal. The house of Cantaber, who is said to have been driven out by the Suevi in 465, has a courtyard with a large pool and flower beds in the shape of a cross. It also has the remains of a suite of private baths in the universal Roman layout of a *frigidarium* (cold baths), a *tepidarium* (warm baths) and a *caldarium* (hot baths). There is a system of hypocausts for the circulation of warm air. The other villa, known as the House of the Fountains, is similarly arranged around a pool but is known for the remarkable floor mosaics laid out in a variety of patterns based both on geometrical and vegetal motifs as well as some panels of realistic renderings of animals, birds and fish and others showing hunting scenes. As for

An external stone wall of the seventh-century Visigothic church at Quintinilla de las Viñas near Burgos. It is plain except for the horizontal friezes which are carved with a bold circular tendril motif containing a variety of designs depicting birds, grapes, shells and other natural forms.

Inside the same church, the voussoirs of the horseshoe arch before the sanctuary are carved with tendril motifs similar to those of the external friezes. Other stones can be seen with angels and Biblical figures carved in bold relief.

The simple exterior of the Visigothic church of San Pedro de la Nave near Zamora expresses the cruciform plan but gives no hint of the rich decorations within.

public buildings and engineering structures such as aqueducts, the city of Mérida has the remains of a theatre, amphitheatre, an aqueduct, a triumphal arch and a villa with mosaics. The aqueduct at Segovia is probably the finest surviving Roman edifice in the Peninsula, and the best preserved theatre is at Sagunto. Many of these structures were used long after the Romans had disappeared, especially the aqueducts. The skilfully shaped masonry of abandoned buildings was often plundered and the stones re-used by later generations.

The Visigoths brought to the Peninsula artistic skills which were merged with the traditions inherited by the majority of the native population from the Romans to form a characteristic style. These can be considered to be based on oriental practices in that the Visigoths appear to have originated from the eastern end of the Mediterranean before their protracted wanderings to the Peninsula. The horseshoe arch is a characteristic feature of the few Visigothic structures that remain. Only the square apse and transepts of what was once a three-nave church remain at Quintinilla de las Viñas near Burgos. It believed to date from the seventh century, and it has a horseshoe arch with carved stone decoration in flowing circular patterns in front of the sanctuary. These patterns are repeated on the outside walls in a number of horizontal friezes which feature flowing tendril motifs containing a series of simple designs depicting birds, grapes and shells. The horseshoe arch has precedent in the churches of Syria and an example has been excavated at Axum in Ethiopia, which dates from as early as the fifth century. The elegant frieze patterns have parallels in Byzantine and Coptic art of the same period.

There are other churches that date from the Visigothic era – San Pedro de la Nave, near Zamora, São Fructuoso de Montelius near Braga in Portugal and São Amaro at Beja, also in Portugal. San Pedro de la Nave, which has a very plain exterior, was originally built in 691 in a river valley but when the

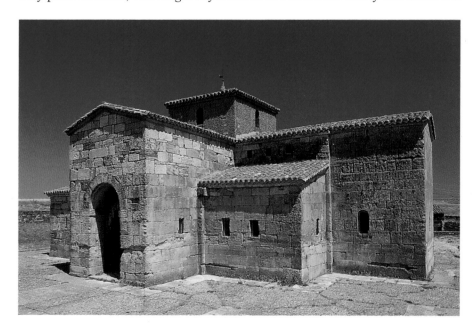

area was flooded in 1934 to allow the construction of a reservoir it was re-erected on a higher rocky platform. The layout is based on a Latin cross with a nave and two aisles. Chapels were added to the ends of the transepts and at either side of the choir. There is a sanctuary at the east end with a horseshoe arch in front of it. There are also friezes similar to those at Quintinilla, as well as bases and capitals that show Byzantine influence. One remarkable capital shows Daniel in the Lions' Den and another depicts the Sacrifice of Isaac. São Fructuoso was built in the seventh century and has a cruciform central plan. On the outside of the east end wall, to the left of the altar, there is a plain arched sarcophagus for the tomb of São Fructuoso. The exterior walls have blind arcading with plain alternating rounded and triangular arches. The square central space is higher than the rest and is lit by small double windows with horseshoe arches, one window to each face. A form of eaves' cornice has small hanging blind horseshoe arches, which are not functional as they do not have keystones to take the stresses from the weight of the structure above in the same way as the other arches. They are decorative and are carved from single self-supporting blocks of stone. Of São Amaro, only the plan form remains as there have been so many later alterations. However it is now a Visigothic museum containing excavated remains from that period, including some architectural elements from the church itself.

ABOVE TOP *This skilfully carved stone capital depicts Daniel in the Lions' Den while above can be seen birds contained in the Visigothic circular tendril motif.*
ABOVE MIDDLE *A similar capital illustrating the Sacrifice of Isaac.*
ABOVE BOTTOM *Another carved capital featuring birds and grapes. There is a horizontal frieze behind the column.*

The Visigothic church of São Fructuoso de Montelius near Braga has a cruciform plan and the central domed tower is lit by a double horseshoe-arched window on each face. The eaves cornice continues the double horseshoe-arched motif combined with an intervening triangle, echoing the triangular pediment below.

An internal view of the dome, pendentives and the four window openings in the same church.

In the eastern Mediterranean, the well-established Byzantine Empire had its capital at Constantinople where a building, important both in symbolic and historical terms, had been erected on the orders of Emperor Justinian in 532 to the designs of Anthemius. This is the magnificent church of Haghia Sophia built on a prominent site overlooking the Bosphorus. A vast dome spans a large square space. On opposite sides of the main dome are two semi-domes which form a main processional axis. Such an axis is an important requirement as an uninterrupted central aisle is essential in a church. The main dome was not only extremely practical, in that it provided a huge clear

The magnificent interior of the church of Haghia Sophia built in Istanbul in 532, viewed from a semi-dome looking towards the central domed space. At the centre is a large circular plaque with a monogram in Arabic script, one of six that were added in the mid-nineteenth century, five hundred years after it had been converted into a mosque. It has been a museum since 1934.

internal space, but it acted as a strong external visual symbol. The original dome collapsed, however, because it was too shallow in outline. The dome that replaced it was taller at the centre with a greater vertical emphasis which not only produced permanent structural stability but also increased its strength as a visual symbol. The interior was richly decorated with many mosaic panels. The multi-coloured marble columns were crowned with stone capitals that were intricately carved and undercut to give the effect of basketry. These, together with the sparkling polychrome mosaics, combined with its soaring height to create a spectacular impression.

When, a century later, the new religion of Islam was searching for a way of expressing a recognisable and beautiful form of shelter for the prayers of the faithful, the talents of the Byzantine designers and craftsmen were already celebrated and well established. At the start of the expansion of Islam the followers of Mohammed were happy to adapt or even share existing churches and temples. When their increasing numbers meant that they had to consider the construction of new mosques, the model was often the arrangement of the Prophet's house at Medina, which he built for himself and his family when he migrated there from Mecca in 622. According to Abdallah Ibn Yazid, quoted by Creswell, it was a walled enclosure about 100 cubits square with a portico of palm trunks supporting a roof of palm leaves and mud on the south side. Outside the east wall were four houses of mud-brick and five of palm branches plastered with mud. All these opened into the courtyard, and at the southwest corner there was a primitive shelter of palm leaves for the poorest of his followers from Mecca. It was simple and unpretentious and Creswell quotes Ibn Sa'd recording the following saying, attributed to Mohammed: 'The most unprofitable thing that eateth up the wealth of a Believer is building.'

At first Mohammed prayed facing the direction of Jerusalem as a gesture to the Jews, who at that time were the leading community in Medina. But after he had made attempts to convert them to Islam, relations became strained between the two groups and he abandoned the idea of Jerusalem as the centre of the world, a belief which, until then, Islam had shared with the Jews and the Christians. After God's revelation to Mohammed, the *qibla*, or direction of prayer, was changed to face the Holy Ka'ba at Mecca, which is south of Medina. After he had recited the revelation which is recorded in the second Sura of the Quran he then turned towards the south and the whole congregation followed suit. Thenceforth the direction of Mecca was the essential factor in the layout of new mosques. This is only one of the differences between the design of a mosque and a church. In Syria, when a church was converted into a mosque, because the direction of Mecca, is south, like that of Jerusalem, and the church faced east, it was a matter of praying facing across the aisles, making a new entrance in the north wall and closing the previous west entrance.

Another characteristic feature of a mosque that is not present in a church is the minaret. Such a structure was unknown in the time of Mohammed. At first there was no preliminary call to prayer, but it was then felt that Muslims should be summoned formally five times a day to pray. The Jews were called to prayer by the sounding of the *shofar* and the Christians by the use of a clapper (later replaced by bells). Mohammed instructed his follower Bilal to give the call to prayer from the highest roof in the neighbourhood. With the passage of time a tower, known as the minaret, was built near the mosque for the muezzin to ascend to make the call to prayer from a platform at the top. It is believed that both the word minaret and the form derived from the lighthouse. According to Creswell, the first written reference to a minaret dates from 673, when square towers were built at the four corners of the mosque of 'Amr at-Fustat (Cairo).

Of the first four Caliphs, three were murdered and two of these were killed inside a mosque. For this reason, according to the historian Ibn Khaldoun (1332–1406), the Umayyad and sixth Caliph Mu'awiyya (d. 680), who had been attacked and was later murdered in the mosque, instituted the *maqsura*, a protective enclosure for the sultan during public prayers. It included the *mihrab*, the niche which was built in the centre of one of the end walls to indicate the *qibla*, the direction of Mecca. The first generation of mosques were simple in form, essentially rectilinear enclosures orientated on the *qibla* and with a roofed columnar hall. The majority of Arabs at that time were nomads, whose main experience of physical shelter was the tent. For at least a generation after Mohammed's death they remained without any architectural ambitions. But eventually for political reasons the talents of the peoples who had been conquered were recruited in the design and execution of new buildings for the Muslims. It was felt necessary to demonstrate that Islam could produce religious and other buildings as impressive as the churches and temples of the occupied countries.

One building demonstrates this next phase to perfection and is the oldest surviving Islamic building. Known as the Dome of the Rock, it is in the Temple area of Jerusalem. Ibn al-Zubayr, a supporter of Ali, had set himself up as a rival Caliph at Mecca. Abdel Malik, the Umayyad Caliph whose capital was Damascus, was possibly motivated by this rivalry when he promoted the construction of the Dome of the Rock, which was begun in 643 and finished in 692. It shelters the rock where Muslims believe the Prophet Mohammed arrived on Buraq, the half-human steed on whose back he journeyed by night from Medina to Jerusalem via Heaven. There is an ancient belief that a cave beneath it was the site of Abraham's intended sacrifice of Isaac, from whom the Arabs consider they are descended.

A view from the outer ambulatory of the Dome of the Rock at Jerusalem looking towards the sacred rock enclosed within the circular drum, supported on twelve columns and four large piers, and around it the wide octagonal inner ambulatory. There is a flight of stairs leading to the cave below the sacred rock.

The Dome of the Rock has a centralised plan, in common with the original rotunda of the Church of the Holy Sepulchre in Jerusalem, and Creswell believed that the dome form was chosen in emulation. It is not directional in plan, like a mosque, because the ritual performed there is based on the act of ambulation similar to those performed at the Holy Ka'ba at Mecca. It has an inner and outer ambulatory; this implies that Abdel Malik may have hoped that it would divert many pilgrims from Mecca to Jerusalem, where there was the additional need to make a powerful statement of the new religion to both Christians and Jews. Externally, it is dominated by a tall dome supported on a circular drum which rests on four piers and eight columns and has a series of rounded arched windows, none of the original grilles of which remain. The central circle of piers and columns is enclosed by the inner ambulatory, the outer border of which is defined by an octagonal arrangement of eight piers and twelve columns. The outer ambulatory and the external wall, which is also octagonal, are contained by this octagon. Externally, the circular dome and its base are seen to rise above an octagonal base. The dome, unlike that of Haghia Sophia, is of double-skinned timber construction and covered with gilded metal. It was reconstructed in the eleventh century. The base of the dome above the window line was originally covered with glass mosaics representing trees, buildings and flowering plants. Below this level the walls are faced with quartered panels of marble.

The exterior mosaics were later replaced by Suleiman the Magnificent with Turkish tiles of the sixteenth century, but the interior mosaics remain in their original state. Inside, below the dome, a wonderful series of polychrome mosaic decorations depicts trees, vine scrolls, acanthus and vases of flowers interwoven with formalised curved linear patterns. The internal surface of the dome is finished with plaster in relief, which is painted with polychrome arabesque linear patterns. The most significant feature is the circular frieze at the base of the dome. This is the earliest example of Islamic architectural calligraphy. It proclaims Sura 4.171 of the Quran which emphasises the oneness of God, as opposed to the Trinity. This Sura, quoted on page 16, is set in gold cursive Arabic against a blue background. The lower mosaics are in blue and green amongst a splendidly glittering background of gold and mother of pearl. These, together with the marble columns and gilt capitals, produced a magical interior that surpassed Haghia Sophia in the magnificence of its polychrome decoration, although not in the size of the dome. The style of the mosaics followed both the Byzantine and pre-Islamic Syrian traditions, and it is likely that designers and craftsmen from Syria, Egypt and Constantinople worked on them. The capitals in the octagonal arcades vary in type, some are Corinthian, some Composites, and the column shafts are not the same height but are disguised with marble collars at the bases. Above each capital is an impost block resting on a wooden tie beam which runs through the arcade. These beams are covered with sheet copper or bronze sheets with embossed curvilinear designs. There are no impost blocks in the arches of the inner circle under the dome, but there are smaller wooden tie beams resting directly on the capitals.

Abdel Malik's successor, al-Walid I (r. 705–15), constructed a mosque which is known as the al-Aqsa mosque near the Dome of the Rock within the Haram al-Sharif (noble sanctuary). Documents from Egypt record that craftsmen were sent from there to work on mosaics for the mosque of Jerusalem. It was severely damaged by an earthquake in the mid-eighth century and rebuilt and extended by the Abbasid caliphate later in the century. Very little remains of the original Umayyad structure, but it was the first mosque to have arcades at right angles to the *qibla* wall rather than parallel to it. This could have been due to the desire to align the *mihrab* aisle, which is wider than the others, on the south entrance of the Dome of the Rock. The prayer hall was wider than it was deep to increase the number of those in the congregation nearer the *qibla* wall.

At al-Walid's capital, Damascus, a structure which had once been a temple of Jupiter and then the Christian church of St John was taken over after a period of joint use. It was demolished except for the four corner towers. A mosque was then constructed and completed in 714. Unlike the al-Aqsa mosque, the prayer hall was divided into three broad aisles with gabled roofs parallel to the *qibla* wall. There is a large central transept with a double-skinned timber dome over the middle bay. The dome was burned down in 1069 and replaced with a stone substitute which in turn was rebuilt

A photograph by Creswell of the courtyard of the Great Mosque at Damascus showing the ablution fountain on the left and the outline of the Treasury on the right. Between them are the façade of the prayer hall and the two-tiered arcades.

after another fire in 1893. The *sahn* or main courtyard was bordered with a two-storey arcade, a device that was also used for the arcades of the prayer hall, the width of which was even greater in proportion to the depth than at the mosque of al-Aqsa. The lower section of the interior walls was lined with quartered marble panels. Above were large areas of mosaics. Only a small part of these remain and some have been restored. The scheme of decoration is similar to that of the interior of the Dome of the Rock, with a naturalistic version of palms, vine scrolls and trees. The most remarkable decoration, however, is to be found around the *sahn*. Here there are remaining fragments of a mosaic frieze depicting a landscape of towns, villages and palaces often shown amongst running water. One panel is named the 'Barada' panel, after the river of Damascus. There is also a rendering of shadows on columns, tree trunks and the sides of buildings but no cast shadows on the ground. Many of the buildings are depicted in three dimensions but in an imperfect form of perspective. Nevertheless a high degree of realism has been achieved. The subject is believed to be the Islamic vision of Paradise but it lacks any trace of human figures. There are also mosaic panels with a similar mix of vegetal patterns, landscape and architecture, which have been recently restored on the gable end of the prayer hall, as well as on the external walls of the first floor of a small building elevated on columns in the courtyard. The latter is called the Bayt al-Mal or Treasury. The arches in the cloister of the *sahn* are not all semicircular, as at the Dome of the Rock, but a medley of several types, including slightly pointed, stilted and slightly horseshoe shaped.

Another innovation to be found in this mosque is the perforated marble window-grille. There are six of them; four at high level give light and ventilation to the northwestern corner of the prayer hall and the other two are on either side of the western vestibule. There are four geometrical designs based on repetitive combinations of the square, circle, triangle, hexagon and octagon. These are the earliest known examples of the sophisticated use of decorative geometry that was to become a characteristic feature of Islamic crafts and architecture, although Creswell maintained that the original window-grilles at the Dome of the Rock were probably of similar design.

Arab trade expanded throughout the known world, as far east as Canton in China and as far south as Kilwa in East Africa. Internal problems, however, mounted and another dynasty, in opposition to the Umayyads, began to grow in power. Abbas (566–652) and his supporters deposed the governor of Persia and then ousted the Umayyad regime in Damascus, thus initiating the Abbasid dynasty. Abbas was succeeded by his brother 'Mansour' who chose Baghdad as his new capital. The only member of the Umayyad dynasty to survive this change of power was Abdel Rahman (731-788), who fled from Syria in 750 and made his way along the North African coast until he reached the Arab Muslim state of al-Andalus and established himself and his followers at Córdoba in 756.

CHAPTER 1

The interior of the prayer space of the Great Mosque of Córdoba. The double arcading is supported on innumerable columns without bases and creates a magical effect of continuous space.

The GOLDEN AGE of CÓRDOBA

The Islamic invasion of the Iberian Peninsula in 711 had been led by Musa Ibn Nuseir (640–717) after he had completed the conquest of the Maghreb and the Berber population had been converted to Islam. A combined force of Arabs and Berbers under the command of Tariq crossed the straits and defeated the Visigoths at Guadalete. The Visigothic king, Roderic, was killed in action. The invading forces quickly captured Seville, Córdoba and Toledo, and by 714 Huesca and Zaragoza in the north had also been occupied. The Visigothic regime had never been popular and resistance to the invaders had not been fierce as many had turned against Roderic. The Jewish community, in particular, had been persecuted by the Visigoth hierarchy and the Christian church. The newcomers promised freedom of worship to both Christians and Jews. Musa's son, Abdel Aziz, married Roderic's widow and an atmosphere of reconciliation was established.

The Arabs later expanded northwards across the Pyrenees into France. In 725 they were defeated by Charles Martel at Poitiers. This was the farthest north the Islamic invasion of Europe reached, and they decided to withdraw behind the natural barrier of the Pyrenees. Christian resistance stiffened and a number of small independent kingdoms managed to survive along the north Atlantic coast and immediately south of the Pyrenees. A balance of power emerged and the Islamic part of the Peninsula, by far the largest, became known as al-Andalus, with Córdoba in the south as its capital. It had been an important city during the Roman occupation and the capital of the province Baetica, which was approximately the same area as present-day Andalusia. For a time in the sixth century it had been annexed by the Byzantine Empire under Justinian but was later re-absorbed into the Visigothic kingdom. It was the seat of a Christian bishop subordinate to Toledo. Its strategic importance was due to its position by the last bridge over the Guadalquivir before the river flowed into the Gulf of Cádiz.

The Arabs, although dominant among the Muslims, were fewer than the Berbers. Friction between the two ethnic groups began to develop and unrest occurred. In the meantime, in 744 the Umayyad Caliphate in Damascus had been overthrown by the Abbasids with their capital at Baghdad. The Umayyad surviver, Abdel Rahman, found his way to Córdoba where he was proclaimed emir in 756. Many Syrian refugees followed Abdel Rahman to al-Andalus, and the golden period of Umayyad rule then began. Córdoba became a capital famed for its support of the arts and culture. At first, because there was no attempt to proselytise the predominantly Christian population, the churches, including the cathedral, were used for worship by both Christians and Muslims. One of these churches, San Vicente, which overlooked the bridge across the river, was taken over by the Muslims after they had purchased the half belonging to the Christians. In 785, however, Abdel Rahman decided that it should be demolished. Before that, the Friday Mosque had probably been another converted or shared church. The first phase of the construction of the new Friday Mosque started on the site of the cathedral. Almost certainly some materials from San Vicente were reused in the mosque, which was probably finished under Hisham at the end of the century. Like the Dome of the Rock at Jerusalem, it was conceived as a visual expression of the prestige of Islam and the symbolic presence of the Umayyad dynasty. It was to be extended in three subsequent phases, as the population of the city increased.

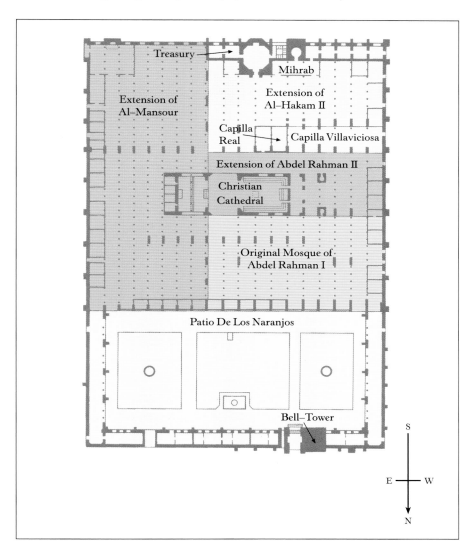

The memory of Syria was still fresh in the minds of the emir and the older generation of many of his courtiers. Abdel Rahman had built himself a country house on the outskirts of Córdoba and in the garden he had planted a selection of trees imported from Syria, including the pomegranate and the palm. He composed a nostalgic poem inspired by the first palm tree in his garden. When it came to the design of the new mosque the memory of the Great Mosque at Damascus was a powerful influence.

The layout of the new mosque was probably based on the precedent of Damascus, but there are some fundamental differences. The interior arcades at Córdoba have a directional emphasis towards Holy Mecca, being at right-angles to the *qibla* wall, as was the case at the al-Aqsa Mosque at

The mihrab of the mosque at Córdoba and the beautiful Kufic calligraphy that frames its horseshoe arch is seen through the interlaced tracery of the multi-lobed arches that define the bay in front of it.

Jerusalem. It also has arches with a shorter span than those in the interior at Damascus, which are parallel to the *qibla* wall. Both mosques have double tiered arcades, but the treatment was very different. At Damascus the arcades were treated as different horizontal bands, one above the other. The width of each arch in the upper arcade (which was the same as that of the timber roof trusses) was half that of those of the lower and taller arcade so a central column was bearing on the centre of each lower arch, resulting in two different scales. At Córdoba the interior arcades are superimposed, with the lower horseshoe arches acting only as cross-bracing to the columns. The upper semicircular and lower horseshoe arches have the same span and are supported roughly on the same columns by means of an impost block. This is a more unified and subtle arrangement than the Damascus composition. Open space between the lower arch and the underside of the upper arch (slightly less than a semicircle) was a master-stroke that creates the powerful impression of interminable space to the interior. Long diagonal perspectives of overlapping arches above the endlessly repeating rows of columns create the illusion of a magical forest. The structural device of the superimposed arcades is said to have derived from the construction of Roman aqueducts, and Spanish historians have cited the aqueduct at Mérida as a precedent. It also solved the problem caused by the fact that the recycled Visigothic and Roman columns were not tall enough directly to support the roof at the height of 13 m. Unlike at Damascus, the arches of both arcades are composed of alternate stone and red-brick voussoirs, and this simple repetitive use of contrasting colours imparts an additional vivacity to this remarkable interior, as well as emphasising the connection between the columns and the arches above. In this mosque it is not possible to perceive the internal space from a single viewpoint. A theological analogy has been made by Fernando Chueca Goitia in that discontinuity can be seen to be the realm of man, and only God is permanent. Thus the impermanence of man and the supremacy of a single deity is expressed in the architectural composition of this unique building.

The roof structure was of timber trusses and tie beams supporting purlins which formed a double-pitched tiled roof over each bay of the naves running parallel to the *qibla*. Gutters ran along the lowest points between the slopes of the parallel tiled roofs. It is believed that there was originally no flat ceiling at the level of the horizontal tie beams, revealing an open timber roof as had been popular in Syrian mosques and was used in the prayer hall of the Great Mosque at Damascus. According to the contemporary poet al-Baloy, there was profuse decoration in gold, presumably of the tie beams and rafters.

The horizontal timber ceiling that spans between the arcades of the mosque reveals the tie beams of the timber trusses which support the double-pitched tiled roof above. The beams and the flat surfaces between them are decorated with interlacing patterns accentuated with dark brown and gold.

In the ninth century, during the reign of Abdel Rahman II (788–852), oriental culture became more dominant as he encouraged poets and musicians to come to his court from the east. The most famous of these was the Persian poet and singer, Ziryab, who came from Baghdad in 822. He is considered to be the founder of the great Andalusian musical tradition, which has continued in both popular and classical music until today.

Abdel Rahman II extended the mosque to the south with eight more bays as well as adding a covered arcade to three sides of the open entrance courtyard. This made the prayer hall almost square in plan, and the continuity of the internal structure was maintained. The *qibla* wall was opened up but the buttresses were retained in order to maintain the stability of the

arcades. Abdel Rahman's son, Mohammed I, completed the work at the same time as building up the west wall, including the gate now called the Puerta de San Esteban. This gateway, with its tripartite division into central opening and two flanking panels in the façade, set the precedent for later entrance doorways. It has a two-tone horseshoe arch within an *alfiz* (see Glossary). An inscription on the tympanum refers to Mohammed I. A rectangular window-grille or *celosia* with a pattern of interlocking circles is placed in the façade above the flanking panels, which have stones carved in relief with floral arabesques. Today there are 30 grilles of white marble of geometrical patterns set in the outside walls; their purpose was to give light and ventilation to the mosque interior and the historian Ibn Ghalib records that there were as many as 54 at one time. They are practically identical with those remaining in the Great Mosque of Damascus. The basic concept of the geometrical patterns of these grilles and other decorative surfaces in Islamic design is the repeating unit. A repeating pattern is generated from squares or polygons inscribed in a circle. In the setting out of geometrical patterns craftsmen used only the compasses and ruler. It is possible to construct any regular polygon from a circle by dividing its circumference equally into the desired number of sections and joining the points with straight lines. At Córdoba either the hexagon or the octagon was the basis of the repeating unit and was often combined with the circle and the square.

The Puerta de San Esteban, in the west wall of the prayer hall of the mosque at Córdoba, was built during the reign of Mohammed I, 852–886. Only the two-toned horseshoe arch and alfiz *remain in a discernible form of the original. There are also two window-grilles or* celosias *in geometrical patterns at either side of the arch.*

A horseshoe arcade in the ruined structure of the royal palace at the settlement of Medinat al-Zahra outside Córdoba. This extensive development was built by Abdel Rahman III at the suggestion of his wife Zahra. It was later reduced to ruins by the Almoravids.

Córdoba continued to prosper, but not without severe political and religious problems; there was an insurrection of Mozarabs in the city as well as rebellions in Murcia and Toledo. In 936 Abdel Rahman III (891–961), at

the suggestion of his wife, Zahra, commenced the construction of a large palace on a site 8 km southwest of the city, known as Medinat al-Zahra. He may have considered that a proper distance should be maintained between his court and a potentially difficult urban populace, in the same way that the rival Abbasid dynasty had ensured at Baghdad. He had already assumed the title of Caliph, 'the defender of the Faith', in 929 in order to demonstrate the base of his power in al-Andalus, as he believed the Shi'ite Fatimid dynasty wanted to invade the Peninsula from North Africa. In 941 the mosque was consecrated and in 947 the process of government and the mint were transferred to this palace complex. It is probable that construction continued until after Abdel Rahman's death in 961. A great number of workers were employed, an estimated 10,000 at the height of the building activity. Ibn Khatib has recorded that 4,324 marble columns were imported, mostly from Tunisia. Marble basins came from Byzantium and Syria as well as twelve golden sculptures inlaid with pearls.

The irrigation system for the gardens and baths and for the houses was fed from the mountains to the north by a long conduit that ran partly underground and at some places on aqueducts supported on horseshoe arches. There were also collecting tanks to store rainwater, which was probably needed to supplement the main supply in the hot, dry summer period. The numerous buildings, practically a town, of Medinat al-Zahra, were arranged along three terraces facing south on the slopes of a range of hills called the Sierra Morena. These terraces were surrounded by a fortified wall with towers which contained an area of some 1,500 by 750 metres. The whole court and council were moved there, and it is believed that a great number of people were involved – figures vary from 1,200 to 20,000. The lower terrace was composed of the mosque, administrative buildings and accommodation for the military. Gardens, pools and pavilions occupied the middle terrace, while the highest position with its magnificent view was given to the various

An overall view of Medinat al-Zahra facing south showing the three levels of the layout. The highest level was reserved for the royal palace.

pavilions of the royal palace itself. The larger houses were arranged around a patio, and reception halls were richly ornamented with marble and glass mosaics and relief patterns carved in stone. At the beginning of the eleventh century the complex was reduced to ruins by mutinous Berber troops of the Almoravid dynasty from North Africa, whose strict religious principles were opposed to the luxury represented by the elaborately decorated apartments and gardens.

Today, only the northern section has been excavated. Some parts of the palace have been restored. The throne room, known as the Salón Rico, where three dates indicating 953–7 have been located in the ornamentation, has been meticulously restored. It has three naves, defined by two arcades of horseshoe arches on columns, and is approached through an open portico with five arched openings. The recessed arch in the centre of the northern wall at the back facing the portico indicates the most likely position of the emir's throne. There are smaller auxiliary rooms on either side of the throne room. An exceptionally beautiful carved panel, one of many in the throne room, has a symmetrical rendering of the traditional oriental 'tree of life' motif within a vegetal border. The trunk is depicted vertically in the centre but the boughs, leaves, and flowers are shown in flowing interlacing curves to produce an almost abstract but recognisable image. Alternate voussoirs of the arches and almost every conceivable vertical surface have similar floral arabesque decoration.

There are many beautifully carved wall panels in the Salón Rico. This particularly elegant example has an oriental 'tree of life' theme within a border of vegetal patterns.

The interior of the Salón Rico, the throne room of the royal palace at Medinat al-Zahra, with typical Umayyad arcades on either side.

Ibn Hayyan, who held an important post in the royal court at Córdoba, relates that a Christian king visiting the caliph was met and accompanied on his way by Christian and Muslim dignitaries. Together they rode between double ranks of Muslim soldiers to the main gate of

Medinat al-Zahra, where they were escorted across the lower level. Here they were received by a senior court official. The group then proceeded with a guard of honour through the reception halls of the next level where they dismounted and rested until the caliph was ready to receive them in one of the splendid halls at the highest level. Thence they proceeded on foot to the hall where the caliph was surrounded by his courtiers. After the audience, the king was taken to the house of the vizier, where he took refreshment and received luxurious gifts for himself and his retinue. On his return to his horse he was given another noble thoroughbred plus a costly harness.

There is also a legend that one of the pools in a reception hall was filled with quicksilver, which was available locally, and when the caliph was entertaining he would instruct a servant to disturb the surface of the pool, so creating a kaleidoscope of the reflecting colours of the surrounding walls, which were said to be of marble inlaid with gold decoration. This taste for exuberant and lavish surroundings, together with the presence of the designers and craftsmen able to execute them so brilliantly, was to prove the spur for the subsequent splendour of the next additions to the Friday Mosque.

Unity within al-Andalus and the consequent prosperity, which had taken Abdel Rahman III twenty years to achieve, had brought a large increase of population to the capital, Córdoba. This created the need for a further extension to the Friday Mosque, which was undertaken by al-Hakam II over the period 961–76. He was Abdel Rahman's son and was reputed to have been a lover of the arts, deeply religious and fascinated by architecture. At first he considered changing the orientation, because it had been realised that the *qibla* was facing south, as was customary and geographically correct in Damascus, and some wanted it to be changed to face the east, the accurate direction of Holy Mecca from Córdoba. However, Abu Ibrahim, faqih or religious scholar, said that from the time of the Islamic conquest up to the present, all Muslims in the Peninsula had prayed to the south and therefore it would be better to continue this tradition. So Abdel Rahman III decided to respect the custom of his ancestors and retain the orientation to the south. The third extension added an area to the south of the prayer hall equal to the area of the first phase, at the same time re-emphasising the sense of depth. It was estimated that the existing entrance courtyard would not be large enough for the enlarged prayer hall so that also was extended to the north. A new minaret was built on the west side of the northern gateway, which was aligned on the *qibla*.

The caliph's architects and designers did not want to destroy the structural unity of the mosque, but some variations in the approach to the design were introduced. New features included trefoil, multifoil and pointed horseshoe arches as well as intersecting versions of them. There were three ribbed domes each with a central octagon, and one lantern ribbed dome over a central square. It is probable that a flat timber ceiling supported on the cross beams of the roof trusses was created at this period in those areas of the

prayer hall without domes. These ceilings were richly decorated with vegetal and geometrical patterns similar to those found at Medinat al-Zahra, and
it is likely that the same artists and craftsmen were responsible for this work
in the Friday Mosque.

The new structure was heightened and the natural lighting was
improved with the addition of skylights. The *qibla* wall was opened up again,
but the arched nave openings were narrower and supported on cross-shaped
pillars. This created a form of visual partition between the new and the old
sections of the prayer hall. The central nave, which is slightly wider than the
others, was stressed by four new domed bays. One of these was at the north
end of the extension, while the other three were aligned in front of the deep
new octagonal *mihrab*, which has a scalloped dome. The four beautiful dark
marble columns that flank the opening were reused from the previous
mihrab, a fact that is recorded on an inscription nearby. On either side of the
mihrab are five square rooms. The five on the east were used as treasuries,
while the others formed a covered way to the palace. The use of the upper
storey of eleven rooms is not recorded.

*The roof structure over the Capilla Villaviciosa
in the Great Mosque at Córdoba consists of a
lantern dome supported on four arches at the
centres of the four sides and four others half-way
between the centre and the corners. The arches
interlink to form a square central space with a
circular dome within an octagon. There are four
openings to each side of the lantern.*

The northernmost of the new domed spaces was defined as square in
plan. There are three bays on the south side with three arches supported on
two columns. It was later known as the Capilla Villaviciosa after the
Reconquest. More cross-bracing was required to sustain the outward thrust
of the lantern dome, which has sixteen windows, four on each side. This was
achieved with the use of a series of interlinked multi-lobed arches. Although
the use of lobed arches has Mesopotamian precedent, the introduction of
interlacing arches in three dimensions in this way seems to be original. The
windows to the three domes in front of the *mihrab* let in less light than those
of the Capilla Villaviciosa because there are fewer of them and they have

marble grilles. In spite of this, the geographer Idrisi (*c.* 1100–64) called the dome at the centre in front of the *mihrab* the Great Dome, probably because it was in the most important place in the mosque where the Quran was read and before the position of the caliph at prayer. The central space of each of the three domes is an octagon contained by visibly interlaced arches. The remaining surfaces are filled with shells, small cupolas and interlacing ribs. The surfaces within the Great Dome are faced with mosaic. The system of ribbed vaulting was later applied in the tenth century in the mosque at Toledo, known as Bab al-Mardum. After the recapture of Toledo by the Christians in 1085, it was extended and consecrated as the church of Santo Cristo de la Luz (see p. 62).

Much of the new decorative work in the Córdoba Friday Mosque shows an extension of the skills and ideas already developed at Medinat al-Zahra, but the use of mosaics was taken to an extreme of sensitivity. Relations between Córdoba and Byzantium had been friendly, perhaps because of the distance, and so al-Hakam asked the Byzantine emperor for help in the supply of materials and design skills. It is said that an expert in mosaics arrived with sacks full of gold mosaics as the gift of the emperor. The visitor then trained a number of assistants who eventually became so skilled that they were able to continue the work unassisted. Nevertheless it

The dome over the bay immediately to the front of the mihrab, *whose mosaic Kufic calligraphy can be recognised to the left of the picture. This consists of a shell dome contained within an octagon created by arches which form two interlocking squares.*

A detail of the mosaics on the mihrab *wall. This shows the gold calligraphy against a blue background and the floral arabesques in gold set in red and blue, as well as blue against gold, on the voussoir shapes of the* mihrab *arch.*

has been claimed that the technical standards at Córdoba are not as high as those demonstrated in the contemporary work in the Haghia Sophia at Constantinople. The front wall of the *mihrab* was covered with mosaic, and the effect of the light from the dome above filtered through the interlaced arches was magical. This space defined the *qibla* and anticipated the *mihrab* where the three domed spaces before it were set out following the same principles. The multi-coloured mosaics covering the vertical surfaces from the capitals of the horseshoe arch upwards were set in a wealth of patterns. The tapering voussoirs were expressed in panels of floral arabesques in intricate detail, while the outer outline of the arch was defined by a curved band of carved stonework. The rectangular *alfiz* consists of two lines of gold calligraphy in the Kufic style against a strong blue background. Below, there is a third horizontal band of blue calligraphy on a gold background immediately above the arch. Above the *alfiz* is a blind trefoil arcade with floral mosaic patterns contained within the arches. The lower wall surfaces to the height of the marble columns at the *mihrab* opening were lined with stone panels exquisitely carved in relief with floral patterns, in a manner very similar to those found at Medinat al-Zahra. The vault over the internal space of the *mihrab* is carved from one block of marble in the shape of a shell. The shell has been described by Burckhardt as an ear of the heart which absorbs the dewdrop of the divine word and is therefore a suitable symbol for the *mihrab*. The shell also became for the Christians the symbol of St James of Compostela. There are blind trefoil arches on marble columns and panels decorated with arabesque patterns in stucco.

At the same time that these sophisticated changes in style were being made inside, entrance doorways to the mosque were inserted in the east and west elevations. One particularly elaborate example in the western façade

FAR LEFT
The mihrab *wall is covered with glittering mosaics that are believed to have been supplied by the Byzantine emperor. The* alfiz *is decorated with Kufic calligraphy in gold on a blue background. There is a horizontal band of calligraphy, just above the arch, where the colours are reversed. Above the the* alfiz *is a blind trefoil arcade that contains floral patterns in mosaic.*

follows the overall pattern set by the Puerta de San Esteban. It has a modest enough rectangular door with a straight arch immediately over the opening but it is contained within a larger horseshoe arch with two-tone voussoirs. This arch has an *alfiz* decorated with red and white mosaics in a geometrical pattern of squares on the diagonal. Above the *alfiz* is an interlacing blind arcade with five panels and six columns. Five pointed horseshoe recessed arches are created by the interlacing of four rounded horseshoe arches in relief which span the distance between every second column. Three of the panels are faced with red and white mosaics in geometrical patterns, while the other two contain stone reliefs of floral arabesques including four carved bosses. On either side of the *alfiz* are modest rectangular *celosias* in a grid pattern of squares and eight-pointed stars. Above these are cinquefoil two-tone arches containing panels of red and white mosaics in geometrical patterns. Surrounding the *celosias* and the arches are many elaborate stone panels with similar arabesque carved patterns. At the level of the eaves is a horizontal carved stone inscription in Kufic calligraphy. Most of the doorways were restored at the beginning of the twentieth century.

The tenth century is considered by historians to be the height of the flowering of the culture of Córdoba. On the authority of the seventeenth-century writer al-Maqqari, Chejne claims that it contained 1,600 mosques, 900 public baths, 60,300 mansions for notables, 80,455 shops and a population of 213,077. The main market was close to the Friday Mosque, the area forming a nucleus at the centre of the city. There were wider streets to the main gates in the city walls, whereas the residential quarters were closely packed. There was an informal layout of courtyard houses with gardens and fountains, the majority having party walls to the neighbours on three sides; this allowed a very high density of residents to be achieved. The houses were inward looking and, in accordance with the Islamic tradition, private in character, allowing no observation of the interior by strangers. They were arranged around an atrium, developed from the Roman model, except that there were normally two storeys with an arcaded cloister giving access to the internal accommodation. This layout provided subdued light to the interior and conditions of comfort during the hot summers within the courtyard, which was paved, often with a central pool and fountain. Beds were planted with flowers and creepers, and more plants were grown in clay pots arranged around the court and hung from the walls. For most of the year the courtyard was used as a living room. This house type can be seen as a development of the best Roman residential planning, except for the informality of the street layout of some quarters which had houses arranged around a cul-de-sac. Hygiene was an important part of the creed of Islam, so the rich had private baths in their residences, while public baths were provided for the rest of the population.

The city boasted an internationally renowned intelligentsia which included philosophers, clerics, scientists, doctors, poets and musicians. Al-Hakam II is said to have had 400,000 volumes in his library. All branches of

A typical courtyard within an urban house at Córdoba. It is planned on oriental principles derived from Roman precedent. The courtyard provides light and ventilation to both storeys, at the same time creating complete privacy.

the arts were encouraged and Córdoba as a result became a cosmopolitan and sophisticated centre. The university was then one of the most famous in the world. Most citizens were literate at a time when in Christian Europe literacy was confined to the clergy. Calligraphy became the supreme art of Islam, and this was widely demonstrated inside and outside the Friday Mosque. The leading role was taken by the Arab nobility. Their language, religion, culture and way of life became the approved norm. Many of Iberian descent had converted to Islam while many of the Arab oligarchy had intermarried with Iberians. The Christians or Mozarabs were often bilingual, speaking a proto-Spanish as well as Arabic. Alvaro, a prominent Christian, complained in the ninth century that they read Arabic poems and romances in addition to the Muslim philosophers in order to improve their style and culture rather than studying the works of the Church in Latin. Towards the mid-tenth century many conversions to Islam occurred and Christian intellectual life seemed to decline in proportion to the increase in military power of the Christian kingdoms in the north of the Peninsula. Non-Muslims lived under their own jurisdiction, with their own leader who was responsible for the collection of the special taxes they were obliged to pay.

The Umayyad state was autocratic from the very beginning, the ruler being the commander of the army and the highest authority in legal matters. From Abdel Rahman III onwards the army of free Muslims was augmented by mercenaries; some were Berbers from North Africa but an increasing number were captured European slaves. On the principle of 'divide and rule', al-Mansour, the powerful chief minister, mixed them up to avoid tribal discontent.

The fourth and final extension of the Friday mosque was undertaken by al-Mansour, in the reign of Hisham II, al-Hakam's young son. Eight aisles were added on the east side running the full length of the prayer hall which now became almost a square in plan. The entrance courtyard and arcade were also expanded eastwards in line with the wider prayer hall. This eastward expansion destroyed the symmetrical balance of the *qibla*, but the new structure followed the previous principle of superimposed arcades and extended eastwards the *mihrab* wall of Abdel Rahman II. The buttresses of the former east wall were replaced with thicker horseshoe arches supported on double columns. This maintained the perception of continuous space, but the line of double columns described the boundary between the new and the old. However, cinquefoil and pointed horseshoe arches were introduced in the lower arcades, while the carving on the capitals is not as refined, either in design or execution, as the former work. Al-Mansour, surprisingly, showed some restraint in not competing with the splendour of al-Hakam's *mihrab* and complementary domed spaces. He was content to leave them in their glory and relish the sheer size of the extended prayer hall, now approximately four and a half times the area of Abdel Rahman's original.

Al-Mansour had arrogated all power for himself and became obsessed with military glory. He frequently invaded the Christian north, attacking Barcelona, León and Santiago de Compostela, where he captured the cathedral bells and brought them to Córdoba as booty. He died in 1002, leaving a power vacuum. Anarchy set in and the provinces soon declared themselves independent, setting up petty kingdoms known as *taifas*. For two centuries, the mosque at Córdoba remained in the state in which al-Mansour had left it. In the meantime the Umayyad dynasty faded away, and Córdoba was no longer the capital of a single Muslim entity in the Peninsula; it had fragmented under a series of *taifa* kings. Other cities, such as Seville, Zaragoza and Granada, grew in significance, Christian power in the north increased and the frontier between the Muslim and Christian kingdoms moved inexorably southwards.

In 1236 Córdoba fell into the hands of the Christians and the mosque was consecrated by the Bishop of Osma as a cathedral with the name of Santa María la Mayor. At first, under Fernando III (1230–52), the new religion was practised discreetly in the corner of the al-Mansour extension. Later the first of al-Hakam's domes was used as the main chapel and became

A view through a multi-lobed arch of the Capilla Villaviciosa in the mosque of Córdoba, revealing the later Christian Gothic insertion.

FAR RIGHT
The Capilla Real, or Royal Chapel which was built in an oriental style for Alfonso X 'the Wise' of Castile within the former mosque. It is even more ornate than the previous Muslim structures. Except for a few shields and heraldic devices it is completely oriental in character.

known as the Capilla Villaviciosa. The structure of the mosque remained undisturbed until Alfonso X of Castile, known as 'the Wise' (1252–84), decided to build a new royal chapel where he could be buried. Alfonso was a tolerant king with a great respect for the culture of al-Andalus. The royal chapel was situated next to the Capilla Villaviciosa and designed in the same style and structure as the mosque of al-Hakam. The decoration is even more ornate than that of the previous chapels and was no doubt executed by Mudéjar craftsmen from 1258 to 1260. It would appear to be a completely Muslim structure if it were not for some shields and heraldic devices. It has a square plan and the dome above is supported on eight arches, the intrados of each having a serpent-like curve, an innovation for this building. The decoration in relief shows the total range of Islamic patterning, and its intricacy anticipates that of the Alhambra at Granada. There are two lions rampant over the arched alcove above a basin.

Since the first building phase of the mosque there had been no boundary wall between the entrance courtyard and the prayer hall. The continuous space flowed from the outside to the inside with no visual barrier. The enclosed courtyard is believed to have been laid out by al-Mansour in 976. This rectangular area is divided into three sections, each with a fountain in the centre. It was planted with orange trees (it is still called El Patio de los Naranjos) watered from irrigation channels which are filled by the fountains.

The Patio de los Naranjos of the former mosque at Córdoba whose orange trees are watered by irrigation channels. In Muslim times the patio would have been used as an overflow as it was a continuous space with the prayer hall. The Puerta del Perdón is seen on the left.

From inside the prayer hall these trees could be seen to echo the forest of columns within. This spatial arrangement also allowed the court to be used as overflow space for prayer on those occasions when the hall could not accommodate an exceptionally large congregation. This was normal practice in the layout of Friday or congregational mosques. But some time after the Reconquest, the Christians decided to close off the roofed space of the hall from the court by a new wall with a doorway (known as the Puerta de las Palmas) on the axis of the main entrance and the *mihrab*. The main entrance was retained but a new gateway in the Mudéjar manner (now called the Puerta del Perdón) was added. The original minaret of 951 commissioned by Abdel Rahman III had been sited just to the west of the entrance but this was later transformed into a six-storey Christian bell-tower in the Renaissance style. Two coats of arms in relief carved on the Puerta de Santa Catalina have renderings of the minaret and the north porch as they appeared before reconstruction. The minaret was not only functional in providing a platform where the muezzin could call the faithful to prayer, but was also considered to be a powerful vertical symbol of the Umayyad dynasty and of their capital city. The large externally dominating dome, as at the Dome of the Rock, was never used in al-Andalus.

Another mosque in Spain survives from the late Umayyad period. It is much more modest in scale and design and was probably not a Friday mosque. Built in Toledo in 999, it was known as the mosque of Bab al-Mardum, after the nearby city gate. The entire construction is of brick and the design elements derive from those of the Friday Mosque at Córdoba. It is square in plan and divided into nine square bays each having ribbed domes of individual design, some based on the square and others on the octagon. The central dome is higher than the others. The higher supporting arcades, at two or three levels, sit on twelve rounded horseshoe arches each supported by four circular columns without bases at ground level. The ground-floor arcades are open on three sides; the fourth side was the *mihrab* wall. After the Reconquest, an extension plus an apse was added on the east side to form a church. There are many simplified versions in brick of features from the Córdoba Friday Mosque. These include multi-lobed arches, blind arcades of interlocking horseshoe arches and rectangular panels of geometrically patterned brickwork.

There are remains elsewhere of mosques from Umayyad times that have been embodied in later Christian churches, which were built without any attempt at continuity of style, such as was achieved at Toledo or in the earlier Christian additions to the Córdoba mosque. At the village of Almonaster la Real, near Seville, there is a church in which a *mihrab* remains in the south wall. Its original square plan has, as at Toledo, later been extended to give the required Christian alignment to the east. At Beja, in the Alentejo district of Portugal, the church of Santa Maria also incorporates the features of a former mosque, including a bell-tower which is obviously adapted from a former minaret.

An internal view of the former mosque Bab al-Mardum at Toledo seen through a cinquefoil arched opening of the external wall showing two of the four columns that support the horseshoe arches and define the nine square bays of the prayer space. It was later extended and transformed into the church of Cristo de la Luz.

CHAPTER 2

The garden and fountain of the Patio de Santa Isabel within the fortified palace at Zaragoza known as the Aljaferia.

The RESURGENCE of CHRISTIANITY in the NORTH

The fragmentation of the Umayyad domain centred on Córdoba led to the formation of a number of petty kingdoms with strong local interests. The struggle between the Christian and Muslim powers in the Peninsula became extremely complex. In the north there were six Christian states – Galicia, León, Castile, Navarre, Aragón and the territory under Catalan domination. South of the line of division, which ran from the river Douro in the west, bent south of Salamanca, curved north to Soria, then skirted the valley of the Aragón north of Zaragoza to the Mediterranean coast between Tarragona and Barcelona, were the Muslim states or *taifas*. There were many, the most powerful being Badajoz, Seville, Málaga, Córdoba, Toledo, Granada, Almería, Murcia, Valencia and Zaragoza. Badajoz and Seville extended westwards to the Atlantic to include what is now southern Portugal, while Galicia incorporated northern Portugal. A period of unrest ensured that many fortresses were built or enlarged. Towns and cities were encircled with new walls and old fortifications were restored.

Zaragoza, the future capital of Aragón, had been one of the most prominent Roman settlements in the Peninsula and was named Caesar-Augusta, after Augustus, who had established a military camp there. It had been captured in turn by the Suevi, followed by the Visigoths. From 716 it became the administrative centre of the northern march of the Umayyad caliphate, and in 864 al-Jaafar began the construction of a fortified palace outside the walls and to the west of the city. This was originally called 'Dar Al Surur' (House of Joy), but came to be known as the Aljafería after the founder. The governors of Zaragoza had a tendency to rebel against the central Umayyad authority, and in the ninth century al-Jaafer became a powerful leader, one of the most important *taifa* kings. The exterior of the Aljafería is characterised by six bulky towers and the whole structure is surrounded by a dry moat.

The severe military character of the exterior of the Aljafería is in contrast to the elaborate and colourful royal quarters within. The horseshoe arch of the main entrance is placed centrally between two of the the circular defensive towers.

The most recognisable section of the first phase of the building of the palace is the Torre del Trovador (Tower of the Troubadour), made famous as the setting for Verdi's opera *Il Trovatore*; this was based on a drama by the nineteenth-century Spanish author Antonio García Gutierrez and was set in the Aljafería, the scene of the declaration of Don Manrico's love for Leonor. The tower is six storeys high and has heavy horseshoe arches at ground and first-floor levels. There are pointed arches on the third and fourth floors. Probably only the two lower floors date from the time of al-Jaafar.

In 1018 Mundir I became the first independent king of the Tuyubi dynasty based in Zaragoza. This dynasty was superseded by Suleiman al-Mustain, who was descended from an important Arab family, the Banu Hud. In 1046 Ahmad Abu Yafar al-Muqtadir succeeded to the throne. He became one of the most celebrated of the *taifa* rulers and was the most brilliant and cultured monarch of the Banu Hud dynasty. He was a poet, astronomer and mathematician and for a relatively short period his court was a magnet for scholars and artists. One of his poems reads:

Oh! palace of happiness! Oh! golden hall!
Thanks to you I achieved the height of my desire.
And although I should have nought but my realm,
For me you are all that I would long for.

The palace is obviously the Aljafería and under his direction its Islamic section was constructed. This comprises the north portico, the mosque, the open courtyard, now known as the Patio de Santa Isabel, and the south portico. At the centre of the north portico was a rectangular hall with an internal pool, known as the Salón del Oro (Golden Room), and on either side were two rooms which were probably private apartments. The mid-nineteenth century writer Paulino Saviron mentions stalactite vaults in these square rooms. However, they and all the carved decorations in alabaster and marble have been lost. A few remaining fragments have made possible the recent restoration of much of the sumptuous multifoil arcades, one of which has interlacing arches with voids between the crossover points. The capitals, some in marble but others carved in alabaster, are similar to those from the time of Abdel Rahman III in the Friday Mosque at Córdoba.

At the eastern end of the north portico there is the doorway into the mosque. This has a horseshoe arch and an *alfiz* containing a blind arcade and intricate floral arabesques and inscriptions in relief. The mosque interior is octagonal in plan and small in dimensions, indicating its private nature, intended for the use of the prince and his court. A jewel set within a severe exterior, it expresses the artistic magnificence of the court in the wonderful intricacy of its wall surfaces where rounded lobes are combined with angular forms. The interlinked cinquefoil arches of the upper gallery and the octagonal dome, supported on ribbed arches, complete the effect. The octagonal

One of the accentuated horseshoe arches within the Torre del Trovador, the oldest part of the Aljafería palace at Zaragoza.

Detail of the capitals of one of the double columns supporting the arcade in the north portico of the Patio de Santa Isabel at the Aljafería. It is remarkable for the intricate carving in deep relief of arabesque floral patterns.

Detail of the horizontal friezes of continuous curvilinear vegetal patterns just below the gallery of the mosque within the Aljafería palace. The upper band continues above the mihrab as Kufic calligraphy. (See p. 50.)

The mihrab *of of the Aljafería mosque where the arcaded gallery of multi-lobed arches allows a limited amount of natural light to enter. A horizontal band of Kufic calligraphy runs between the gallery and the horseshoe arched opening of the* mihrab.

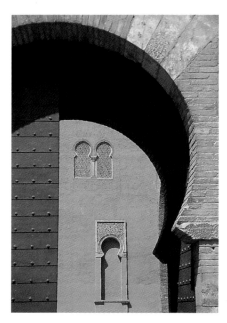

The celosias *of the* ajimez *window to the upper level of the mosque in the Aljafería are seen above a blind horseshoe-arched opening which is contained within a panel of arabesque decoration. This view is framed by the arch of the main entrance to the palace. (See also p. 78.)*

mihrab which faces southeast has a horseshoe arch with alternate plain and floral arabesque voussoirs. The *qibla* is not geographically accurate but follows the orientation of Mecca as from Damascus. In this and other ways it is modelled on the *mihrab* at Córdoba. Above the arch is a frieze of quotations from the Quran in Kufic calligraphy which is continuous at the same level along the other seven sides of the mosque.

A restricted amount of natural light reaches the gallery through two *celosias* which when seen from the main entrance patio, appear to be set in an *ajimez* at high level. This is a sophisticated development of the window-grilles of the outside walls of the Great or Friday Mosque of Córdoba. The *ajimez* is the only opening in a plain wall surface, and the double window with its single column, carved capital and the interlacing hexagonal grid of the two horseshoe-arched openings provides an exceptionally beautiful example of this Islamic element of design which gains from the simplicity of its setting.

At the southern end of the Patio de Santa Isabel is a portico, with six openings spanned by multi-lobed and interlocking arches, which are supported on piers flanked with single columns. The arches have here attained a degree of abstraction from their strictly functional purpose. The network of criss-cross braided patterns produces an overwhelming display of complexity, in sharp contrast to the simple paving and planting of the court, which would probably also have been provided with a pool in which the arcade would have been reflected. Al-Maqqari, an Arab man of letters, in his description of al-Andalus in the seventeenth century, compares it with a patio garden of the eleventh century:

> This garden is one of the most marvellous, beautiful and perfect places. Its patio is of pure white marble; a jet of water crosses it like a wriggling snake and there is a pool into which the running water flows. The ceiling of its pavilion, and its walls, are decorated with gold and lapis lazuli. The garden has rows of plants aligned symmetrically and its flowers smile in their buds. The sun cannot reach its damp earth, the breeze spreads their perfume in waves, day and night, as if they were formed with the glances of lovers or had been taken from the pages of youth.

Those parts of the palace that date from the Islamic period were neglected for many centuries, particularly when it was used as a military barracks. It is now possible to experience these magical spaces as they were at that time because of the thorough investigations of Christian Ewert and the recent restorations carried out under the supervision of Francisco Iniguez Almech and Angel Peropadre Muniesa. This work is particularly important because the La Aljafería is the only palace in the Peninsula to have survived in any recognisable form from the era of the *taifa* states. Its regional significance has now been reasserted as it has become the seat of the regional government of Aragón and a modern assembly hall and administrative offices have been sensitively inserted within the ancient walls to the east of the Patio de Santa Isabel.

The simple rectangular layout of the paving and planting complements the elaborate carving and curves of the arcades of the Patio de Santa Isabel.

A detail of the complex braided patterns of the interlocking and multi-lobed arched portico at the southern end of the Patio de Santa Isabel of the Aljaferia. Natural light is reflected from the white marble paving of the courtyard.

The Abbadid dynasty was established at Seville, and al-Mutamid (1069–91) built a palace there called al-Qasr al-Mubarak (now known as the Alcázar). A garden has been discovered there which once belonged to it, and a later garden, known as the Crucero, was built over it to the same layout. As the name implies, it had raised paths in the form of a cross within a rectangle with the four remaining spaces made into sunken beds. There were arcaded galleries at the short sides with pools in front, and there was a fountain at the intersection of the arms of the cross. This layout is an early example of what came to be seen as the prototypical Islamic garden created in the Iberian Peninsula and Morocco. A seventeenth-century description speaks of another garden here, at a much lower level, which was divided into quarters and planted with orange trees in such a way that the tops almost reached the level of the paths above.

Málaga was the main port for the state of Granada and an important city in its own right. In the Alcazaba or royal palace, which is on a prominent fortified site overlooking the harbour, there remains a group of rooms dating from the eleventh century, which enclose the west courtyard. An open pavilion faces the sea, and a portico is composed of three exaggerated horseshoe arches on slender columns. The voussoirs are alternately smooth and decorated with incised arabesques. The under surface of each intrados is also decorated in this way. The composition owes much to Cordoban precedent, but the decoration lacks the conviction and flair shown by the craftsmen of the Great Mosque. This palace was later extended and developed during the Nasrid period.

Many Christians continued to practise their religion in the Muslim territories and used Arabic as their first language. They became known as Mozarabs and developed their own characteristic ritual. But some wished to leave and travel north to live in states where Christianity was the official religion. Alfonso III (866–910), king of León, encouraged monks and other Christians to emigrate and settle in the north. One of the earliest Mozarabic monasteries was built at San Miguel de Escalada, in León near Gradefes, in 913 on the site of a Visigothic church that had been destroyed during the first Arab invasion. An inscription refers to Abad Alfonso and his companions

from Córdoba and their beautiful new temple. Although it is possible to discern Islamic influence in the design of Mozarabic churches, they are quite different from a typical mosque. The layout of a mosque places no emphasis on sight lines but in a church it is considered desirable for all the congregation to be able to see the priest, especially when he is preaching. Separation of the chancel, the altar, the clergy and the choir from the body of the congregation in the nave is normally the basis of the layout. It was usual to have a change of level between the chancel and the nave, and the pulpit, at a higher level, would be accessed by a flight of steps. This resulted in a plan that is directional, hierarchical and compartmentalised, often with the addition of transepts and chapels. At Escalada the plan is of the basilica type with three naves and a three-horseshoe-arch screen before the chancel. Its most remarkable feature is the open gallery of twelve horseshoe arches that runs the full length of the church on the south side. Here there are carved capitals decorated with palm leaves and arabesques.

FAR LEFT, TOP
The Mozarabic monastery of San Miguel de Escalada in León has a basilica type plan and was constructed on the site of a Visigothic church by monks who had fled from Córdoba at the beginning of the tenth century. It has an unusual lateral gallery of horseshoe arches.

FAR LEFT, BOTTOM
The horseshoe-arcaded gallery at the monastery of San Miguel de Escalada.

Alfonso III of León also conquered the region of Beira, now in northern Portugal, and populated it with Galicians and Mozarabs. In 912 the monastery of São Pedro de Lourosa in Portugal was founded. It has had an eventful history. Al-Mansour destroyed the east end in 987 but it was rebuilt in the thirteenth century. In the 1920s it was restored to its original form. The plan is similar to that of Escalada but without the screen at the east end.

The exterior of the church of São Pedro de Lourosa in northern Portugal which also has a basilica plan. The Mozarab origin of the church is demonstrated by the ajimez window in the gable wall of the nave. The porch with a semi-circular arched entrance is a later addition as is the fifteenth-century free-standing belfry. To the left are some recently excavated graves.

The plain interior of the nave of São Pedro de Lourosa viewed from the north aisle reveals the simple dignity of the horseshoe arcades.

The continuous development of the church of San Pedro de la Nave near Zamora is illustrated by this interior view. The Visigothic beginnings of about 650 (see p. 18) were supplemented by Mozarabic additions dating from 950. The horseshoe arch before the rectangular sanctuary is in the Mozarabic manner as are the arcades of the nave. Visigothic carved capitals can be seen supporting the arches of the central crossing. (See pp. 18 and 19.)

The naves are formed by horseshoe arches supported on recycled Roman columns. There are *ajimeces* at a high level in the gable walls of the nave. The porch, probably a later addition, has a simple semicircular arch, and there is a free-standing belfry with Gothic arches to the north of the chancel which dates from the fifteenth century. The interior has a dignified beauty and must have much the same appearance today as a millennium ago when it was first used for worship. Recent excavations have revealed ancient graves and the remains of a baptistery. It continues in use as the local church.

The church of San Pedro de la Nave, near Zamora, was founded in Visigothic times about 650 and was continuously developed until 950. Its original location was flooded by the construction of a dam, so in 1934 it was re-erected on a new site. Within its structure it is possible to discern the relation between the Mozarabic style and its predecessor. The simple exterior appears Visigothic, and inside there are characteristic horizontal carved stone friezes, similar to those at Quintinilla de las Viñas, as well as carved capitals on such biblical themes as the Sacrifice of Isaac and Daniel in the Lions' Den. The plan is in the form of a Latin cross, but the horseshoe arch before the rectangular apse is in a Moorish manner and implies the presence of Mozarab craftsmen.

Although the isolated church of San Baudelio, near the village of Berlanga de Duero, is generally accepted as Mozarabic, the layout of the nave is similar to that of a mosque or synagogue. The nave is almost square in plan with a gallery at one end, supported on sixteen piers carrying horseshoe arches. Opposite the gallery is a small square chancel behind a horseshoe archway. The nave roof is carried on eight horseshoe arches radiating from a single column which stands like an exotic tree at the centre. The walls were covered with frescoes which were stolen in the 1920s but have now been returned in a faded state. It seems possible that this building could have been a mosque or synagogue and later converted for Christian use with the addition of the chancel.

In the northernmost part of Aragón, just south of the Pyrenees near the original capital, Jaca, is the monastery of San Juan de la Peña, hidden in the foothills with a spectacular view north across the valley of the river Aragón. This was a refuge for Mozarabs who, with the support of Galindo Aznarez, count of Aragón, founded the monastery in 920. It escaped the depredations of Abdel Rahman III but more Mozarabs fled there for shelter when he sacked Pamplona to the west. They built the church and council chamber in a Mozarabic style at a lower level set into the rock face. The monastery became the spiritual home of the expanding kingdom of Aragón and the site of the royal pantheon. When monks from the abbey of Cluny in France arrived, the Roman ritual was introduced for the first time in the Peninsula at the end of the eleventh century. The monastery was extended upwards by King Sancho Ramirez and consecrated by his son Pedro I (r. 1094–1104) in 1094. From the eleventh century the Holy Grail, the legendary chalice from the Last Supper, was kept at San Juan de la Peña in safety from the Muslims for three hundred years (it is now in Valencia Cathedral). Wolfram de Eschenbach's *Parsifal* was based on the theme of the Holy Grail, a subject later exploited by Richard Wagner in his sacred

The remarkable central column of the church of San Baudelio near Berlanga de Duero which supports eight radiating arches which carry the roof of the square nave. The faded remains of a fresco can be seen on the front of the gallery above the horseshoe arches and piers.

A Mozarabic horseshoe archway at the monastery of San Juan de la Peña in Alto Aragón. This arch was originally at the lower level of the monastery but was re-erected at the upper level when it was extended at the end of the eleventh century. An inscription in Latin was also added over the arch. The rest of the structure was built in the Romanesque style.

musical drama of the same name. When the upper floor at San Juan de la Peña was constructed, a horseshoe-arched doorway was moved from below to the higher level to give access from the larger church to a new cloister under the cliff face. An inscription in Latin, translating as, 'This door opens heaven to all the faithful who combine the faith with God's commandments', was added to the Mozarabic arch. Otherwise the new work was carried out in a Romanesque style with many beautifully carved capitals in the cloister. Although the royal pantheon remained here, the monastery waned in importance as Aragón expanded southwards and the capital was transferred first to Huesca and then to Zaragoza.

To the east of Jaca lies a district called the Serrablo. It is a valley near the French border where the river Gallego flows south from the Pyrenees. At the end of the eighth century there were Muslim garrisons in Huesca, Pamplona and Zaragoza. The Muslims were active farther south along the Ebro valley, leaving the area to the north to Conde Aznar Galindez, who founded Aragón as a political entity. The daughter of Aznar II married the Wali (the Muslim governor) of Huesca who was able to offer protection to the monastic orders that had been established in the Serrablo during the second quarter of the tenth century. This protection diverted the attention of al-Mansour westwards to the pilgrimage centre of Santiago de Compostela in Galicia, which he attacked after his sacking of Barcelona in 985.

A number of Mozarabic churches have survived in this area, and an association known as the Los Amigos de Serrablo has been responsible for their care and study. A typical example, San Pedro at Lárrede, has a tall square minaret-like bell-tower in stone with windows at the top on all four sides, each consisting of three vertical openings with small horseshoe arches within a simple *alfiz*. The main door to the church has a wider horseshoe arch and the western wall of the rectangular vaulted nave has a simplified *ajimez* at high level, the openings in the stonework being closed with translucent alabaster sheets. The plan is in the shape of a Latin cross, with a semicircular apse, and the tower is built over the north transept. There are no openings or windows in the north walls.

Due to the increasing influence of the Cluniac clergy and their beliefs, the Mozarabic style was soon replaced by the Romanesque in architecture. Features that could be seen to be oriental in origin were abandoned as being too reminiscent of Islam. Textiles with geometric patterns of patent oriental derivation must have continued in use because pieces of such cloth have been found in the tomb of San Ramón at the cathedral of Roda de Isábena in northern Aragón. An embroidered fragment from a shroud is believed to be of Egyptian Coptic origin and from the tenth or eleventh century; another incorporating Kufic calligraphy is probably of Persian design. Perhaps the most interesting find was the mitre of San Valero, which had borders of woven silk with oriental designs made by craftsmen from al-Andalus, probably in the twelfth century. Muslim textiles at that period were superior to anything that could be produced in Northern Europe, and they were often

A simple double window within an alfiz in the Mozarabic church of San Pedro at Lárrede in the Serrablo district of Alto Aragón. The windows are made of translucent alabaster sheets set in two horseshoe-arched openings.

presented as gifts to notables, both clerical and lay, so it would not have seemed so unusual for them to be used for burial and liturgical purposes.

The kingdom of Castile had been steadily increasing its power and territory. Ferdinand I (r. 1035–65) united Galicia, León and Castile. He expanded his territory southwards, reaching Coimbra on the river Mondego in present-day Portugal in 1064 and took Avila and Segovia. In 1085 Alfonso VI (r. 1072–1109) of León and Castile made the strategic capture of Toledo, the former Visigothic capital, from the Muslims. In 1094 he advanced south to the river Tagus but was thrown back by the Moors at Lisbon. In the following year he established the county of Portucalia, named after the town of Portus Cale (now Oporto), between the rivers Douro and Mondego and granted it to his son-in-law, Count Henry of Burgundy. This is the early beginning of the state of Portugal. Following a long struggle with the kingdom of León and Castile, and after a brilliant victory over the Moors at Ourique in 1139, Afonso Henriques, the son of Henry of Burgundy, was proclaimed King Afonso I of Portugal (r. 1128–85).

Navarre and Aragón, however, did not make so much progress south. Huesca was hotly disputed by the Muslims and was not taken until 1096 by Pedro I of Aragón. The rich valley of the river Ebro was stoutly defended by the Muslims until 1118, when Zaragoza was captured by Alfonso I of Aragón (r. 1104–34). The inexorable southward expansion of the Christian kingdoms, which was gathering momentum during the first half of the twelfth century, was to falter due to rivalries and intrigue between them and the Muslim *taifa* kings. This complicated pattern of political relationships, however, did not hinder to any great degree the interchange of trade and ideas within the Peninsula or beyond.

CHAPTER 3

An interior view of the twelfth-century former synagogue in Toledo now known as Santa Maria de la Blanca. Three of the horseshoe arcades are shown supported on columns with carved capitals with designs based on pine cones tied with palm leaves. (See also pp. 74–5.)

CONFRONTATION
and the RECONQUEST

When Alfonso VI, king of León and Castile, captured Toledo from the Muslims in 1085, he found a city that had been prospering, both economically and culturally, since the beginning of the century. This was no surprise because he had spent nine months there during 1072 when he was fleeing from his brother, Sancho II, after defeat in battle. Toledo was then ruled by al-Mamoun, one of the *taifa* kings who had come to power after the disintegration of the Cordoban caliphate when al-Andalus broke up into a number of petty states based on the previous administrative districts. The rulers of these petty *taifas* sought to emulate the luxury and artistic eminence of old Córdoba.

Al-Mamoun was the most able of the *taifa* kings of Toledo and his court attained an outstanding level of culture. In 1075 he was succeeded by al-Qadir. Alfonso VI had made a secret agreement in 1082 whereby al-Qadir was to cede Toledo and the surrounding territory to him, handing over the fortifications and the royal palace undamaged, on the understanding that Alfonso would install al-Qadir as the ruler of Valencia and help him to capture Albarracín. But al-Qadir could not surrender without an honourable struggle, so Alfonso and his troops, after attacking the surrounding countryside to the north, besieged the city but allowed any Muslims to leave if they so wished.

The superior military strength of the northern Christian kingdoms was not only a consequence of the weakened condition of the Muslim states of al-Andalus, but was also due to the fact that the start of the Christian Reconquest of Spain had attracted attention from powers elsewhere, both temporal and ecclesiastical. Pope Alexander II had called on European knights to repel the Muslims from the central zone south of the Pyrenees; in this way the Reconquest was becoming a holy war. There was a particularly strong response from Burgundy and other states north of the Pyrenees. With Alfonso VI came many so-called Franks (Provençals, Burgundians and Gascons), who were the majority, but there were also English, Germans, Flemish, Normans and Lombards. Years of comparative prosperity in Northern Europe had resulted in a population increase which, combined with improvements in agricultural methods, had created urban migration. With greater peace and security came the development of religious pilgrimages to Rome, to the Holy Sepulchre at Jerusalem and to Santiago de Compostela. Economic growth followed the pilgrim routes, and the pilgrimage to Santiago brought thousands of visitors across the Pyrenees through Navarre, León and Castile. The shameful memory of the sacking of Santiago in 997 by al-Mansour and his plunder of the cathedral bells, reinforced by the complaints of the Mozarabs at the treatment that they had experienced in al-Andalus before they fled to the Christian north, must have inspired many to regard the Reconquest as an almost obligatory religious mission, similar to the First Crusade which was soon to be promoted.

The capture of Toledo had an important strategic significance: it lies at the geographical centre of the Iberian Peninsula and it represented the then southernmost extension of the Reconquest, although Huesca to the north was still occupied. It also had a powerful religious significance as the former Visigothic capital of the Peninsula. Moreover, during the 374 years of Muslim rule, there had remained a significant Mozarabic community who had maintained a religious continuity with the Visigoths but had nevertheless adopted Arabic as their normal language and were not to abandon it until the thirteenth century. The important situation of Toledo was emphasised when Alfonso VI adopted the title 'Imperator Totius Hispaniae'. He also liked to be referred to as 'Emperor of two religions' as, although there was no question of his dedication to the supremacy of both Castile and Christianity, he was prepared to be tolerant of the remaining Muslims, whose cultural development and skills were to a large extent superior to those of the invading Christians. They were granted religious freedom and allowed to keep their main mosque, but in 1086 the former Visigothic church of Santa María was reconsecrated after having served as a mosque. The Christian bishopric had until then been in the hands of the Mozarabs, but a new appointment as bishop had already been promised by Alfonso to Don Bernardo, a Cluniac monk of French origin who wished to introduce a new Roman rite. In 1088 the Pope confirmed Don Bernardo as bishop and also granted Alfonso's request that the primacy of the bishopric of Toledo be restored. At the same time the status of the Muslims was defined in that the king became directly responsible for his Muslim subjects and no Muslim could be imprisoned or sentenced to death without royal permission.

The Castilians came from a tough and inhospitable environment and had acquired a scale of values based on physical strength, personal valour and religious faith. Knight errantry of this kind was satirised some centuries later by Miguel de Cervantes in *Don Quijote de la Mancha*, whose hero is unable to face up to reality. Cervantes himself lacked confidence too, as when the first part of *Don Quijote* was published in 1605 he pretended he was not the author but had translated an Arabic account by the wise Cidi Hamete Benengeli. Most Castilians lacked the skills and aptitudes appropriate to business, economics and the crafts. In cultural matters they owed much to alien ideas.

The skills of the remaining Muslims were therefore complementary to the desired social roles of the Castilians, and it was in the king's interest to protect those who elected to stay. They did not, however, have the same legal rights as Christians and were expected to pay extra taxes as well as being debarred from holding public office. This situation they shared with the small Jewish community. Although there was tolerance of the three religions of the 'Book', discrimination was practised in favour of those who followed one, Christianity, and separate development for those who followed the others. In due course the Muslims and Jews were forced to live in separate quarters, usually outside the city walls. There were certain restrictions on their employment but the Muslims were permitted to practise their skills in the building industry as masons, carpenters and plumbers as well

The impressive fortified gateway to Toledo known as the Puerta del Sol dates from the twelfth century. It is a prominent Mudéjar structure of stone and brickwork incorporating a variety of arch types, including semicircular, horseshoe (both rounded and pointed), interlacing and multi-lobed.

as in the crafts of leather and textiles. Their expertise in agriculture and market gardening was also essential for the development of the new Christian kingdom and they were encouraged to continue in these activities.

Although it would seem from assessment of surviving tax documents that at no time did the Muslims exceed more than 5 per cent of the total population of Toledo, their influence in the shaping of the built environment was out of all proportion to their numbers. The most pressing demand for public building was the need for new churches, as Alfonso VI was content to use the existing royal palace. The clergy seemed to have had no objection to the employment of 'infidels' on the construction of buildings for Christian worship and they used materials and techniques that had been familiar to them for centuries. Now there were new necessities and different planning requirements. A Christian church has different spatial demands from those needed for a mosque. Although they both have a symbolic value, a bell-tower serves a function different from that of a minaret and requires relatively large openings at the top to allow the dissemination of the sound of the bells in all directions. The Christians had originally adopted the basilica form for their places of worship, and as the separate full-time clergy increased in number and power, so the plan lengthened in a hierarchical and directional form with the space closest to the altar reserved for the use of the clergy. French influence had led to the frequent introduction of a semi-circular apse used for ceremonial purposes and the placing of side chapels. Both the church and the mosque have a directional emphasis in the plan. The mosque interior space is relatively simple, normally wider in proportion to its length. It is frequently approached via a courtyard where a fountain is provided for the ablutions required in preparation for prayer.

In Portugal, when the Arabs settled and became the rulers, they did not impose Islam on the population, although there probably was pressure to convert during the Almoravid period. In 1147 when Lisbon was finally recaptured by the Christians, they found toleration of the three religions, and there had been no declared official religion. At first both Moors and Mozarabs were held captive but after much protest the Mozarabs were released, many deciding to flee to the north and settle in Coimbra. The Moors were expelled but the Jews were allowed to stay. In 1170 there was a charter for enfranchised Moors who were permitted to settle in a northern suburb outside the city walls and form their own community served by two mosques. This area of the city is now called the Mouraria. By the end of the century the Christians were the majority in the city proper, dominated by the former Moorish Castelo de São Jorge, and in the area at present known as the Alfama.

Because the proportion of Christians increased as the Muslim population decreased, demands for the conversion of mosques into churches followed. A surviving example in Toledo is the small church of Santo Cristo de la Luz, which as the foundation inscription reveals, had been built as a mosque in 999. In 1187 Archbishop Don Gonzalo Perez added an apse,

The church of Santo Cristo de la Luz at Toledo (see also p. 45). The original brick mosque is to the right and the Christian apse was added in 1187 to the left in a style that harmonises with it, an early example of the Mudéjar.

which continued the pattern and construction of the original – a simple brick structure with stone elements and square in plan. The arcade and friezes were replicated in the apse to create a satisfying harmony of old and new. The two-storey façade, with blind arcades of interlacing horseshoe arches and decorated brickwork above, the internal arcades and the nine square-ribbed vaults are in the Umayyad tradition of al-Hakam's extension to the Great Mosque at Córdoba. Inside there are remains of Romanesque wall paintings.

This church is probably the earliest surviving example of what is now called the Mudéjar style. The word is said to originate from the Arabic word *mudayyan* meaning 'those who have submitted', and is used by architectural historians to refer to a style that, with historical perspective, is clearly recognisable as a uniquely Iberian phenomenon. This has not been accepted without some controversy. Goitia regards it as a continuation of Islamic art in the Iberian cultural sphere after the disappearance of Islamic political power, while others have not thought it worthy of consideration as a style in

its own right but rather a perversion of the Christian styles of Romanesque and Gothic, maintaining that the Christian concept and construction have been merely decorated with bastard Islamic patterns and features. If, as Lamperez claims, style means the conformity of form with material, then Mudéjar is a recognisable way of building that was executed by assimilated Muslims and derived from Islamic precedent. It was accepted by both Christians and Jews as normal for their religious buildings, but it can be regarded as a hybrid, in that it has dual roots. This duality creates a tension which when resolved can create a true work of art.

The church of Santiago del Arrabal in Toledo is cited by Goitia as an example of perfect harmony in the Mudéjar style. The oldest part is the tower, which dates from the eleventh century and has a square plan and a central core supporting a staircase lit by very small windows in the external wall. About half-way up is a double-horseshoe-arched opening with a central marble column (*ajimez*), while its top is crowned with a pyramidal tiled roof immediately above the bell platform, which is lit by two openings with pointed arches on each of the four faces of the tower. The construction is of brick and rubble stonework with brick quoins. The main building dates from 1265 and has three naves and three apses, which have external bands of blind arcades in brickwork. The dignified use of proportion blends harmoniously with the tower, which is placed to the east of the south transept with its plain façade of rubble masonry. There is also a remarkable pulpit in the Mudéjar style.

Another early example of the Mudéjar in Toledo is the church of Santiago del Arrabal. The square bell tower dates from the eleventh century and has an ajimez *window about half-way up. The structure is random stonework with brick quoins.*

The main façade of the same church has a variety of patterned brickwork set in the random stone walling. These include horseshoe, pointed, multi-lobed and interlacing arches, as well as three circular windows.

San Román is another Mudéjar church in Toledo. It was consecrated by Archbishop Don Rodrigo Jinerez de Rada in 1221. Three naves are separated by Roman and Visigothic columns carrying wide horseshoe arches.

The roof over the central nave is supported on walls punctuated by groups of three windows each centred over an arch below. The east end was much altered in the sixteenth century, but some parts of the single apse, which is the oldest part of the church, remain. The interior is of special interest as it contains frescoed religious scenes of Romanesque character surrounded with geometrical patterns and plant motifs in stucco, suggesting Islamic precedents. The interiors of most Mudéjar churches have undergone considerable later modification so it seems probable that in their original state they contained similar paintings.

The increasing power of the Christians caused alarm amongst the *taifa* kings, and many Muslims felt that their military weakness was a consequence of too much attention to luxury and the pleasures of life. A more ascetic and strictly Islamic attitude was demanded. Help was sought from the Almoravid emir, Yusuf Tashfin, who in 1086 crossed the straits to al-Andalus, which was then united with North Africa, and a balance of power with the Christians was achieved. His subjects were Berbers from the borders of the Sahara desert, hardy nomads who practised a more austere form of Islam. By 1102, the Almoravids' rule stretched from the borders of Aragón to Senegal, and they fought many successful battles against Alfonso VI, who lost some of his reconquered territory in the south. They were never able to regain Toledo, however, which was to remain permanently in Christian hands.

Although the puritanical outlook of the Almoravids can be seen as they expressed it in the restrained and simple exteriors of the few surviving buildings of this period, Andalusian influence can be detected in the refined ornamentation of the Great Mosque at Tlemcen now in Algeria. Here there is a subtle contrast between the rounded horseshoe arches of the aisles and the transverse multifoil pointed arches leading to the *mihrab*. The multifoil arches are intricately decorated in carved stucco and in front of the *mihrab* is an elegant rib-vaulted cupola with a filigree of arabesques. These forms can be interpreted as a three-dimensional expression of the Andalusian laxity that overcame the later Almoravids. At least that appears to have been the opinion of the Almohads, the dynasty that succeeded them. The Almohads had been founded in protest; they were influenced by the mystical movement of Sufism, wished to restore what they perceived to be the true Islam and affirmed the unity of God. They took Marrakesh in 1141, established it as their capital, crossed to al-Andalus and restored order, adopting Seville as their main centre in the Peninsula in 1147.

Their approach to the design of public buildings was typified by the three splendid minarets at Marrakesh, Rabat and Seville. The celebrated minaret at Seville, by Ahmed Ibn Baso who also designed the Marrakesh minaret, was completed in 1196. It is now called La Giralda after the bronze statue of La Fé (Faith) which acts as a wind-vane at the summit of the elaborate Renaissance-style lantern, which was added in the sixteenth century to accommodate the bells of the cathedral. The former minaret is the most

La Giralda in Seville was originally the minaret to the Great Mosque that was demolished to make way for the cathedral. The Renaissance style lantern with its crowning bronze statue was added in the sixteenth century to house the bells for the cathedral.

The central section of La Giralda is part of the original minaret designed by Ahmed Ibn Baso and completed in 1196. It incorporates panels of interlacing patterned brickwork and four double-arched openings, two with cinquefoil and two with rounded horseshoe arches.

The fountain at the centre of the Patio de los Naranjos is believed to date from Visigothic times and was probably used for ablution before prayers in the days of the Great Mosque. The Mudéjar horseshoe arch of La Puerta del Perdón can be seen beyond.

A view of the Patio de los Naranjos at Seville as seen from La Giralda.

important structure from the Almohad era in Seville and constitutes the major part of La Giralda. It has a square plan and above a relatively plain lower section, each of its four faces is divided horizontally into two sets of three vertical panels. The central panel on both levels has a series of superimposed double-arched openings with columns, some of Visigothic origin. The other two panels contain elaborate interlacing brickwork with blind arcades at the base. The uppermost level, just below the Christian addition, is composed of an interlacing arcade forming a flat cornice that may have been the terminating feature of the minaret. The corners are accentuated by flat quoins in contrast to the decorated and moulded surfaces of the rest of the upper part of the tower. It is a noble and well-proportioned composition that reflects the restrained but imaginative taste of the Almohads.

In 1220, Abdallah, the governor of Seville, added some outworks to the city walls next to the Alcázar (Royal Palace). Part of this was the Torre del Oro (Tower of Gold), a tall, twelve-sided structure of uncut stone and brick with a central hexagonal staircase. It was sited on the river bank opposite another tower on the other side which has long since disappeared, and a chain was suspended between the two towers to defend the entrance to the harbour. It has a twelve-sided lantern with yet another, circular, lantern which was added in the eighteenth century. The older lantern has blind pointed horseshoe-arched windows with some remaining blue and white glazed tile decoration. Its name derives from the fact that its upper storey was once faced with golden lustre tiles. It is not only a remarkable work of fortification but a striking expression of Almohad power, and second only to La Giralda in the Seville skyline.

The Great Mosque was demolished in 1401 to make way for the largest Gothic cathedral, as well as the third largest, after St Peter's in Rome and St Paul's in London, of any style in Europe. In the centre of the *iwan*, the large entrance courtyard, now called the Patio de los Naranjos (court of

the orange trees), is a fountain which dates from Visigothic times and was used by the Muslims for ablutions before prayer. The chapel of the cathedral beside La Giralda was part of the mosque and part of its structure is of the Almohad period. There are nineteen horseshoe arches in the courtyard, which are also Almohad, but the main north gate, La Puerta del Perdón, was built later under Christian rule in Mudéjar style.

Further west at Mértola, in the Alentejo province of Portugal, which is on a spectacular hill site overlooking the Guadiana river and its small tributary the Oeiras, there is architectural evidence of the Moorish period. Remains of a Roman forum survive, and it is believed that the settlement dates originally from Phoenician times. The castle at the peak of the hill has some Visigothic elements and various later additions. The parish church, Igreja Matriz, which was formerly a mosque, has a square plan, the interior is divided by numerous columns into five aisles, and the former *mihrab* can be recognised behind the altar. The central aisle is wider than the others and both this aisle and the ridge of the double-pitched tiled roof are aligned on the axis of the central front buttress; the entrance door is immediately to the right of the buttress. The present altar and the *mihrab* are on the east, at right-angles to this axis, which appears to have been the main orientation of the church. The *mihrab*, which is believed to be from the Almohad period and has traces of a multifoil arch over it, is set within an arch with a shell pattern recessed in the wall. This wall must be very thick because there is no external trace of the *mihrab*. There are also two doorways with horseshoe arches in this wall. Later additions to the church from the Manueline period include capitals, possibly the vaulting and buttresses as well as the parapet wall. These demonstrate later oriental influence. The original minaret collapsed, and the replacement belfry is in a different position, at the corner of the main elevation.

A flying buttress which frames a rounded horseshoe-arched doorway in the former mihrab *wall of the Igreja Matriz at Mértola.*

A view of the Igreja Matriz (parish church) from the castle at Mértola in Alentejo. It was formerly a mosque and overlooks the river Guadiana on the right. The present and the former mihrab, *which is believed to date from the Almohad period, are aligned at right-angles to the ridge of the roof.*

The Ermida de la Senhora das Neves (Chapel of Our Lady of the Snows) in the architectural form of a Muslim tomb is on the summit of a hill overlooking Mértola. Immediately to the left can be seen the castle, and the church to the far left of the picture.

The Ermida de Nossa Senhora da Nazaré (Our Lady of Nazaré) at Sitio, overlooking the beach of Nazaré, also has a form similar to a Muslim tomb with its pyramidal roof over a plain cube. Its roof is faced with multi-coloured azulejo tiles.

There are also structures built within the river bed of the Guadiana that have survived from Moorish times. These are former water mills, simple stone barrel-vaulted rectangular rooms grouped where they will gain maximum benefit from the river flow. They are typical of many on this river and are submerged when the water is at its highest level in the winter. But the most striking building to show a typical and pure Moorish form is the Ermida de la Senhora das Neves (chapel of Our Lady of the Snows), which is on the summit of a hill opposite the castle. This consists of a hemispherical dome on a pure cube with vertical merlons at each of the four corners and a single doorway. The cube and the corner features are painted white, and the dome is covered with red clay tiles. If it were not for the cross surmounting the dome this could be a *qoubba* or tomb of a Muslim holy man or marabout in Morocco or Algeria. According to Georges Marçais this is a typical structure of the nomad, Arab or Berber. Another ermida or small church which shows a form similar to that of a Muslim tomb is the Ermida de Nossa Senhora da Nazaré in the village of Sitio which overlooks the fishing village and resort of Nazaré on the Atlantic coast of Portugal. It is built into a rocky escarpment so that from one side it has the appearance of a cube with a single doorway surmounted with a pyramidal roof faced with polychrome *azulejos* or tiles. This simple form is also cited by Marçais as typical of a *qoubba*. In the crypt is a small window with a spectacular view of the shore below. The chapel commemorates a miracle of Our Lady who intervened to save a hunter's life when he chased a deer over the cliff.

Seville had been an outstanding centre of culture when ruled by al-Mutamid, the *taifa* king, who was not only a poet but also a great patron of the arts. The royal palace was, no doubt, then in existence, and was later extended in the Almohad era. The present entrance to the Alcázar is the Puerta del León or Lion's Gate, so-called because of the ceramic panel, showing a heraldic lion with a cross held in its claws and a banner in its teeth, mounted

The Patio del Yeso is the oldest section of the Alcázar complex at Seville, dating from the Almohad period. The portico to one side of the patio and parallel to the rectangular central pool has an intricate display of interlacing trelliswork in stucco.

A detail of the azulejo dado of the opening archway to the Patio del Yeso with a band of interlacing geometric pattern set in a background of floral decorated multi-coloured tiles. Above the dado the wall is lined with a blind arcade and muqarnas with elaborate arabesque patterns in stucco.

over the gateway on the wall which is part of the original eleventh-century enclosure. There was a complex of prayer halls, reception rooms, baths and family quarters. Calvert believed that justice was dispensed in the Patio de la Montería and that the Patio del Yeso (gypsum plaster) is the only surviving Almohad section set amongst the later Christian additions. It is a long rectangular garden courtyard with a pool at the centre and a portico along one of the long sides which is divided into three sections. The central section consists of a single tall pointed multi-lobed arch leading to a double-horseshoe-arched opening beyond, while the other two sections each have three smaller multi-lobed arches supporting interlacing trelliswork above. This complex display of intricate modelled stucco decoration does not show the austere approach to design that might be expected from the Almohad public pronouncements on religious and other matters, but it is within the palace where some private surrender to Andalusian luxury was presumably permitted.

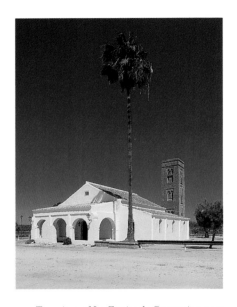

Two views of La Ermita de Cuatrovitas near Seville, originally a mosque of the Almohad period but later converted for Christian worship. Instead of accommodating the bells at the top of the brick minaret, as at La Giralda, a small arched belfry as well as a simple porch and aisles in plain Romanesque style were added.

Near Seville, a few kilometres outside Bollulos de la Mitación, there are the remains of a mosque now referred to as La Ermita de Cuatrovitas. The free-standing brick minaret is a smaller and simpler version of La Giralda, but the central columns of the double-lobed arches at the upper levels are missing. This modest and restrained treatment of the public face of the mosque is more in line with Almohad principles. The square prayer space is now used for Christian worship, and a few of the arches in the nave are horseshoe in form. The access was probably changed when it was adapted from use as a mosque and, unlike La Giralda, when a bell was added a separate structure was built in the form of an elevated brick wall with a round-arched opening for the bell and a pediment and cross above.

At the small village of Villalba del Alcor, between Seville and Huelva, there is a unique building, the parish church of San Bartolomé. It was originally constructed in the twelfth century as a fortified mosque and later converted to a church, with additions and alterations between the thirteenth

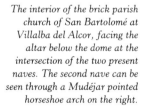

The interior of the brick parish church of San Bartolomé at Villalba del Alcor, facing the altar below the dome at the intersection of the two present naves. The second nave can be seen through a Mudéjar pointed horseshoe arch on the right.

and sixteenth centuries. The mosque was built in the Almohad manner of dignified simplicity and the later Mudéjar craftsmen have extended it in a sensitive and sympathetic way. Today the main space of the church is L-shaped, and there is a dome above the altar where the two naves intersect. The south nave was the *iwan* of the mosque, whereas both the east nave and the unifying domed space are of Mudéjar construction. The south nave is divided into seven bays by diaphragm arches. The central bay is narrower than the others and contained the *mihrab* but is now the principal entrance to the church. The Mudéjar nave is shorter and divided into four slightly wider bays. In both naves each bay is a double square and the height is twice the width of the nave. The inner side of the older nave consists of double arches opening into a patio which had previously been the ablution court-yard of the mosque.

Each nave possesses a special intimacy because it is not possible to see from one to the other but only to the altar under the dome. In this way, the Christian congregation in both naves faces the altar through a succession of arches, whereas the praying Muslims had faced the *mihrab* in a direction parallel to the spans of the arches. There is little decoration and no tracery, but there is a variety of arch types, including both rounded and pointed horseshoe and a few three-centred arches. The bell-tower, like La Giralda, is a former minaret that has been heightened to accommodate the bells with arched openings on each face and a crenellated parapet at the top. The exterior is plain except for a Gothic doorway in the east façade which is decorated with geometrically patterned *azulejos*, combined with the heraldic arms of the Archbishop Don Diego Hurtado de Mendoza dating from the end of the fifteenth century, between the *alfiz* and the arch. The oriental origin which is so evident inside is only revealed externally by one blind horseshoe arch high in the wall of the dome on the principal elevation. Here the builders did not rely on large areas of rich decoration, yet the interior is unmistakably Muslim and Mudéjar in concept.

The exterior of the same church. Originally built as a mosque in the twelfth century, it was converted into a church in the thirteenth century. A nave was added, forming an L-shaped plan with a dome over the intersection of the nave and the former iwan *of the mosque where the altar is now located. It has become an integrated composition of Almohad and Mudéjar styles with Gothic additions. There is a blind horseshoe arch high in the wall of the dome.*

The fifteenth-century Gothic arch over the doorway in the eastern façade is decorated with azulejos *in geometric patterns incorporating the heraldic arms of the then archbishop on either side.*

The revival of Muslim power meant, however, that the Mudéjars were sometimes seen as enemies within Christian society serving loyalties elsewhere. Nevertheless, their reputation for reliability and good craftsmanship must have been high, because some internal migration within Castile occurred. Some moved to Burgos and Salamanca in Old Castile to the north, where little or no Islamic influence had been experienced previously. This influence was later demonstrated in the twelfth century when the convent of Las Huelgas, near Burgos, was founded by Alfonso VIII (r. 1158–1214). Mudéjar work is evident in the interior face of the main cloister and the chapel of Santiago de la Asunción. The full complement of Islamic decoration and structure, including a timber ceiling with geometrical patterns, carved stucco vaulting, ribbed domes and multi-lobed arches, is to be found within this large complex which is predominantly designed in a style containing elements of Romanesque and Gothic.

A general view from the corner of the remains of the stone cloister of the thirteenth-century monastery of San Juan de Duero at Soria. The angled opening at the corner has a pointed horseshoe arch.

TOP
A section of the cloister with Gothic arches supported on quadruple columns with carved capitals.

BOTTOM
Another section of the cloister with an unusually simplified interlacing pointed arcade supported on pilasters with vertical fluting.

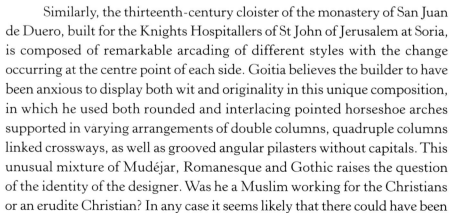

Similarly, the thirteenth-century cloister of the monastery of San Juan de Duero, built for the Knights Hospitallers of St John of Jerusalem at Soria, is composed of remarkable arcading of different styles with the change occurring at the centre point of each side. Goitia believes the builder to have been anxious to display both wit and originality in this unique composition, in which he used both rounded and interlacing pointed horseshoe arches supported in varying arrangements of double columns, quadruple columns linked crossways, as well as grooved angular pilasters without capitals. This unusual mixture of Mudéjar, Romanesque and Gothic raises the question of the identity of the designer. Was he a Muslim working for the Christians or an erudite Christian? In any case it seems likely that there could have been a collaboration between Muslim masons and Christian sculptors who carved the capitals in the Romanesque manner.

Farther west in the region of León at the small town of Sahagún is one of the finest examples of Mudéjar brickwork. It is the church of San

Lorenzo, built in the thirteenth century. It has a nave, two aisles, three apses and a transept, but the most striking feature is the huge square tower over the crossing of the nave which has four storeys of arcading. The lower two arcades are blind with rounded arches; the bottom arcade has five arches to each face while the other has four taller arches. The higher two arcades have pointed arches to the bell openings. Although the local monastery was occupied by Cluniac monks and is near the pilgrimage route to Santiago de Compostela, the building work was carried out by Moors working for the Catholic church. The plan and the use of rounded arches shows Romanesque influence which has been blended with Mudéjar brick detailing.

The Jewish community of Toledo was treated differently from the Mudéjars; because the Jews did not appear to have loyalty to an external enemy and they flourished with the king's approval, particularly in the economic field. Like the Muslims, the Jews were confined to their own quarter (Judería) and towards the end of the twelfth century they constructed a synagogue there. This was later converted to a church with the name of Santa María de la Blanca. It has five naves defined by four colonnades of rounded horseshoe arches which in turn support blind arcading above. The interior is very rich in the Mudéjar manner with a wealth of geometrical patterning and vine scrolls. The column capitals are carved in three-dimensional perforated arabesques in hard plaster with the shapes of pine cones and palm leaves.

The church of San Lorenzo at Sahagún in the region of León has a large square tower with four storeys of brick arcading constructed by Mudéjar craftsmen demonstrating Romanesque influence.

FOLLOWING PAGES
The interior of the former synagogue at Toledo known as Santa María de la Blanca. It was built at the end of the twelfth century and has remarkable carved stone capitals and incised geometric patterning and blind arcading in the parallel walls above the main horseshoe arches. (See also pp. 58–9.)

The Jews did not have a distinct architectural heritage and were content to adapt a current form for their own purposes but in a particularly rich and sophisticated way. By the twelfth century the Jewish population of Toledo had risen to 12,000, making it the most important Jewish community in the Peninsula. Another synagogue, in Segovia, had a plan similar to that in Toledo, but the interior was simpler in expression. It too was converted to Christian use under the same name of Santa María de la Blanca.

To the east and north of Toledo, the Christian kingdom of Aragón had also been expanding southwards. The only *taifa* kingdom that did not immediately submit to the Almoravids at the end of the eleventh century was Zaragoza. It was, however, absorbed by 1110, only to be captured eight years later by King Alfonso I of Aragón (r. 1104–34). In spite of its northern location, Zaragoza had been Islamicised to a considerable degree. King Pedro I of Aragón (r. 1094–1104) had also granted the remaining Muslims religious freedom and certain property rights. It would seem that a greater proportion stayed in Aragón than in Castile because it is recorded that in 1610 when they were finally expelled they constituted 15.2 per cent of the total population of Aragón. The majority were settled in rural areas where they were farmers skilled in the use of irrigation. The proportion was lower in urban centres, probably only 5 per cent in the city of Zaragoza where they were eminent in the building crafts. The Aljafería, the royal palace, became the alcázar of the Christian royal house and was a powerful influence in the shaping of attitudes to design. The sophistication of its sumptuous interior and intricately decorated surface patterns in a variety of materials, not only pleased the new occupants but set a standard by which new buildings were judged. It must have been a great contrast to the bare simplicity of the Romanesque churches of upper Aragón.

The new areas of Aragón, particularly the fertile valley of the Ebro, did not have ready access to supplies of building stone, so brick had been the normal building material since Roman times. A system of geometrical

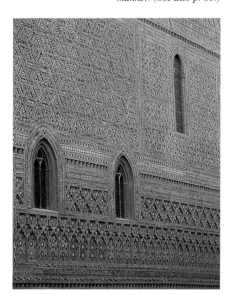

The huge area of decorated brick walling at the cathedral of La Seo at Zaragoza. It embodies interlaced brick patterning with a variety of azulejo *tiles in the Mudéjar manner. (See also p. 81.)*

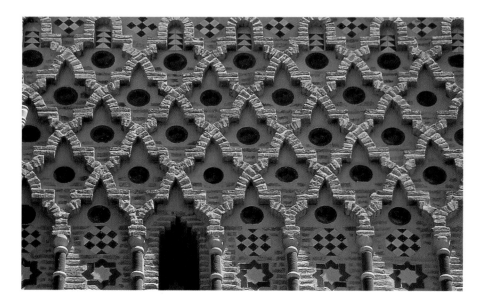

A detail of the interlaced brick patterning combined with azulejo *tiling in green and white from the bell-tower of San Salvador at Teruel. Some of the tiles are circular while others are cylindrical. (See also p. 79.)*

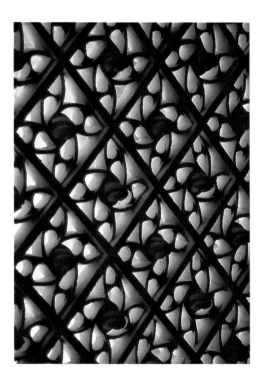 

Details of the intricate pierced fretwork of these celosia windows.

The cloister at Tarazona cathedral showing the full range of celosia windows that it contains. (See also p. 82.)

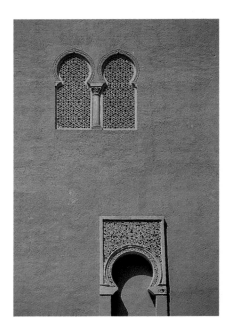

RIGHT
Geometric celosias *within an* ajimez *at high level and floral arabesques enclosed by an* alfiz *below in the entrance courtyard of the Aljafería at Zaragoza. (See also p. 50.)*

FAR RIGHT
One of the angled external walls to the apse of the church of San Pedro at Teruel. It is decorated with separate panels of brick and azulejo *patterning. The turrets are also decorated with* azulejos.

A view of the bell-tower of the church of Santo Domingo de Silos at Daroca showing the transition from ashlar stone construction with two cylindrical columns to brickwork with rectangular brick pilasters. Stone is retained only for the quoins at the higher level.

patterns was developed by the skilful manipulation of a standard brick known as the *rejola*. It was twice as long as it was wide, theoretically two hands by one hand, and approximately 35.3 cm x 16.8 cm x 4.6 cm thick. It was supplemented by a wide variety of moulded specials. In due course, glazed tiles of green, purple and brown were added to give a more colourful effect. The climate here is relatively dry, providing generous hours of sunshine which gives strong shadows to the projecting brick patterning and life to the colours of the glazed tiles. Some of the large-scale walled surfaces are so rich in effect that they seem like vast exotic hanging tapestries. Striking examples are the external wall of La Parroquieta of the cathedral of La Seo at Zaragoza and the bell-towers of Teruel. Another Islamic precedent is the pierced window made from gypsum (*celosia*) to provide ventilation and reflected light. The prototype in Aragón was probably the twin window to the upper level of the mosque in the Aljafería but the most varied Mudéjar examples are those in the cloister of the cathedral at Tarazona where there is an extensive range of geometrical and arabesque patterning.

The earliest example of Aragonese Mudéjar is to be found in Daroca, which was captured by Alfonso I of Aragón in 1120 and repopulated with Christians by him to create a bastion against the Muslims to the south. The tower of the church of Santo Domingo de Silos, at Daroca, was initially built from stone but was completed in brickwork to imitate stone forms. It has a square plan and each face is divided into three bays separated by two small stone columns at the base. These columns convert into rectangular pilasters when the wall changes to brickwork at a higher level. At mid-height there are double windows with interlacing arches but the tower is crowned with a projecting roof supported on a cornice of small superimposed arches of Romanesque precedent.

Teruel is the city with the most spectacular display of Aragonese Mudéjar architecture. The oldest of the famous towers, all of which are square in plan and of exceptional height, is that of the cathedral of Santa María de Mediavilla. It was built in 1257 and the four walls have a rich patterning of projecting brick and coloured glazed medallions. At the top of the tower there are two double-arched openings on each face. Above these are

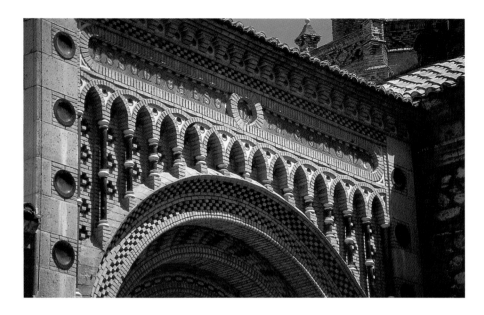

The square bell-tower of the Mudéjar cathedral of Santa Maria at Teruel is surmounted with an octagonal lantern.

The portal of the same cathedral was added in the early twentieth century in an attempt to match the Mudéjar style, without creating an exact reproduction of existing elements of the cathedral. (See pp. 200–1.)

The bell-tower of San Salvador at Teruel spans the street below with its magnificent array of brick and azulejo patterns.

superimposed two quadruple-arched openings. There is a massive brick cornice and the tower is surmounted by an octagonal lantern with openings for the bells. This is, in turn, crowned with a smaller hexagonal lantern and finial. At the lower level there is a blind arcade of interlacing rounded arches and above this arcade are two recessed arched openings. Within the cathedral is a beautiful painted *artesonado* ceiling over the nave. It is in three planes, the central section being horizontal while the others slope with the pitch of the roof. Immediately below are huge tie beams spanning the full width of the nave. The ceiling and beams are decorated with geometrical strapwork combined with a variety of paintings representing hunting scenes, celebrated figures of valour, artists, potters and other craftsmen at work. Carpenters and wood carvers are shown in the shaping of the roof structure and ceiling on which their portraits are painted. The cathedral was extended with a new transept and polygonal chapel at the east end in 1335, the work of a Moor, Yusuf of Zaragoza. The crossing of the nave and transept was completed in 1538 with a dome similar to the one at La Seo at Zaragoza. Three hundred years of developments in the Mudéjar style are to be seen in this unique building.

The bell-towers of Teruel, including that of the cathedral, have one special characteristic in common; they were built over the street, each allowing passageway through two wide pointed archways with parallel thick walls on either side to take the weight of the structure above. The towers of San Martín and El Salvador appear slightly taller than those of the cathedral and San Pedro and are believed to have been derived from earlier structures.

The tower of San Martín with similar pointed archways at the base closes the vista along a street in Teruel but is actually free standing. It also has an impressive succession of brick and azulejo panels.

RIGHT
A detailed view of brick and azulejo panels and arches at the middle level of the tower of San Martín at Teruel. Unfortunately much of the cylindrical and flat tiling is missing.

FAR RIGHT
The arched bell openings in the tower of San Salvador with the incredibly rich variety of brick and azulejo patterning below.

There is a traditional story that two leading Mudéjar architects of the region, called Omar and Abdala, as they were strolling through the Moorish quarter, were having a friendly discussion about the proposal of the Christians to erect two towers which would be the pride of the city. The choice of designer was to be decided by competition. At that moment, an upper window opened to reveal the face of the beautiful Zorayda and both men immediately fell in love with her. Some days later, Omar was awarded the contract for the tower of San Martín while Abdala was given the contract for the tower of San Salvador. Time passed and the two young rivals in love pursued their case with Mohammed, the father of Zorayda. He decided to settle the question by saying that the one who first completed the most beautiful tower should have the hand of Zorayda. They rushed to finish their building at speed, but both put up screens to hide their work from their rival. Omar managed to finish first by working day and night. His tower was much admired for its beauty but then it was noticed that it was leaning to one side. Omar, deeply upset by his failure as a practical constructor, climbed to the top of the tower and crying out Zorayda's name, preferring death to a life without honour or love, jumped to his death. Later Abdala completed the tower of San Salvador and because it was both beautiful and vertical was allowed to marry Zorayda. Each tower is distinctive in its use of Mudéjar decorative elements, and they dominate the urban landscape, giving the city an individual exotic quality.

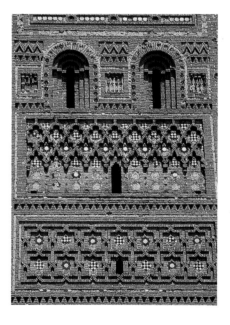

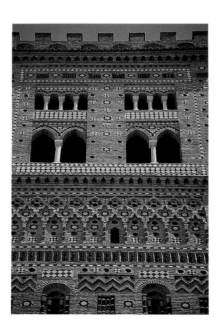

Alfonso I had wanted to rid Valencia and other eastern ports of the Muslims so that the Aragonese could set sail to Jerusalem for the Holy Crusade. Alfonso II (r. 1162–96) saw Teruel as the strategic key to the conquest of the Levant. Although the original settlement seems to date from before the Reconquest, it was probably only a small village of potters benefiting from the nearby seam of red clay before Alfonso II chose the ridge of high ground on which to build his garrison city with walled fortifications. It was a new frontier town built from almost nothing. Separate quarters for the Mudéjar and Jewish minorities were established, with seven parishes, within the walls. There were therefore seven churches, one mosque and one synagogue. The potteries continued to provide an important activity and the manufacture of bricks and tiles was dominated by the Mudéjars who were also farmers, gardeners, butchers, shopkeepers, smiths, shoemakers and medical doctors. The Jews were not engaged in agriculture but were also active in trade and medicine. Their special role was in business, and the first bank in Teruel was founded by a Jewish family. The techniques used in ceramics had been introduced by the Arabs and the red clay, containing iron oxide, when fired with a transparent lead glaze produces a strong and lively red-brown (*royo*), typical of the simple traditional pottery still made for domestic purposes. The colours of the ceramic tiles, cylinders and medallions used to decorate the walls of the bell-towers were olive green (produced with copper oxide), dark purple (manganese oxide) and red-brown. White and green were used in the two later towers, San Martín and San Salvador, but for some reason the dark purple was discontinued. A small proportion of tin was added to the lead glaze to produce a brilliant opaque white, and tiles in the shape of an eight-pointed star were introduced.

Mudéjar builders were also active in Zaragoza. The construction of the church of San Pablo was started during the second half of the thirteenth century, and its tower follows the usual Aragonese model except that it is octagonal in plan, has an uncharacteristic plain treatment to the lower half and is terminated with a pointed timber roof. The main body of the church is composed of three naves, with additional side chapels on both flanks, resulting in a complicated plan and many geometrical variations. Another Mudéjar church in Zaragoza is Santa María Magdalena, which dates from the fourteenth century, but only the tower and the apse survive from that period. The tower is in its original state, still decorated in its brick and vivid green and white ceramics.

The most important building in Zaragoza at that time was the cathedral church of La Seo. Its construction began in the fourteenth century on the site of an early Christian church which had been converted to a mosque during the Islamic period. It is predominantly Gothic in style but it has some important Mudéjar features. Benedict XIII, the antipope at Avignon, a member of the Luna family, originated from the valley of the Jalón in Aragón and was an important patron. He employed Mahoma Rami, a Mudéjar, as his master of works for the additions to La Seo as well as at the church of San Pedro Mártir at Calatayud and another at Cervera de la Canada. The magnificent patterning of brick and coloured ceramics to the exterior wall of La Parroquieta, already mentioned, was also applied to the exterior of the apse. The dome suffered structural failure in 1498 and was subsequently completely reconstructed under the supervision of Juan

By contrast the bell openings in the tower of the cathedral of Santa María at Teruel are framed by a relatively simple arrangement of azulejo decoration but some of the tiles are coloured purple, a colour that was later discontinued.

A close-up of the brick and azulejo of the external wall of the cathedral of La Seo at Zaragoza. The heraldic shield with a crescent moon at its centre is the emblem of Pedro de Luna (Benedict XIII), the first archbishop. (See also p. 76.)

RIGHT
*The exterior of a single bay
of the cloister at the
cathedral of Tarazona
showing the range of
patterns in the pierced
stucco windows.
(See p. 77.)*

FAR RIGHT
*A detail of one of many
patterns used in the pierced
windows in the cloister at
Tarazona.*

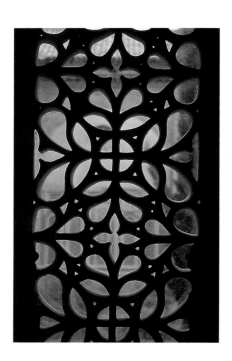

Botero, a master-mason who was assisted by Mudéjar masons. It consists of an octagonal lantern supported on arches spanning a large octagonal opening in the form of four sets of double parallel ribs. This type of construction derives from Islamic precedent and follows the Mudéjar approach to the original problem. It was used as a model by Juan Botero for the domes of the cathedrals at Teruel and Tarazona, where he adopted a more complicated solution which produced a particularly beautiful silhouette. The cloister at Tarazona Cathedral is another outstanding example of Mudéjar craftsmanship. The windows facing the courtyard have a series of pointed brick arch frames separated by decorated brick buttresses. Each frame is divided horizontally into two panels, the lower consisting of an elaborate tracery of gypsum plaster and stone contained within five vertical semicircular arched windows, the central one being wider and taller than the others. The space above the four shorter windows is filled with square windows with similar tracery. The upper panel is solid but pierced with a roundel window with two small vertical rectangular windows on either side. The design of this cloister is unique.

Many churches were built in the Mudéjar manner in Aragón between the thirteenth and sixteenth centuries. The majority had a single nave, a polygonal apse, side chapels and a characteristic bell-tower of decorated brickwork which is a special feature in the landscape of the prosperous agricultural valleys of the rivers Ebro and Jalón. The tower at Tauste is 72 metres high and has recently been restored. It has an octagonal plan and is of particular elegance and beauty. Two towers at Calatayud, San Andrés and Santa María la Mayor, also have octagonal plans but with the corners strengthened and visually accentuated. A vertical pilaster is used at San Andrés while Santa María la Mayor has a bolder modelled buttress at each corner. The most elaborate example is to be found at Utebo. Known as the 'Campanario

FAR LEFT
The handsome octagonal brick bell-tower of the church of Santa María at Tauste. It is 72 metres high and has recently been restored. The panels of decorative brickwork are typical of many examples of Aragonese Mudéjar church towers.

LEFT
The brick tower of Santa María la Mayor at Calatayud also has an octagonal plan but with bold modelled buttresses at the corners. There are many intricate brick panels in the wall faces and the tower is crowned with a steeple which has a metal-covered roof shaped in a Baroque manner.

de los Espejos' (Bell-tower of Mirrors), because of its profusion of glazed tile decoration, it is octagonal in form but rises from a square base, severely classical in expression. Above this, three octagonal storeys with buttresses at every corner are set back at each level. A variety of pattern and shape of opening is expressed in an uninhibited way, resulting in a highly modelled and richly decorated composition of great vigour.

Although their influence in architectural design persisted, the social and political situation of the Mudéjars steadily worsened in Aragón and Castile. Proselytism by Muslims was forbidden and any Christian becoming a Muslim was liable to the death penalty, whereas Muslims were encouraged to convert to Christianity. From 1242 the mendicant orders in Aragón were given permission to make as many conversions of Muslims and Jews as possible. The practice of Islam was tolerated for the time being as long as it was not public, and there were only small and discreetly sited mosques. Two have survived, at Tortoles (a suburb of Tarazona) and Torrellas. In Portugal a law was passed in 1366 allowing sentence of death on any Moor who was caught receiving a Christian woman. In Spain, mixing within households was not supposed to happen but there are descriptions in the fifteenth century of Jews and Mudéjars acting as servants in Christian homes and taking meals with Christians. Muslims were expected to avoid anything that would make them conspicuous, such as bright colours, luxurious materials like furs or silks and the wearing of jewels, gold or silver – in fact anything that could imply social distinction or any appearance that could indicate that they were above their 'station' in life. Later they were expected to carry the distinguishing sign of a blue *luneta* (crescent) on their right shoulder. In Portugal, from 1468 onwards, Moors were required to wear special clothing, open cowls and red crescent badges. The Jews were treated better, having been allowed to stay in their own quarter and possess

Moorish slaves, but were nevertheless expected to wear a distinguishing star on the breast.

That the Mudéjars were in a state of cultural assimilation is illustrated by the development of a dialect of Castilian Spanish which was written in Arabic script called Aljamiada. It was used by Castilian-speaking Muslims who were illiterate in Latin script but had been educated in the remaining Quranic schools using the Quran and other literature in Arabic script. These books were imported from Islamic countries with which contact was still maintained. All kinds of texts were translated into Aljamiada, maintaining the phonetics of Castilian, and it continued in use until the seventeenth century. It even persisted for one or two generations after immigration to Tunisia, where many Muslim refugees from Aragón eventually settled.

The economic situation in Aragón had fluctuated from the beginning of the twelfth century when Alfonso I had expanded his territory to the south. Repopulation of the Ebro valley had been interrupted by the political crisis that followed his death in 1134, but the marriage of Petronilla, Queen of Aragón, to Ramón Berenguer IV, count of Barcelona, and the consequent union of Aragón and Catalonia heralded a new phase of economic expansion. Barcelona became the port for increased overseas trade through the Mediterranean and the subsequent acquisition of territory to the east – first Sicily, then Sardinia and Corsica. There was, later, a slow decline in trade. The conquest of Valencia by Jaime I of Aragón in 1238 created another centre of attraction for settlers from the Christian north. The fertile irrigated land, or *huertas*, in the surrounding areas of Valencia, which had produced crops of sugar, rice and fruit, needed labour to replace those Muslims who had fled, although some stayed and worked successfully with the newcomers, many of whom came from Aragón.

In spite of the centuries of Islamic rule in Valencia there is little or no architectural evidence surviving from this period. All new buildings were in the Gothic style, and the only Mudéjar craft skills that were fully developed were ceramics and carpentry. The timber roof of the Capilla del Cristo de la Pas de Godella, near Valencia, is an example of Mudéjar carpentry. It is supported on rafters sitting on large purlins which rest on a series of diaphragm arches spanning the single nave. An unusual feature of this ceiling is the formation of a horizontal section (*alminate*) below the intersection of the purlins at the ridge. This is achieved with a series of small tie beams joined to the rafters with another series of beams at right angles, thus forming a grid which sits on a double row of elaborately carved brackets. The overall effect is of three planes of rectangular coffers finished with multi-coloured decoration incorporating geometrical patterns, floral motifs, exotic animals and Christian heraldry. Many of these themes were used in the ceramics produced in the celebrated potteries at Manises.

In the meantime, Córdoba, which had been the capital of Muslim Spain for over three centuries, declined politically and was incorporated in the *taifa* kingdom of Seville. The intellectual life of the city nevertheless continued to flourish. Ibn Rushd (1126–98), born there and known as Averroës in the Latin languages, was a celebrated scholar and polymath (physicist, astrologer, mathematician, philosopher and doctor) who did much to bring the teaching of Aristotle to Europe but the king, Yacoub al-Mansour, a doctrinaire Muslim and opposed to his theories, prevented him from teaching. A contemporary was Maimonides (1135–1204), the Jewish scholar who became famous for his wide learning in medicine, theology and philosophy. He wrote in Arabic and his works included his *Guide to the Perplexed*. He later went to Cairo, where he became personal physician to the great Saladin, the conqueror of Jerusalem, and taught at the Ibn Ezra synagogue in Fustat. An inscription (*mezuzah*) was placed on the jamb of the entrance doorway to the former synagogue in 1985 to celebrate the 850th anniversary of the birth of a worthy son of Córdoba.

The Jewish community, though small in number, was important in business and the professions and remained so after the Reconquest. The synagogue was built in 1315 by Isaac Mejeb. It is modest in size and almost square in plan, with a rich interior in Mudéjar style. There is a gallery with three large openings intended for the use of women, and in the centre of the east wall the position of the tabernacle is suggested by a recess. A niche in the west wall opposite is crowned with a multi-lobed arch. The upper sections of the walls are decorated with elaborate arabesque patterns in carved gypsum which were originally painted in a variety of primary hues. There are Hebrew inscriptions, carved in the stucco of all four walls, consisting of quotations from the Psalms and one recording the name of the founder and the year of construction. The lower parts are now of rough brickwork but H. A. Meek suggests that these might originally have been decorated with tiles.

The eastern migration of Maimonides shows that contact between the Muslim states in the Mediterranean was close and was no doubt strengthened by the third Crusade, which was initiated in 1189. This was followed six years later by a campaign against the Muslims in the Iberian Peninsula which was part of a wider confrontation in Europe, Asia and Africa. The southwards pressure of the Christian crusade, combined with the dwindling power of the Almohads, led to the defeat of the Muslims at the battle of Las Navas de Tolosa by Alfonso VIII of Castile in 1212. This altered the balance of power in the Iberian Peninsula for good, and the Christian ascendancy was never to be seriously challenged again. Among the many treasures now on display at the royal monastery at Las Huelgas, near Burgos, the old capital of Castile, is the beautiful multi-coloured embroidered banner of the Miramolin which was captured during this battle. There can be few such exquisite works of art created solely as a military symbol. The Muslims in the south continued to lose territory to Castile, Aragón and Portugal. Córdoba was lost in 1236 and, finally, Seville in 1248 to Castile, while the forces of Aragón continued their advance down the east coast, reaching Alicante in 1266. By far the largest area had been gained by the Castilians and, in 1246, the Muslim kingdom of Granada was allowed by Ferdinand III to continue in a form of semi-independence as a vassal state of Castile.

Another magnificent example of Mudéjar design for the royal house of Castile that is entirely oriental in concept and construction is the Capilla Real (Chapel Royal) which was built within the Great Mosque at Córdoba in 1258–60. It is difficult to imagine that it was built for a devout Catholic king, Alfonso X (1252–84), for whose burial it was intended. The only clue to its Christian origin lies in the display of some heraldic shields and emblems. It is square in plan and covered by a dome that is typically Almohad in form and supported on eight arches the profile of which is serpentine. Otherwise, the arrangement is similar to the dome of al-Hakam II (see p. 37). Every surface of the walls and dome is covered with rich interlacing decoration in carved stucco, a precursor of the wonderful filigree work of the Alhambra a century later. There seems little doubt that the chapel was designed and executed by Mudéjars who had stayed in Córdoba. Their work harmonises well with the previous construction of the Cordoban caliphate and presumably pleased the Christians (at least for a century or two) because later kings of Castile, Ferdinand IV and Alfonso XI, were also buried there.

A detail of the stucco work and azulejo *dado in the Capilla Real (Royal Chapel) in the former mosque at Córdoba. This was built by the Christian King Alfonso X in a more complicated version of the style of the earlier Muslim dynasty. (See also p. 43.)*

CHAPTER 4

Geometric patterns based on the eight-pointed star produced by a grid of horizontal, vertical and diagonal white glazed strips with the interstices filled with a variety of coloured cut azulejos. This type of mosaic was frequently used for the surface of dados in Moorish and Mudéjar buildings. These two examples are from the Alcázar in Seville.

COEXISTENCE and CULTURAL INTERACTION

Castile became the most flourishing cultural centre of medieval Europe and Toledo was a great attraction for scholars from the new centres of knowledge at Paris, Bologna, Oxford and the expanding cities of the German states. Ferdinand III (r. 1217–52) encouraged the interaction of the three religious cultures, particularly in literature and philosophy. Much of the ancient knowledge of the Greeks and Romans had been translated into Arabic when the Greek philosophers left Alexandria for Damascus and Baghdad. The Arabic had been translated into Latin, which was the official language in Toledo and of the rest of the Christian areas of the Peninsula. Ferdinand's son, Alfonso X (known as 'the Wise', r. 1252–84), however, made Castilian the official language and established the celebrated School of Translators. Scientific knowledge increased, especially in mathematics, astronomy, geography and medicine. Poetry and music were promoted at the royal court and Alfonso himself compiled 417 melodies under the title *Cantigas de Santa María*. They divided into two groups, the first consisting of narratives describing the miracles of the Virgin Mary and the second was made up of songs in her honour. The sources were troubadour songs, often from the Provençal, traditional airs sung by pilgrims and some melodies specially composed by Alfonso and his minstrels. They demonstrate the influence of Arabic culture in the verse form, the style and lively rhythm of the music and the form of the instruments used to play it. In his dress, Alfonso favoured the rich Oriental textiles and was portrayed in a contemporary manuscript wearing Arab costume while playing chess, a game of Arab origin. The prominence of mathematics was the research background to the development of sophisticated geometrical patterns in brickwork, carved stone, stucco, glazed tiles, mosaic, timber and all kinds of inlaid work carried out by Muslim craftsmen. In carpentry, craftsmen created *artesonado* patterned ceilings with increased intricacy and skill. The art of calligraphy, which is so important in Islamic culture, was extended to Latin, Castilian and

The opulent artesonado *ceiling to the former synagogue of El Tránsito in Toledo. The horizontal surface is decorated with geometric patterns based on the eight-pointed star while the sloping planes have narrow panels created by the exposed rafters. Double horizontal tie beams are exposed and decorated while below them is a continuous band of Hebrew calligraphy which runs above an arcade of multi-lobed pointed arches.*

Hebrew, and was used extensively for inscriptions on public buildings. In pottery the range of colours widened leading to a growing use of glazed tiles.

The Jewish community in Toledo continued to prosper and a splendid proof of this was the building in 1366 of the Sinagoga del Tránsito by Samuel Levi, the treasurer of King Pedro I, 'the Cruel', (r. 1350–69) and a member of a prominent Jewish family. The interior of the temple, a clear rectangular space, is richly decorated in the Moorish style. There is a gallery for the use of women along the south wall. The niche at the centre of the opposite wall has a triple arcade on slim columns marking the position of the ark; here stood the altar when the former synagogue was used as a church after the expulsion of the Jews in 1492 (this has now been removed). Above

The intricate stucco decoration to the ark wall of the Tránsito synagogue.

the arcade is a stucco panel composed of elaborate curvilinear patterns in relief, and at a high level, just below the ceiling, is a pair of windows. On either side of the niche are inscriptions on the panels: one embodies a shield featuring a castle and a lion, which symbolise Castile and León and the associated royal protection it was hoped it would bring. There are two friezes in Hebrew calligraphy bearing quotations from the Psalms, one immediately below the ceiling and the other below a continuous arcade of multifoil arches on double columns. Some of these arches are blind while others act as window frames. Below the lower frieze is a continuous panel of floral arabesque patterns as well as inscriptions in Arabic, heraldic shields and quotations from the Hebrew Bible, as if to make an historic gesture to *convivencia*. Tragically, this hope was to prove too optimistic because Levi was later executed by Pedro I and his wealth confiscated. The ceiling is an elaborate sloping version of *artesonado* with geometrical patterning below a double pitched roof supported by timber trusses with exposed and decorated double-tie beams.

A frieze of complex curvilinear and vegetal themes with bands of Hebrew calligraphy above and below.

The austere exterior of the Tránsito synagogue at Toledo is in complete contrast to the luxurious surfaces of the interior.

The Jews did not have a recognisable architectural heritage. They were content to follow current trends and used them with great skill and sophistication. A typical synagogue in the Peninsula was a relatively simple building from the outside and one that did not need a tall structure equivalent to the minaret or bell-tower. The main temple space was usually a rectangle or square in plan which was approached through a vestibule. It contained a raised dais with a lectern for the reading of the Torah. The floor level of the temple was required to be no higher than the street. This helped to reduce the apparent bulk, as seen from outside, in accordance with the desire to avoid an overbearing presence in the urban fabric. The Jews shared many elements of Moorish culture, often preferring reading or writing in Arabic to Latin. The Talmud calls for both a ban on the visual representation of the human form and the segregation of the sexes in the place of worship. A special gallery for the use of women was often provided, as in the Tránsito at Toledo.

There had been a Jewish community in Tomar in Portugal from the early years of the fourteenth century, and it came to prominence during the following century. A synagogue, which is believed to have been built between 1430 and 1460, survives and is currently used as a Luso-Hebraic museum. Externally, it is indistinguishable from other houses in the streetscape of the old Jewish quarter. Internally, it is very simple with plain stone walls, square in plan and roofed with stone Gothic vaulting supported on four columns symmetrically placed with carved stone capitals of simple leaf patterns. These are the only decorated features in an austere space which is in complete contrast to the rich interior of the Tránsito in the Moorish style. It has a remarkable characteristic in the provision of acoustic devices to increase the reverberation time and volume of the voices of the cantor and congregation. These are in the form of earthenware pots embedded high in the wall plaster at the corners, with the neck openings exposed. It could have been used as a place of worship for only a relatively short period because of the edict of 1496, issued by King Manuel I (r. 1495–1521) at the insistence of his wife, Isabella of Castile, that all Jews must convert to Christianity or leave Portugal by October 1497. In the sixteenth century it was converted into a prison and was later used as a warehouse. Only in the early 1920s was its original function revealed, and it was then classified as a national monument.

Valencia was taken by the forces of Aragón under James I in 1238 after a period of uncertainty that followed the rule of Rodrigo Diaz, whose legendary name was 'El Cid'. Gothic then became the predominant architectural style in Valencia and Islamic influence in architecture quickly faded. In agriculture the situation was different. The intensive system of irrigation introduced by the Arabs has lasted to today and the area continues to be famous for its abundant production of oranges. The strict rules governing the timing and the flow of water in the irrigation channels are the same as in Moorish times.

Ten years later Seville was captured by the Christians under Ferdinand III. While ruled by the Berber regime of the Almohads, it had for a time enjoyed a reputation in the arts and science that rivalled that of Córdoba. The Patio del Yeso at the Alcázar dates from that period. Seville continued in importance for at least two centuries, first under Alfonso X, and then under Pedro I (r. 1350–69) who remodelled the Alcázar using craftsmen and materials from Granada, which was still under the Muslim rule of the Nasrids. Mohammed I, the founder of this dynasty, had come to power in the city and province in 1231, and its long survival until 1492 as an independent Muslim entity was due to the persistent rivalry between the Christian kingdoms of Castile and Aragón. Many of the Muslim elite of Seville fled to North Africa, including the forebears of the North African historian, Ibn Khaldoun, who settled in Tunis.

The upper level of the central section of the façade has a unique frieze of Kufic calligraphy that runs horizontally above the three cinquefoil-arched widows. Some of the vertical strokes of the letters are crossed with horizontal bars. These bars have no significance in Arabic and are believed to represent the Christian cross.

The elevation of the Alcázar palace at Seville that faces the Patio de la Montería is divided into three distinct sections. The central section with the main entrance is surmounted with projecting eaves and a roof pavilion.

Pedro I first rebuilt the Sala de Justicia in the Alcázar in a more lavish version of the Almohad Patio del Yeso with a beautiful *artesonado* ceiling in geometrical patterns before turning his attention to the larger complex centred on the Patio de las Doncellas (Maids of Honour) which is the most luxurious example of Mudéjar architecture. The Alcázar has been used by the royal family of Spain since the time of Pedro, and there have been additions and alterations to the palace over the centuries. Sufficient remains, however, of the Mudéjar work to show the unity of the king's apartments, which he shared with his mistress, María de Padilla. The main two-storey façade to the entrance courtyard, the Patio de la Montería, is divided into three and the entrance doorway is in the central section, which has overhanging eaves. The simple horizontal arched door opening is flanked by two blind multifoil arches with elaborate tracery. At first-floor level there is a central window composed of three cinquefoil arches and two double-arched windows on either side. Below the eaves is a horizontal panel in blue and white glazed tiles which form an inscription in Arabic written in angular Kufic script. This reads: 'There is no victor but Allah'. Some of the vertical strokes have a superfluous horizontal bar at the top, thus forming a cross, presumably to please the Christian king who could not read Arabic. Another horizontal inscription in Latin script flatteringly praises the king in Spanish and records the date of the reconstruction, 1364. Above this panel there is a cornice and a blind arcade of lobed arches on double columns. The two outer sections of the façade consist of open arcades at both floor levels. The entry is indirect in that the visitor must turn at right-angles before proceeding further into the building. This is an Islamic tradition to maintain privacy and avoid the possibility of direct vision into the house from outside. It also has an advantage from the point of view of security and defence.

A corridor off the small entrance vestibule leads to the arcade of one of the shorter sides of the Patio de Doncellas, opposite the arched opening to the Salón de los Embajadores (Hall of the Ambassadors) at the far side. The patio has arcades on all four sides and a fountain in the centre. The upper floor was added in the sixteenth century in a simplified Renaissance style that attempts to match the elegance of the lower storey. The lower arcades are composed of pointed multifoil arches on double columns with the central arch being taller and stilted. The Salón de los Embajadores is square in plan with triple rounded horseshoe-arched openings into the adjoining royal apartments, one of which, opposite the patio, is known as the Comedor de Felipe II (Hall of the Ceiling of Philip II). It is a long rectangular space and its ceiling is vaulted and composed of coffers containing a variety of geometrical patterns. It was designed by Martin Infante, a master-carpenter of the late sixteenth century.

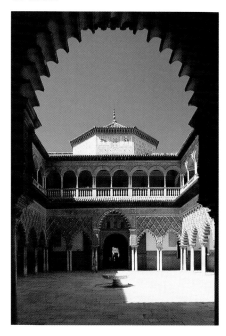

The Patio de las Doncellas in the Alcázar at Seville. The central fountain is framed by the main multifoil arches of the arcade.

The magnificent Salón de los Embajadores within the Alcázar at Seville. The view through the triple horseshoe opening is of the Dormitorio de Felipe II and the Patio de las Muñecas beyond.

Another space, the Dormitorio de Felipe II (Bedroom of Philip II), opens into a small courtyard which is called the Patio de las Muñecas (Patio of the Dolls) named after the tiny medallion doll faces at the spring of one of the smaller arches of the arcade. This patio was the centre of the living

The later additions above the Patio de las Muñecas restrict the natural light reaching this small courtyard, which was the nucleus of the private royal apartments.

quarters of the royal household and its proportions were changed in the nineteenth century by the addition of a second storey. A passageway leads from this patio to the entrance vestibule to allow informal family access. On the axis of one of the short sides of the patio is a room which connects with the Dormitorio de los Reyes Moros (Dormitory of the Moorish Kings), an elongated rectangle with openings on one of the long sides to the Patio de las Doncellas and on the other to a smaller bedroom. The main space has an exceptionally beautiful wooden ceiling with geometrical patterns, and doors, carved with plant motifs by artists from Toledo, which are designed to fold back against the wall to give the effect of a beautiful tapestry but with interlacing arabesques in wood. Another long rectangular room known as the Salón del Principe (Hall of the Prince) opens off the long side of the Patio de las Muñecas opposite the Dormitorio de Felipe II.

The domed ceiling over the Salón de los Embajadores is a masterpiece of Mudéjar carpentry. It was made by Diego Ruiz in 1427 from interlocking timber sections with complicated geometrical patterns in the form of a hemisphere (or half-orange, as it is known in Spanish) which is supported on interlocking timber *muqarnas* (stalactites). The innumerable polychrome facets of the domed surface catch and reflect the light, suggesting the stars in the heavens.

The quality of the workmanship of those parts of the palace built during the time of Pedro I is quite overwhelming. The craftsmen were the best available and came from Seville and Toledo as well as those from Granada sent by Mohammed V, who is said to have been a friend of King Pedro. The standard of the Mudéjar work of the later monarchs, until the time of Philip II, was also maintained to a high degree. The complete repertoire of Moorish finishes and materials, especially the *azulejos*, the carved plasterwork and the magnificent joinery was used lavishly throughout the Mudéjar sections of the palace, but with the degree of control and discipline necessary to prevent the effect descending to the level of garish vulgarity reached by some workers in later centuries when they tried to emulate the glories of the Alcázar and the Alhambra.

There can be little doubt that Pedro I appreciated the aesthetic qualities and the outstanding skills that were exercised on his behalf. Like Alfonso X, he valued the Moorish heritage; indeed he was accused of being a lover of Moors by his political enemies during his lifetime, and this accusation was even maintained after his death by his successors from the house of Trastámara. They alleged too that he was the son of a Jewess, and his employment of Jewish administrators was resented by the Christian petty bourgeoisie. He also appears to have been unscrupulous and bloodthirsty as his nickname, 'the Cruel', implies. Apart from the killing of Samuel Levi, as already mentioned, he is credited with the deaths of his half-brother, Fadrique, and a guest from Granada, Abu Said, who was killed for his jewels, one of which – a ruby – is believed to have been presented by Pedro to the Black Prince of England. It now adorns the imperial crown of the United Kingdom.

Another Pedro, Pedro IV of Aragón (r. 1336–87), was also deeply interested in Moorish art, architecture, poetry and science. He was nicknamed 'the Ceremonious' and even appeared at court in oriental dress but was ambitious at the expense of Castile. He intrigued on behalf of Enrique of Trastámara, the bastard half-brother of Pedro I. This struggle between the two rivals involved France and other European countries, including England whose Governor of Aquitaine, the Black Prince, was directly implicated in the complex negotiations, no doubt the explanation of the gift from Pedro I. It all ended with the murder of Pedro I himself, but not before he had completed the transformation of the Alcázar at Seville. This was done at a time following the Black Death and the consequent European economic depression and when, in spite of the war between Castile and Aragón which was devastating the frontier regions to the north, some of the most beautiful buildings in the world were being created in Andalusia in cooperation between theoretical enemies.

The successors to the Almohads in North Africa, the Marinids, a dynasty of Berber origin, few in number and without an overriding religious drive, had made Fez their capital. In the thirteenth century they laid out a new city alongside the old, where they established the royal palace. This is

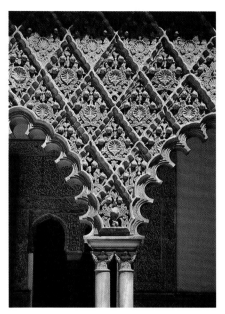

A detail of the richly decorated stucco work above a multi-lobed arcade in the Patio de las Doncellas in the Alcázar at Seville. The panels are centred on a shell motif while the arabesque in the panel above the double capitals rises from a clenched fist.

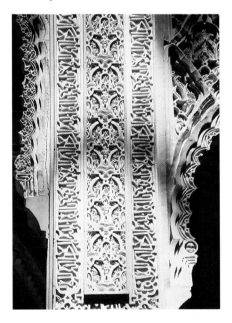

A detail of calligraphy enclosing a vertical band of interlacing arabesques above one of the columns in the Patio de las Muñecas.

FAR LEFT
The domed ceiling of the square Salón de los Embajadores is a multifaceted hemisphere mounted on a support of interlocking muqarnas. This masterpiece of sophisticated joinery, made by Diego Ruiz in 1427, matches the splendour of the stucco walls below.

now a huge complex with the addition of many later palaces and pavilions. The Marinids had invaded al-Andalus in 1275 but never succeeded in expanding their territory there in spite of a long military campaign. They were eventually defeated by the Christians at the battle of Rio Salado in 1340 and never attempted to intervene again but continued to maintain close relations with the Nasrid court at Granada.

Their attitude to religion and architecture was far less puritanical than that of their predecessors and they built many elaborate mosques and madrassas (religious colleges). The most celebrated example is the Bou Inania Madrassa in Old Fez. It was planned around a paved marble courtyard with a fountain at the centre for ablutions; the prayer hall takes up one side, the other three consisting of cloisters where student rooms were arranged both at ground and first-floor levels. At the centres of two sides are square lecture halls which rise two storeys high and are approached from the cloister corridors through pointed horseshoe arches. This courtyard layout also became the norm for the colleges of European universities, a chapel taking the place of the prayer hall.

Almohad restraint was abandoned and Andalusian luxury reasserted itself with the elegant use of repetitive patterns worked into many contrasting materials, as well as flowing calligraphy set into glazed tiles. The workmanship is superb, the proportions are perfect and the balance between the vigorous colouring of the glazed tiles and the textures of natural cedar wood, stone and carved plaster is exactly judged. Here was a perfect environment for study and contemplation. There is also an elegant minaret with green tiles, the tallest in the city of Fez, but opposite the entrance to the madrassa is a remarkable structure. It is the water-clock which consisted of thirteen projecting wooden blocks, on which rested brass bowls, below a similar number of windows. It is no longer complete and there is speculation

RIGHT
Details of the delicately matched textures of timber, azulejos and carved stucco to be found in the courtyard of the Bou Inania Madrassa in Old Fez. The band of cursive Arabic calligraphy with a circular motif is exceptionally beautiful.

FAR RIGHT
The entrance lobby of the Bou Inania Madrassa at Fez has a flight of steps leading up to the main courtyard whose level is expressed by a narrow ledge. Above and below this the dado is faced with multi-coloured cut azulejos patterned with a grid of twelve-pointed stars and octagons at the intersections. Above the dado the walls are lined with delicately carved stucco including a horizontal band of cursive Arabic calligraphy.

concerning its exact method of operation, but its purpose was to draw attention to the madrassa and sound the times for prayer. It was therefore accessible to the minaret by means of a corridor at the upper level.

The scholar Ibn Khaldoun was invited to Fez by the sultan, Abou Inan (after whom the madrassa was named), and stayed there from 1354 to 1363. In 1362 he was dispatched to Seville to meet Pedro I on a diplomatic mission. As he was a member of the ruler's personal circle there seems little doubt that he must at some time have held discussions at this wonderful madrassa. After leaving Fez, he visited Granada and then wandered from court to court in North Africa during very difficult times, eventually settling in a remote part of Algeria in the province of Oran. He decided to write a monumental history of the world. The introduction, which is called the *Muqaddimah*, is a major work in itself and dedicated to a lengthy discussion of the interaction between man, society and the physical environment. He anticipated many ideas that have been sources of controversy in recent times. He divided the known world into seven climatic zones and claimed that climate affected both human character and skin colour. When dealing with architecture, which he described as the first and oldest of the crafts, he emphasised the need for a building to protect its occupants from the extremes of heat and cold. He was insistent on the importance of ventilation, cleanliness and flowing water. He also believed that bad air was a cause of disease; this might have been due to the fact that both his parents died from the plague in Tunis. He wrote about the history of the Berber people and discussed the social bonds that the Almoravids and Almohads had acquired. He used the word *asabiyya* to define their tribal solidarity, which he maintained had resulted from the exigencies of life in the harsh conditions of the desert. He indicated the stages whereby this quality faded as they settled and enjoyed the gentler existence in the easier conditions of al-Andalus. However, Granada did manage to retain some degree of *asabiyya*, in spite of intrigue and bad faith, perhaps because of the constant external threat on its frontiers.

The eastern section of the city of Fez contains an Andalusian quarter which was settled by refugees from both Córdoba and Qairouan in Tunisia. Tradition has it that the doorway to the el-Azhar mosque built in 1357 by Sultan Abou Inan in the new city was brought from Andalusia. Its minaret carries horizontal panels of *azulejos* on all four faces at the top of the external walls, tiles that are supposed to have originated from Andalusia. There had been a continuous interaction between Córdoba and Fez. The twentieth-century French scholar Terrasse believed that the carved timber *mimbar* of the Qairouyyin mosque was made in Córdoba as early as 1144 and that the Córdoba tradition had some influence on the Almoravid style. The tiled courtyard of the mosque dates from the sixteenth century and has two end pavilions and a fountain which share the magical richness of the Patio de los Leones at the Alhambra (Granada) and demonstrate the aesthetic influence of Andalusia and may even be the work of Andalusian craftsmen. The *mimbar* in the Qoutoubia Mosque at Marrakesh is also said to be an example of Cordoban craftsmanship.

The use of the term *azulejo* in both Spanish and Portuguese to describe a form of glazed tile is further evidence of the cultural interaction between the Peninsula and North Africa, Morocco in particular. It probably derives from the word *zillij*, an Arabic word for a small, cut monochrome glazed tile, used to decorate architectural surfaces and assembled in a variety of shapes and colours to produce a predetermined geometrical pattern. In combination they formed horizontal bands of pattern on the upper surfaces of minarets, when the tiles were of relatively large dimensions. Smaller tiles were assembled in geometrical patterns to line the lower sections of walls and to pave floors. At least three colours were normally used, the predominant ones being blue (produced with cobalt), green (copper), purple-brown (manganese) and yellow ochre. *Azulejos* seem to have appeared simultaneously in Morocco and the Peninsula, though apparently blue first appeared in the Peninsula and with a greater variety of shades. As *azul* means blue in Spanish and Portuguese, it is frequently given as the origin of the term. *Azulejos* do not appear to have been used in the buildings of the Umayyad dynasty, when mosaics in glass, different coloured stone and gold were employed as wall finishes in the Byzantine tradition, as in the Great Mosque of Córdoba.

From the thirteenth century to the fifteenth polychrome patterning created by the use of *azulejos* in a variety of shapes and techniques was increasingly used. White and turquoise tiles are present on the Qoutoubia Mosque at Marrakesh, and the Almohad minaret of la Giralda and the Torre del Oro at Seville were surfaced with a limited number of glazed tiles. In the latter, a lustre-finished tile was used. The technique of lustre glazing is believed to have been introduced to Spain from Egypt in the thirteenth century, Málaga being the main centre. An iridescent metallic surface is obtained by applying a mixture of a metallic oxide and ochre, after the tile has already been glazed, and then fired for the second time. Silver would produce a golden effect while the use of a copper oxide resulted in a rich metallic red. The final appearance depended on a blend of the two glazes and great skill and artistic judgment was therefore required.

The Nasrid dynasty in Granada and the Mudéjar builders at Seville, Córdoba and Teruel used glazed tiles in a glittering array of colour, pattern and finish. The tiles were often cut into geometrical shapes before assembly in complex star patterns, in the same way as the Moroccan *zillij*. The Spanish term is *alicatado*. Curvilinear shapes also were assembled in interlacing patterns. White tiles, obtained by the use of tin in the glaze, became common in the creation of white interlacing strapwork on a polychrome background. The cutting and assembly of these intricate shapes was labour intensive and time consuming so the logical step of creating similar patterns on simple single tiles became the next development. The patterns were painted on square or rectangular tiles, which would then be glazed and fired.

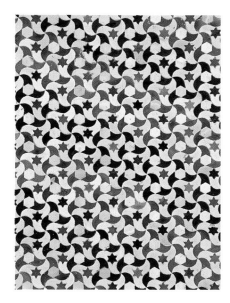 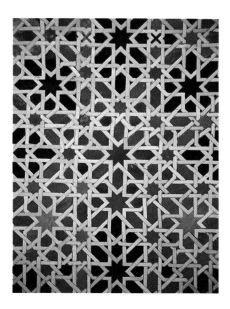 

A technique usually called *cuerda seca* (dry cord) was introduced. This enabled a fine black, or almost black, line to be drawn to define a border between two strong colours in much the same manner that the junctions between the separate pieces of *zillij* had done. The lines would be painted on the tile using a mixture of manganese and grease or oil before firing. An alternative was to use a cord treated with the same mixture which burnt away leaving a permanent black line on the surface of the tile. Another technique was called *cuenca* (hollow), when the pattern was formed in the tile in three dimensions, before it had hardened, so that the different colours were confined to the desired shape by the raised ridges in the body of the tile. An alternative involved the forming of grooves to receive the coloured glaze to delineate the lines of a pattern.

The term *azulejo* was then used to describe the larger tiles and is at present applied to glazed tiles in general. The technique of *zillij* is still practised in Morocco, and the tiles and skilled craftsmen are in demand in many countries in the Islamic world. The Portuguese discovered, or rediscovered, the glazed tile, as it is probable that they were used in buildings of the Moorish period, which have since disappeared, when the decorative attractions of the *azulejo* became popular following the capture of Ceuta in 1415. They were imported from al-Andalus or North Africa until the end of the sixteenth century, when local manufacture was started. Although the bulk of *azulejos* in the Peninsula were decorated with geometrical patterns, some had floral designs. From the seventeenth century the vogue for realistic scenes of hunting and open-air idylls became dominant and large panels of specially made tiles were assembled to form murals. *Azulejos* became extremely popular in Portugal and the walls of churches, palaces, fountains and kitchens were lined with them. Mass production began in the eighteenth century and their use was extended to middle-class houses and commercial and public buildings. A well-known example dating from the seventeenth century is to be seen in the garden of the Palácio dos Marqueses da Fronteira

Three detailed examples of wall surfaces faced with azulejos *in varying geometric patterns. The first, from the Patio de los Arrayanes at the Alhambra, is based on the hexagon, six-pointed star and interlocking curved elements. The second, from the Alcázar at Seville, has an interlocking repeat pattern based on the eight-pointed star while the third, from the Palácio Nacional at Sintra, has the eight-pointed star combined in a repeat pattern with the twelve-pointed star. This example shows the* cuerda seca *technique.*

in the northwest of Lisbon. Here, surrounding a pool, are blind arcades with panels of *azulejos* made in Lisbon depicting horsemen and other figures. The craze for *azulejos* was exported to Brazil, where they are still very popular. In Spanish America the *azulejo* was not so extensively used but these tiles were manufactured in Mexico at Puebla, to which the skills were brought from Seville.

Contemporary with the regime of the Marinids in Morocco and Algeria, their allies against the Christians, the Nasrids, had been steadily losing territory to the kingdoms of Portugal, Castile and Aragón. In 1373, because the Portuguese had been attacked by Castile as a result of a dynastic quarrel, King Fernando decided to rebuild a defensive wall around Lisbon, which had prospered and expanded beyond the boundary of the old Moorish walls. The new wall, known as the Fernandino wall, excluded the Mouraria, presumably because the Moors were regarded as potential enemies, especially as the Castilians had been known on occasions to side with the Muslims against the Aragonese.

At Ronda in Andalusia a tower is the only part of the church of San Sebastian to survive. It is built in brick and stone and was formerly a minaret from the early Nasrid period.

The Nasrid dynasty that was to rule Muslim Granada until the final stage of the Christian Reconquest in 1492 had modest beginnings in the small town of Arjona in the present province of Jaén. Mohammed I (d. 1272) led a revolt and soon established power over the surrounding area, including Jaén. He was a strong-minded chieftain with a frontier mentality. He managed to extend his influence to Córdoba, but this was short-lived and he became involved in the complicated and often treacherous dealings between the Christians and the *taifa* kings. In 1237 he succeeded in taking over Granada, a year after the Christian capture of Córdoba. Ferdinand III of Castile went on the offensive, captured Arjona and began to lay siege to Jaén. Mohammed decided that he was not strong enough to defend it and, coming to terms with the military strength of the Castilians, relinquished Jaén in a peace treaty in 1245 that allowed him to build up his forces in the mountainous territory centred on Granada. In 1252 Ferdinand III was succeeded by Alfonso X who was as unwise in his activities relating to political and military matters as he was wise and successful in matters cultural. Instead of pursuing the elimination of the state of Granada, rather than face the risk of fighting in the mountains he turned his attention to a disastrous campaign against the Muslims of North Africa. There was also an insurrection of the Mudéjars in those parts of al-Andalus that had been recently occupied by the Castilians. This was to a large extent orchestrated from Granada. It came dangerously near to success but Mudéjars in Old and New Castile and Navarre did not join the revolt because they realised that Granada would not be able to come to their aid. From then onwards the Mudéjars understood that discretion would be their best policy and they quietly accepted a secondary role within the Christian states. When Mohammed I was succeeded by his son Mohammed II in 1273, Granada was a well-established state, in spite of its precarious position, and many Muslims emigrated there from Castile.

Meanwhile, the Portuguese had continued their advance down the Atlantic coast to the Algarve, reaching Mértola in 1238, Tavira the next year, and finally Afonso III captured Faro in 1249. In the last stages of the Christian occupation of Muslim territory, which was centred on the petty state of Niebla, now in southwest Spain, the land was divided between the Portuguese and the Castilians, who retained the area east of Seville as far as Huelva. Very few Muslims remained in Portugal; most had fled to North Africa. The majority of the Mudéjars were active in the building trades and in ceramics. No complete buildings in Portugal remain from that period that were designed in a comprehensive Mudéjar manner but some religious buildings do contain isolated details, such as *artesonado* ceilings and panels of *azulejo* tiling. There are, however, some small churches, or *ermidas*, which are often described as Mudéjar. These display characteristics that are unique to Portugal – the use of cylindrical buttresses crowned with conical pinnacles and set in thick external mud and stone walls, which often have battlemented parapets, giving the appearance of fortresses. The exteriors are plastered and painted with limewash. Their plan is usually a simple rectangle with a barrel-vaulted roof. It is believed that they were built by Mudéjar craftsmen who were familiar with the technique and materials. The Ermida Santo André at Beja and the Ermida São Bras at Évora are examples of this remarkable type of church.

The Marinids eventually withdrew their forces across the Straits, and the rivalry between Castile and Aragón, in which Castile for a period was the weaker of the two, led to an agreement between Aragón and Granada whereby the latter was given a free hand in al-Andalus. Ceuta, on the North

The Ermida Santo André at Beja is an example of a small Mudéjar church with cylindrical buttresses and conical pinnacles that is peculiar to Portugal. This ermida was built to commemorate the capture of Beja from the Moors in 1162.

A general view of the Alhambra from the north. The square Torre de Comares can be seen on the left while the buildings of the Alcazaba are centre right.

The principal gateway to the Alhambra was built in 1348 by Yusuf I and is named the Puerta de la Justicia because courts of justice were held in front of it. Over the massive horseshoe arch of the porch is a representation of an open hand which is believed to have symbolised the five fundamental principles of Islam.

African coast, was then disputed between Granada and the Marinids and this led to a tripartite combination of the interests of Castile, Aragón and the Marinids. When Nasr (r. 1309–14) succeeded Mohammed III of Granada, he decided to reach an accord with the Marinids and gave up claims to Ceuta as well as ceding them Algeciras and lands as far inland as Ronda. Military struggles between Granada and Castile continued. Both the next two rulers of Granada were treacherously murdered, but despite all the difficulties the regime remained viable. It was not until Yusuf I (r. 1332–54) became king that Granada developed into a centre of artistic and literary creativity. At the Alhambra, which had become a palace-city independent of the city below, his construction of the principal gateway, the Puerta de la Justicia (Gate of Judgment), in 1348, is commemorated by an inscription, but his greatest achievement, the Madrassa, has completely disappeared.

The gateway is so named because it was the custom for the Nasrid kings to hold courts of justice in front of it. From the outside the horseshoe archway of the porch, set at the centre of a massive tower, leads, through a second arch with the original timber doors, to an impressive interior consisting of two lofty halls arranged to form a double right-angle entry. Above the second arch is seen the inscription of Yusuf I, which is surmounted by a niche containing an image of the Virgin Mary later placed there by Ferdinand and Isabella. At the top centre of the arch to the porch, which is twice the height of the inner arch, where a keystone might have been expected, is a small representation of an open hand. This is believed to have symbolised the five fundamental principles of Islam in parallel to the four fingers and thumb. These principles are, faith in God and in Mohammed as his prophet, prayer, the giving of alms, fasting, particularly during Ramadan, and the pilgrimage to the holy city of Mecca. The Arabs also considered the hand to be a powerful symbol of defence against the enemies of the Quran. James Murphy, in his commentary to the engraved plates illustrating his volume, *The Arabian Antiquities of Spain* (1815), says on the authority of Pedraza, a historian of Granada, that the Mudéjars, after the reconquest of Granada, used to wear a small badge showing the shape of a hand, thus indicating solidarity with their fellow Arabs. The Inquisition naturally took exception to this and the use of the symbol was formally abolished by law.

Behind and above the Puerta de la Justicia is another smaller gateway, which was probably the connection between the palace and the administrative section of the palace-city, called the Puerta del Vino (Wine Gate). This two-storey structure was built by Mohammed III and later altered in the time of Mohammed V. The western façade is plain but the eastern elevation is later and has a double window to the guard room above. The spandrels to the horseshoe arch below are decorated in relief with interlacing vegetal patterns centred on a medallion. Unlike the Puerta de la Justicia, both arches are aligned on a tunnel-vaulted space with benches on either side for the waiting guards or visitors, allowing a direct view from outside to inside.

A gateway known as the Puerta del Vino was probably the checkpoint for entry to the palace of the Alhambra in Granada with the guard room over the archway where there were benches for waiting guards and visitors.

The Christian victory of Rio Salado in 1340, in which both Castilian and Portuguese troops were involved, was followed by an attack on Algeciras which initially failed, but after a long siege it was surrendered in 1344 in exchange for peace for ten years. In 1354 Yusuf was stabbed to death in the Great Mosque of Granada in mysterious circumstances, so bringing to an end a reign that had succeeded in achieving both the survival of the last Muslim state in the Peninsula as well as establishing Granada as a centre of artistic brilliance. He was succeeded by Mohammed V at the age of sixteen, whose reign, although interrupted twice, was eventually to last for 37 years, until 1391. He took the opportunity of a civil war in Castile to recapture Algeciras in 1369, but his chief triumph was the subsequent use of diplomacy to keep a balance of relative peace with Castile. This was the period of continued cultural excellence, epitomised by the magical extensions to the palace of the Alhambra which were developed from the promising beginnings of Yusuf.

CHAPTER 5

The lavishly decorated timber ceiling to the Salón de los Embajadores (Hall of the Ambassadors) within the Torre de Comares. There are five finely wrought celosia windows to each wall face at high level below the ceiling.

The FINAL FLOWERING
of GRANADA

The founder of the Nasrid dynasty, Mohammed I, had come to power in 1231 and started the construction of a fortified palace on the Sabika hill, an outcrop of the Sierra Nevada overlooking the city of Granada. His son, Muhammed II, completed the external walls, which were built from a mixture of red earth and stone. This combination was extremely hard and durable. The red colour led to the name 'Alhambra', derived from the Arabic for 'the red'. These walls were the beginning of a huge complex that was to become world renowned as the most beautiful palace of all time and later the most famous tourist attraction of Spain. It has been a source of inspiration for poets of many languages, beginning with the Arab poets who wrote numerous inscriptions on the surfaces of the buildings. It charmed all visitors, not least the Christian royal family who lived here, but later, as in the case of the Friday Mosque at Córdoba, made new additions in a style that broke the continuity with the past. At the Alhambra, Charles V (Charles I of Spain, r. 1516–56) commissioned an extension which was designed by Pedro Machuca in a severe Renaissance style. It was also on a more grandiose scale than the Moorish palace and intended for large-scale ceremonial use only. Charles continued to be charmed by the older buildings and occupied them for his family's personal use and their pleasure at the

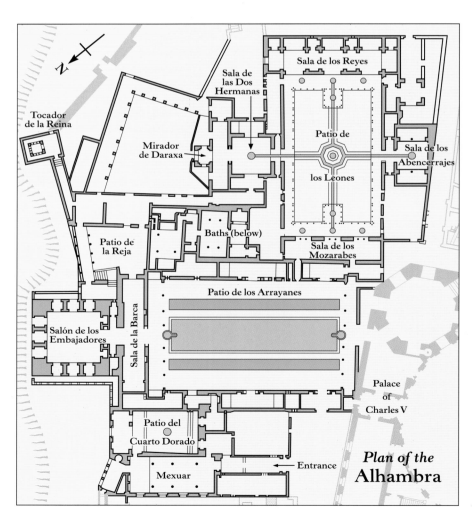

Plan of the **Alhambra**

beautiful surroundings. However, it is only those parts of the palace that were in the Andalusian and Mudéjar styles that have touched the hearts of visiting poets, writers, artists and musicians of many nationalities who have celebrated it in their work.

A view looking west of a model of the Alhambra which clearly shows the layout of the palace. On the right is the Torre de Comares aligned with the Patio de los Arrayanes to the left of it. At right-angles and parallel to the south portico of the Patio de los Arrayanes opposite the tower is the Patio de los Leones. In front of this is the octagonal pitched roof over the Sala de las Dos Hermanas (Hall of the Two Sisters). Aligned with this towards the foreground is the Mirador de Daraxa and the garden patio. Between the mirador and the Patio de los Arrayanes can be seen the roofs of the royal baths.

The walls enclosed a self-contained town. It had twenty-three towers and four gates. It was, like Medinat al-Zahra, an administrative and military centre as well as a royal palace. There were once seven palaces, dwellings for all classes, barracks, innumerable offices, workshops, a mint, a number of mosques, public and private baths, a madrassa, gardens and a royal necropolis. The ordinary buildings have disappeared but the most beautiful palaces have been preserved, maintained and in some cases restored. The Puerta del Vino and the Palacio del Partal (Partal Palace) are believed to date from the beginning of the fourteenth century, the time of Muhammed III. The Partal Palace consists of an arched gallery, which acted as an anteroom

A view across the pool to the portico of the Palacio del Partal at the Alhambra. This is to the east of the Patio de los Leones and is probably the oldest surviving section of the palace. It dates from the beginning of the fourteenth century.

to the Torre de las Damas (Tower of the Ladies), now reflected in the large rectangular pool on the south side. Water to fill it flows from the mouths of two lion statues, believed to have been moved from the Maristan, the city hospital, when it was demolished in the nineteenth century. They are similar to those of the famous fountain in the Patio de los Leones (Court of the Lions). Both the palace and the tower are of brickwork, and the five arched openings of the gallery are supported on slender stone columns. Above the arches are decorative panels in stucco. Along the gallery is a carved and painted wooden ceiling laid out in geometrical patterns in which the octagon predominates. At the centre on the axis of the central archway there is a multi-faceted domed ceiling. The gardens were restored in the 1920s in a sympathetically Islamic manner by Torres Balbas, who was then the architect in charge of the conservation of the palace.

A close-up of the portico of the Palacio del Partal showing the brick and stucco construction of two of the arches.

Yusuf I and Mohammed V were the Nasrid emirs responsible for those marvellous buildings which created the world reputation of the Alhambra. Three gates and four towers were rebuilt during the reign of Yusuf I. The prominent massive Torre de Comares contains his throne room, or Salón de los Embajadores (Hall of the Ambassadors), as it is normally known. This is a magnificent space worthy of its purpose. Square in plan, it forms a cube with a cornice consisting of *muqarnas* upon which sits a superb cupola with seven levels of intricate marquetry based on repetitive twelve-pointed star patterns. This complex ceiling is said to consist of more than 8,000 polygonal wooden pieces. There is one central arched entrance which is entered from the Sala de la Barca, a smaller rectangular space at right angles to the axis of approach to the throne room. The derivation of the word 'Barca' is a matter of uncertainty. In Spanish it means 'boat', and some say this refers to the shape of the centre section of the timber ceiling, while in Arabic *baraka* means 'blessing' and could therefore indicate that it was used as an anteroom. Goodwin, however, believes it to have been the emir's

The vaulted timber ceiling of the Sala de la Barca with geometric patterns based on the twelve-pointed star. The two ends are shaped as semi-domes.

private room for both day and night, as it has alcoves at either end. At the centre of the long side opposite the throne room there is another arched opening to a portico which acts as a link to the northeast end of the rectangular Patio de los Arrayanes or Myrtle Court. This courtyard is named after the myrtle bushes which are planted in two long rows on either side of a long rectangular pool.

The Patio de los Arrayanes seen from the Sala de la Barca through the elaborate pointed archway of muqarnas. Above the two storeys of porticoes can be seen the roof line of Charles V's Renaissance extension to the palace.

FOLLOWING PAGES
A diagonal view of the Salón de los Embajadores showing the deeply set full-height window openings, three to each wall face, whose natural lighting is supplemented by the celosia windows at high level.

The other three sides of the throne room each have three arched openings in the massive walls, giving an effect of deep recession. The central recession is slightly wider than the other two and a central slender column supports two slightly stilted arches at the outer edges. The other two openings have single wider multi-lobed external arches. Above these external arches there are two smaller simple arched openings. The lower openings reach down to floor level, so there is a metal balustrade for safety. As a result of these openings there is direct natural lighting on three sides as well as magnificent views of the city below and of the Sierra Nevada beyond from the northeast-facing windows. There is another row of rounded arched openings at a high level just below the horizontal calligraphic frieze beneath the cornice. There are five of these arches to each side, two of which are blind. Below this are two deep friezes of surface decoration. The upper has

This colour lithograph of 1837 by Girault de Prangey shows the distant view towards the west through an ajimez window opening set in the depth of the external wall of the Salón de los Embajadores at the Alhambra. There appears to have been no protection at that time from the sheer drop. Metal railings were later added but at present there are perforated screens covering the opening down to floor level. (See pp. 112–13.)

repetitive twelve-pointed star patterns while the lower is covered with intricate tracery with smaller repeated units and horizontal lines of calligraphy at the top and the bottom. The calligraphy is in cursive Arabic, except for the middle band which has medallions of cursive alternating with lozenges of linear Kufic. There are similar lozenges above the coloured tile dados and there is a continuous band of cursive calligraphy around the *alfiz* of the lower window openings.

The visitor today is guided through a hall of audience, or Mexuar, which was used for centuries as a Christian chapel. It has been altered considerably since the Reconquest, but the gallery was retained, as was much of the decorative surface, including some polychrome tiled dados in geometrical patterns based on the octagon and sixteen-pointed stars. At one end is the prayer room, which has two rows of window openings on one side. The upper windows are *celosias* while the lower are larger, clear openings which have the same magnificent views as the Salón de los Embajadores. The *mihrab* is polygonal and exquisitely decorated. A doorway leads directly from the Mexuar into a rectangular patio paved with marble, in the centre of which is a circular bowl for a fountain in a small octagonal pool. It is known as the Patio del Cuarto Dorado and was built in the Mudéjar style after the Reconquest.

At the south end of the Patio del Cuarto Dorado is the façade of the Palacio de Comares. This, however, dates from 1370 and has expansive overhanging timber eaves. Below the eaves is a modelled cornice of *muqarnas* over an arcade of five arches consisting of a single central arched window with an *ajimez* on either side. The windows are made from timber latticework. Three steps up from the floor level of the patio are two rectangular door openings on the centre lines of the *ajimeces* above. The dados and architraves are finished with polychrome glazed tiles, while the remaining wall surface is decorated with an intricate but refined mixture of curved and

A detail of the azulejo *mosaics and carved stucco work of the central panel of the southern façade of the Patio del Cuarto Dorado in the Alhambra.*

linear interlacing patterns in relief. The upper windows are contained in bands of inscriptions of cursive Arabic script. The composition of the façade is a sensitive balance of proportion, colour and texture. It is believed that Mohammed V received visitors here and that the overhanging eaves were for his protection. The left-hand door was intended for the use of the emir, as it gave relatively easy access to the royal quarters. The right-hand door, on the other hand, served as the entrance for the public and the administrative staff whose offices were to the east of the palace. It is probable that a temporary throne was placed between the two doors at royal audiences.

The Patio de los Arrayanes is a wonderful space, a rectangle with a single axis aligned with the central arches of the seven-bayed colonnades and the single-jet fountains at either end. The pool is the main element and the tranquil effect of its slightly shimmering surface reflecting the elegant arcade on slender columns is complemented by the green myrtle hedges bordering the long sides. These side walls are simple flat surfaces punctuated now and again by doorways, the arches and *alfiz* of which were intricately decorated in relief as well as being crowned by an *ajimez* at the upper level. Whereas the Cuarto Dorado was for day-to-day business and the personal requests of ordinary citizens, who all had the right of access to the emir, the Patio de los Arrayanes was for the reception of distinguished visitors of state who might eventually meet the royal personage in the throne room.

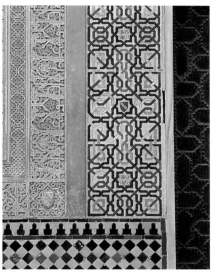

A detail of the geometric azulejo *decoration to the jamb of the right-hand door in the façade.*

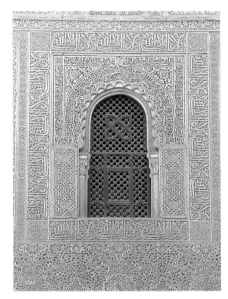

The timber trellis work of the high-level window in the same façade and the elaborate carved calligraphy that surrounds it.

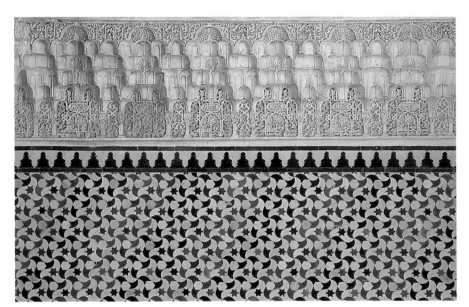

A detail of the horizontal junction between the azulejo *dado and the carved stucco above that incorporates arabesques, calligraphy and* muqarnas. *It occurs in an alcove at the end of a portico in the Patio de los Arrayanes. (See also p. 101.)*

LEFT
The two-storey elevation of the Palacio de Comares seen through the central arch of the portico at the northern end of the Patio del Cuarto Dorado which was the audience chamber of the palace.

FOLLOWING PAGES
A long view of the Patio de los Arrayanes in the Alhambra showing the doorways in the side walls which are accentuated with decorative stucco panels set in the plain white surface of the wall.

The Nasrids were skilled in the arts of diplomacy, preferring persuasion and negotiation to the violence of war. Perhaps they had no choice as they clung to the last part of the Peninsula to remain in Muslim hands surrounded by overwhelmingly powerful Christian enemies to the north. Their architecture expressed the desire to charm and reassure rather than to intimidate by the expression of strength, as was so often demonstrated by the grandiose and heavy structures of the palaces of Northern European monarchs. Such an example was the extension to the palace built by Charles V, replacing former accommodation believed to have been the harem. Construction started in 1526 to designs by Pedro Machuca of Toledo, but building continued for over a century and it is still not absolutely complete. Although the style is Classical in an austere and heavy manner, the attention to pure geometry remains, but at a much larger scale. The plan is a large square which contains a central circular patio and an octagonal chapel at one corner. It is said that bullfights used to take place in the central patio.

Near the southeast corner of the Patio de los Arrayanes is a doorway which leads to the Sala de los Mozarabes, an anteroom that opens into the colonnade of the Patio de los Leones (Court of the Lions). This courtyard, the construction of which was started in 1378, is almost the same size as the Patio de los Arrayanes, but is at right-angles to it. It differs in other ways. There are paved colonnades to all four sides, with two open porticoes projecting into the courtyard at the centres of the short sides. The patio was set out as a paradise garden, divided into four quarters in the traditional Islamic layout.

A view of the Patio de los Leones from one of the end pavilions. The water channel leads to the fountain supported on the sculpted lions after which the courtyard is named.

The garden is frequently cited in the Quran as a symbol for Paradise associated with shade and water. It is an idealised form of the pattern of irrigation. Water channels representing the four rivers of life cross in the centre. Together with the fountains, they symbolise water as the source of life. The priorities of water usage are carefully defined for the Muslim. Drinking is obviously the first, with free access for all. Then in the urban situation comes bathing, organised separately for the sexes, and direct access is given for ritual ablutions at the mosque. After these basic demands have been met, comes the distribution of water for land use. Individuals are responsible for the channels within their gardens and courtyards. The water is usually obtained from a fixed point and is normally paid for. The maintenance and supply is the responsibility of the community. The four rivers of life are symbolically defined in the Quran as one of water, one of milk, one of wine and one of honey. The quarters were usually filled with trees and flowers. The desert origin of the Arabs and Berbers provided the image of the oasis and the need for a surrounding wall to exclude the dust-laden winds and to give privacy and protection. The presence of water helped to cool the atmosphere of a hot and dry climate and the feeling of comfort was augmented by the psychological effect induced by the moving water of the fountains. To the Muslim the beauty of the garden, as part of the whole of creation, is seen as a reflection of God.

Today, the horizontal surfaces of the Patio de los Leones that are neither paving nor water are gravel, except for four small orange trees at the corners, a rather sad reminder of what was once a luxurious medley of cypresses, palms, oranges, pomegranates and flowers. The level of the original planting was lower than the paving, presumably to prevent the flowers and shrubs from obstructing the view of the fountain and the delicate decoration of the porticoes, and at the same time creating the effect of a carpet of flowers.

At the centre of this wonderfully proportioned space stands the Lion Fountain, from which the court gains its name. There are twelve small

A close-up of the Lion Fountain showing the verse by Ibn Zamrak carved on the rim and details of the sculpted lions.

James Murphy's engraving of the Lion Fountain dated 1815 shows a circular basin which had a powerful jet. This was supported on a pedestal at the centre of the twelve-sided basin which now has a weaker jet in its place.

carved stone lions mounted on a twelve-sided stone base. Each lion, centrally placed on one of the twelve sides, is facing outwards. In the centre of the exposed teeth of each lion is a spout, out of which water flows into a flat stone channel enclosing the base. Above the lions is a twelve-sided stone basin at the centre of which is a single jet fountain. The water from this basin feeds the lion spouts. James Murphy, who made a series of measured drawings of the Alhambra palace between 1802 and 1809, eventually published a number of black and white engravings, *The Arabian Antiquities of Spain,* in 1815. Plate number XXXIV clearly shows another circular basin on a pedestal above and at the centre of the present twelve-sided basin. In his close-up of the fountain, a powerful central vertical jet is shown discharging into the higher circular basin, whence the water overflows around the rim into the lower basin.

The play of water, if skilfully designed, is a form of kinetic sculpture and can be a work of art in its own right. The flow and motion of water was controlled by the force of gravity. Change of level was the simplest method of creating a play of water, but pressure was needed to produce the defiance of gravity shown by the vertical jet of a fountain. John Brookes says that the pressure in early fountains was obtained by building up a reservoir of water at a higher level, which fed the water through pipes of ever-decreasing diameter so that the weight of water acting on a narrow aperture increased the force of the water at the fountain head to produce a single plume. From this plume the water could later be distributed in sprays or dribbles, creating a variety of pleasing sounds in addition to a cooling effect.

A poem in Arabic by Ibn Zamrak carved around the rim of the basin extols the beauty of the court, the garden and, in particular, the fountain and the play of its jets of water.

> *Behold this mass of glistening pearl,*
> *falling within a ring of frothing silver,*
> *to flow amidst translucent gems*
> *than marble whiter, than alabaster more translucent.*

This poem is one of many written by Ibn Zamrak that adorn the surfaces of the Alhambra. He was the chief minister of Mohammed V. Although he composed verse of great delicacy, much of it in praise of the emir as well as descriptions of the natural beauties of Granada and the magnificence of the architectural surroundings, he was also an expert politician and intriguer. He was the instigator of charges of heresy made against his predecessor and teacher, Ibn Khatib, who fled to North Africa, where he was executed after a trial in the prison of Tlemcen. Ibn Khatib was also an outstanding literary figure who wrote many works of history, poetry, philosophy and medicine. The modelling of the lions has been criticised by some observers, who have maintained that it is rather crude in comparison with the refined and sensitive treatment of the surrounding environment. The lions are believed to signify princely power and Oleg Grabar believes they symbolise a luxurious setting associated with Solomon, of Jewish and Muslim legend. The Jewish poet Ibn Gabirol (*c.* 1021–57) refers to a throne erected in honour of the Queen of Sheba, which was inlaid with gold and supported on twelve lions. It is true that the carving of the lions is stylised rather than realistic, and some scholars have maintained that the sculptures are Byzantine in origin, but they possess a certain dignity and strength that complements the simplicity of the paved surfaces of the court, the water channels and the secondary fountains. They are also integrated by contrast with the intricacy of the colonnades and the complicated sophistication of the multifoil arches and their decoration.

Théophile Gautier, the French journalist and poet, wrote of his four-day sojourn there when he and his friends camped in the courtyard during a tour of Spain in 1840. He described how he kept his bottles of sherry cool in the fountain and wrote of an incident early one morning when he and his friends were still asleep in their beds and they were drenched by the fountains suddenly springing powerfully into action. This was due to the need to test them before a visit by a prince of Saxe-Coburg-Gotha, a suitor of Queen Isabel II, whose retinue arrived soon afterwards, to the consternation of the campers. On his return to France, Gautier wrote that it would be difficult to find anything less like lions than these works of African fancy. He continued to observe that:

> the paws are more like those rough pieces of wood that are put into the stomachs of cardboard dogs to preserve their equilibrium; the faces, rayed with cross-bars, no doubt intended to figure the moustaches, are exactly like the mouths of hippopotami; the eyes are of such primitive drawing that they recall the shapeless attempts of children: and yet these twelve monsters, if considered not as lions but as chimeras, as caprices of ornamentation, produce, with the basin which they support, a picturesque and elegant effect which enables one to understand their reputation and the praise contained in the Arabic inscription ...

The two axes of the court, at whose intersection the Lion Fountain is placed, are defined by four water channels which terminate with smaller single-jet fountains. The longer axis has two fountains at each end: one at the centre of the portico and the other in the colonnade. The channels on the shorter axis extend through the colonnade into two separate halls, the Sala de las Dos Hermanas (Hall of the Two Sisters) on the north side and the Sala de los Abencerrajes on the other. At the eastern end is the Sala de los Reyes (Hall of the Kings). This complex of apartments arranged around the Patio de los Leones is generally considered to have been the residence of the royal family. Although they are formally related in plan, there is no direct arched

A beam of sunlight enlivens the network of tracery of arabesques and calligraphy on the upper wall of one of the three roof lanterns of the Sala de los Reyes.

FAR RIGHT
The reverse view to the picture on p. 120 of the Patio de los Arrayanes with the fountain set in the water channel at the centre of the pavilion.

A column and wall panels of floral patterns in the Patio de los Leones.

or visual connection between the two large courtyards in the Alhambra, making it easy to control access and maintain privacy. The rhythm of the colonnades is unusual in that the columns are grouped down the sides as alternate double and single but in threes at the eastern corners of the courtyard and the outer corners of the two square porticoes, whereas groups of four occur at the western corners of the courtyard and the internal corners of the porticoes. This multiplicity of slender columns gives a vertical emphasis which is counterbalanced by the circular bases and capitals and the incredible medley of fragmented decoration above. This consists of impost blocks, *muqarnas* and panels of stucco in complicated repetitive curvilinear patterns and medallions frequently contained within bands of Arabic calligraphy.

RIGHT
A detail of the fabulous carved stucco work of the arcade of one of the pavilions in the Patio de los Leones.

FAR RIGHT
Another detail of the stucco decorations in a pavilion of the Patio de los Leones.

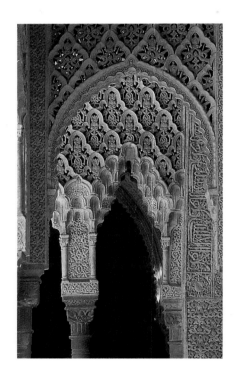

ABOVE
A detail of the stucco patterns over one of the smaller arches in the arcade.

RIGHT
A similar detail of stucco work over a central semicircular arch in a lateral arcade of the Patio de los Leones.

But the most intricate stucco and timber decoration is to be found in the square Sala de las Dos Hermanas where the domed ceiling is composed of a mass of fragmented surfaces in the form of *muqarnas* which hang like stalactites above the twin windows in the octagonal drum. The geometrical setting-out is based on a central star motif. This complex vaulted ceiling hangs from a wooden roof truss; thus the repetitive use of the *muqarna* is purely decorative, although the form of the *muqarna* developed originally as a device to meet the problem of finding a shape to transfer the weight of a circular dome to an octagonal or square structure below. This is an exception to the common assertion that decoration in Islamic architecture is always subordinated to the expression of the structure. Here the means of the support to the ceiling is completely disguised with exceptional skill. Below the octagonal gallery there is further use of the *muqarna* to give decorative form to the transition at the corners from the octagon to the square plan below. At the centre of the room there is a single jet fountain in a circular bowl set flush with the floor paving. This bowl is connected by a straight water channel at floor level to the twelve-sided channel at the base of the Lion Fountain outside.

An intricate composition of muqarnas *above and below the octagonal lantern light over the square Sala de las Dos Hermanas appears like a galaxy of shooting stars.*

FOLLOWING PAGE
A general view of the Sala de las Dos Hermanas showing the central fountain and the water channel leading to the Patio de los Leones behind the photographer.

127

This straight water channel continues to the centre of the Hall of the Abencerrajes, where it also ends in a single jet fountain, exactly opposite the Sala de las Dos Hermanas. Here there is another fantastic domed ceiling composed of decorative hanging *muqarnas*. In this case the gallery has sixteen faces forming eight triangular projections above the square plan below. There is one projection at each corner and one at the centre of each side of the square. Again, multiple *muqarnas* are used to make the transition from the projecting gallery above and the square below. The south wall is flat, with no openings, while the north side has a single arched opening facing the Patio de los Leones. The east and west sides have twin arched openings into rectangular alcoves. James Murphy recounts a legend that explains the name of this room. The Abencerrajes were one of the noblest tribes of Granada, and Boabdil, the last king of Granada, is supposed to have here beheaded 86 members of the tribe. The fact that these executions were held within the domestic quarters is explained by the charge of illicit intercourse with the queen which was made against one of them. She is said to have committed her defence to four Christian knights who fought and overcame each of her accusers and so vindicated her character and those of the Abencerrajes.

In his comprehensive study of Granada Ibn Khatib paints a glowing picture of the way of life of the people of all classes and occupations. He describes the extent of personal adornment, listing precious stones such as sapphires, topaz, emeralds and fine pearls. The most common form was the use of necklaces, bangles, bracelets and ankle-rings made from silver. He was particularly enthusiastic in his account of the ladies of Granada. After describing their personal attractions he comments that they were especially skilled in the arts of toilette and coiffure. These enticements were matched with the wearing of multi-coloured layers of fabric set off by embroidered cloth-of-gold, brocade and other finery. If the display of exquisite jewellery is added, the total effect of figures, movement, costume and setting must have been of overwhelming splendour, a scene of luxury that European orientalist painters of the nineteenth century attempted to reproduce. Overhead, the glittering assembly of the interlocking parts of the dome of both the Salas de las Dos Hermanas and de los Abencerrajes, surrounded by the hanging *muqarnas*, echoed the geometrical filigree of the jewellery worn by the reclining figures below. The polychrome display of fabrics and costume was complemented by the clear bright colours of the patterned glazed tile dados, while the variety of flowing and interlacing patterns of the carved stucco of the upper wall surfaces was reflected in the design of the fabrics and woven carpets.

To the north of the Sala de las Dos Hermanas lies the Sala de los Ajimeces and beyond is the Mirador de Daraxa, so called because it overlooks a garden patio of the same name. This garden has at its centre a Moorish fountain with a bowl in the shape of a lotus which was taken by Charles V from the Mexuar and mounted on a Renaissance pedestal. The planting is the traditional pattern of paths bordered by box hedges and the

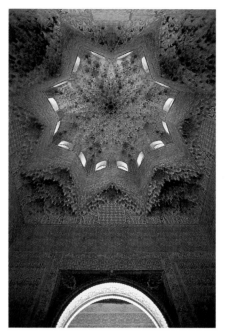

The muqarna *ceiling of the Sala de los Abencerrajes, whose lantern has sixteen faces based on an eight-pointed star, is smaller than the similar ceiling to the Sala de las Dos Hermanas but is equal in magnificence.*

A view through the double window of the Mirador de Daraxa to the garden court of Lindaraja beyond.

beds are occupied with orange and cypress trees. The layout was probably planned by Charles V whose apartments opened off it on the east side. Previously the mirador enjoyed a direct view of the river Darro and Albaicín from the *ajimez* opening on the north side. It has a particularly beautiful medley of *muqarnas*, calligraphy and decorative stucco. On the western side of Charles V's apartments alongside the Comares tower is a small garden patio known as the Patio de la Reja (Iron Grille). Although this was created as late as 1654, it has typically Islamic features. The floor is decorated in flowing interlacing geometrical shapes echoing the star of Islam and at the centre is a bowl fountain supported in an octagonal pool. The planting, however, is confined to large clay pots.

The Sala de los Reyes (Hall of the Kings), at the eastern end of the Patio de los Leones, is a long room divided into five bays defined by a series of pointed arched openings with elaborate *muqarna* treatment of the intrados. A series of alcoves opens off these bays, three of which retain their painted ceilings. The largest of these consists of a lozenge-shaped composition painted on leather of a gathering of ten Muslim dignitaries who may have been intended to portray the Nasrid dynasty. They are depicted in a semi-realistic style with strong colours and gilt. It is believed that it and other paintings in the hall are the work of Christian artists commissioned by Mohammed V. The other paintings illustrate tales of hunting and chivalry, including one which is said to show a Muslim noble winning the heart of a maiden from her Christian lover.

The ceiling of one of the alcoves to the Sala de los Reyes at the eastern end of the Patio de los Leones has this multiple portrait of ten regal figures painted on leather. It is believed to be the work of Christian artists.

In the right-angle formed at the junction of the complex of the Patio de los Leones and the Patio de los Arrayanes lies the suite of rooms that comprises the *hammam* or royal baths. In the first, bathers undressed and washed and then passed to the *calidarium* or steam room where they would be sprayed with cold water by attendants. After that they would move to the rest room, which has a musicians' gallery. All these spaces are lit from above.

Except for the rest room, they are lit from star-shaped apertures lined with green glazed tiles in the stone vaulted roofs. These openings also served the important function of ventilation. The *calidarium* is a large square central space with two alcoves on either side of a triple arcade of horseshoe arches on slender marble columns. James Murphy measured the baths in some detail and his drawings show where the boilers and steam conduits were situated. He also has two plates showing perspectives of the king's bath and the queen's bath, respectively. Each shows a single naked figure. In the case of the queen it is an obviously female figure exposed from the waist upwards, whereas in the king's bath only a diminutive head appears above the bath panel and this gives the impression of a child. He offers no explanation in the comments attached to the plates except that he describes the queen's bath as the most richly ornamented, with gilding and porcelain, and states that the basins containing water are in white marble. In the king's bath there is a small alcove with a multifoil horseshoe arch and two slender columns. This is set in the far wall at the side of the bath.

The rest room is very different and is in the form of a lofty square patio with a central fountain. A first-floor gallery is supported on four white marble columns and at the highest level there is a lantern with a row of round-arched *celosia* windows. On opposite sides of the central space at the lower level are two raised recesses with twin arched openings and a central column. These were for the rest and relaxation of the royal family, while the court musicians performed above at gallery level. Throughout the baths area and rest room the dados are finished with a rich tapestry of glazed tiles in a variety of shapes and sizes. These simple and durable finishes ease cleaning and resist damage from water and steam. The floor of the rest room is paved with a similar geometrical pattern of coloured glazed tiles and the area around the fountain is based on star shapes. The colours of the tiles are

An engraving of 1813 by James Murphy of one of the royal baths in the Alhambra. He named it 'the King's bath' and portrayed what appears to be the head of a child in the water. Over the arched opening to the alcove can be seen two of the star-shaped apertures in the vaulted roof which provided light and ventilation.

The rest room in the royal baths of the Alhambra. The balustrade of the first-floor gallery where the court musicians performed can be seen over a raised alcove where the royal personages rested before the central fountain.

131

black, white, golden brown, green and blue assembled in many permutations. It is said that they were made in the potteries of Málaga. Above eye level in the rest room every surface is decorated with carved stucco in the usual mixture of subtle patterning and bands of inscriptions. Much of the colouring remains, and is believed to be part of the redecoration carried out by the Christian kings after the Reconquest.

Ferdinand and Isabella of Castile were overwhelmed by the beauty and luxury of the interior of the royal apartments and used and enjoyed them. So did Charles V, who is reputed to have spent his honeymoon there and added his own apartments as well as renovating the baths with new glazed tiles. By then the mosque had been demolished and other parts of the Moorish palace were destroyed to make way for the neo-Classical extension. The baths, in particular, must have been a revelation. Although the wearing of multi-coloured finery was commonplace in the Christian courts of Europe, personal cleanliness was not emphasised. Indeed washing in the nude was considered immoral by many medieval churchmen. The Moorish public baths were seen by the same clergy to be shameful centres of sin and consequently most of them were closed or demolished after the Reconquest.

The experience of moving through the internal spaces of the Alhambra is a memorable progression through space and time. At no one point is it possible to perceive the whole. Although at most positions the space is contained, without a direct view of the outside, there is never an effect of claustrophobia. There is a sequence of self-contained units, usually courtyards, aligned on a number of axes, an arrangement that allows the perception of one or more subsequent spaces from one point of view. Odd numbers are important in the spatial composition. Triple recession is common, looking from one major space to another through an intermediary which is frequently an arcade. If observing the fountain in the Patio de los Leones from the Sala de los Reyes the picture is framed by the arcades of the intervening pavilion and portico. Similarly, if the Patio de los Arrayanes is seen from the Salón de los Embajadores, it is framed by the archways of the Sala de la Barca. Screens of receding planes are often a preliminary to the climax of the external view of the landscape. The number seven is also used as the basis for composition, as in the arcades of the Patio de los Arrayanes, or five, as in the case of the Partal Palace. As such members of elements are always arranged on a symmetrical axis, a central arch is emphasised by greater width or height or both. An even number of arches cannot achieve symmetry if the arch is the dominant motif, and is only used in the case of the Sala de los Ajimeces, where two arches are coupled together to emphasise the central column.

Another view of the Patio de los Leones and the Lion Fountain seen through the colonnade of one of the two end pavilions.

RIGHT
The Patio del Cuarto Dorado, showing the central fountain and the triple portico at the north end.

It is important to understand that the residents and visitors at the Alhambra usually sat or reclined on carpets or cushions on the floor. The sills of any window openings, where a view of the outside gardens or landscape was desirable, were kept low or at floor level in order to give observers a wider range of vision in the vertical and horizontal planes. A low seat on the floor also meant a greater awareness of the finishes of the ceiling and the undersides of the arcades than if residents were standing or moving about the building or using Western-style furniture with elevated seats. These surfaces were decorated with exceptional care and skill because of the lower angle of vision. The throne, the level of which was only slightly above the floor, was normally placed symmetrically; however, access and approach were not directly in front of it but at right-angles. In the Salón de los Embajadores the window embrasures are grouped in threes, and it seems likely that the throne was placed in the central recess to the left or the right as the visitor approached from the Sala de la Barca. Above, the hemispherical dome signified the universe and its myriad stars. The emir and his courtiers

A close-up of a muqarna *arch in the Sala de la Barca revealing traces of the original colouring. To the right the wall surface is decorated with an incised circular pattern of tendrils and fruit.*

Three successive muqarna *arches in the Sala de los Reyes seen in perspective. This and the previous view of intricate detailing of* muqarnas *would have been seen at their best when the observer was seated at ground level. (See also p. 135.)*

were therefore at its centre in a position of earthly power. Here, where the dome is placed over a cube, the equal relationship of height to width and breadth means that the floor area is not excessive and the distance of the monarch from his visitors and courtiers is not intimidating. On the other hand, the height is great enough to create an impressive space in three dimensions around him. The balance of the expression of power with the creation of a human environment of peace and relaxation is the secret of the success of the design of the palace as a whole.

Outside the Alhambra, the Nasrids built a summer villa on the main water conduit to the east and at a higher level than the Alhambra. As there is an inscription recording the name of the Emir Ismail I (r. 1314–25), it is believed that it dates from the early fourteenth century. Its name, Generalife, supposedly derives from the Arabic for 'Architect's Garden', the legend being that Ismail bought it from one of the original designers of the Alhambra who had built the villa for his own occupation. It is a clever composition of pavilions, fountains, running water and planting on a sloping

The extended view of the Patio de la Acequia in the Generalife gardens which are separate from the royal palace but a part of the total Alhambra complex. It is celebrated for its long perspective of regularly spaced fountain jets.

site. On the hilltop above there is a mirador known as the Silla del Moro (Moor's Seat). Just beyond the Generalife proper is a raised garden and from here a flight of steps with fountains and flowing water in channels at balustrade level ascends to the Silla del Movo. Because of the ubiquitous shade and presence of flowing water it is possible to be cool and comfortable outside at the height of the summer heat in July and August, at the same time as enjoying spectacular views down to the Alhambra, over the city and across to the snow-covered mountains of the Sierra Nevada.

The Generalife is now approached over a bridge, which spans the ravine separating it from the Alhambra, then through an avenue of cypresses. It consists of a number of gardens and pavilions arranged on all four sides of a long garden court called the Patio de la Acequia (Patio of the Canal). This court presents a view in deep perspective of the royal apartments at the north end. Although there is only one long water channel there is a cross axis half-way along that is expressed by a path, at one end of which there was a small mosque. Although this path does divide the court into four long sections in the Islamic garden tradition, it is not very obvious and the visual emphasis is definitely unidirectional. The original entrance was through a smaller courtyard at the southwest corner. The portico of the northern pavilion has

A close-up of three of the arches in the portico at the end of the Patio de la Acequia. They are decorated with bands of cursive calligraphy enclosing panels of floral stucco work.

five arched openings with a wider central archway. It is similar in style to the porticoes of the Patio de los Arrayanes and is aligned on the axis of the long water channel which is now flanked by two rows of single-jet fountains, and on either side are numerous flowers and shrubs in colourful array. James Murphy in plate XCV, entitled 'Perspective View of the Garden of the Generalife', shows a different scene. Here the only fountains are in circular bowls at each end of the water course with one half-way along.

The movement of water was probably more restrained and tranquil in the days of the Nasrids. The contemporary scene is more lively than it was in Murphy's day, when he showed a relatively flat surface either side of the water-course in his perspective, although in plan he has drawn standard repetitive symbols to represent small-scale planting. In the accompanying text he expatiates on the fertility of the vegetation, mentioning the cypress trees and the lofty and spacious bowers. He expressly describes the enchanting effect of the Patio de la Acequia, where the water makes the space appear longer than it really is. 'At the side of the gardens is planted the blooming laurel, a tree to which the Moors were extremely partial, while box fences enclose beds of roses. The whole is in perpetual bloom, as most of the trees are evergreen, sheltered on three sides, and exposed to a southern aspect.' Presumably these comments were specifically referring to the Patio de la Acequia rather than those gardens of the estates outside the enclosing walls of the patio.

Another perspective of the play of fountains in a setting of flowers and greenery within the gardens of the Generalife.

The harem was at the northern end of the long patio overlooking a small water court known as the Patio de la Sultana. Here a U-shaped canal encloses two central islands. It is intimate and alive with the murmuring sound of fountains. The square beds are planted with flowering oleanders the pink flowers of which stand out in summer in contrast to the dark green background of the cypresses. From this level the next stage leads upwards to the famous water stairway. On both sides of the flights of stairs the balustrades are formed with tiled channels. Here the water runs into basins, each of which has a fountain jet, at the top and the bottom of each flight. There are three landings, each with bowl fountains at the centre and pergolas for shade. A few steps from the top of the last flight is the wonderful viewpoint, at one time known as the Silla del Moro (Moor's Seat) but called the Mirador of the Sultana by others.

The laurels of the Generalife also inspired Théophile Gautier. He wrote of the canal turning a right-angle, which it does at the southern end of the water-course where it leads to other enclosures adorned with ponds. 'In the centre of one of these ponds blooms, like a vast bouquet, a gigantic rose-laurel [oleander] of incomparable beauty.' Later he wrote his celebrated romantic poem on the same theme. In a series of illustrations of Granada and the Alhambra, published in 1837, only five years before Gautier's visit, Girault de Prangey shows a succession of arched bowers of some climbing plant straddling the central water-channel in the Patio de la Acequia at regular intervals, a very different impression from that recorded by Murphy about 30 years earlier. De Prangey also depicted more planting in the Patio de los Leones than is present now.

Due to the lack of any pictorial representation from medieval times of the Alhambra and its gardens, it is impossible to be certain of the appearance of the courtyards when at the height of the glory of al-Andalus. Manuscript illustrations show warriors and monarchs at court, with little attempt to depict the architectural context, but none show courtiers or the

De Prangey's romantic lithograph of the Patio de la Acequia in the Generalife garden at the Alhambra shows a planting arrangement very different from the present scene. (See p. 137.) Also there appear to have been no jet fountains lining the water channel in 1837.

royal family relaxing in their private apartments or gardens. Unfortunately, there seems to have been no Andalusian equivalent of the Persian or Moghul miniature, or if there were, none have survived the Reconquest. Most of the colours of the painted stucco and timber decorations have faded or were disfigured with coats of whitewash in later centuries. Owen Jones and Jules Goury tried in the nineteenth century to analyse and reproduce what they considered to have been the original colours of the decoration in relief.

In 1359 the reign of Mohammed V was interrupted, due to palace intrigue, by the short reigns of Ismail II and Mohammed VI. He was restored to the throne in 1362 with the help of Pedro I of Castile who had Mohammed VI killed in Seville. Mohammed V continued in power until 1391. Meanwhile in Castile the dynasty of the Trastámaras, which had been founded in 1369, ruled for the next century. Although Navarre in the north had remained independent, even for a year or two allied with Granada against Castile, it was eventually absorbed into Aragón by marriage. The Hundred Years War between France and England created a division between Castile and Aragón because the latter favoured the cause of England and Castile allied itself with France. Rivalry between the Christian kingdoms diverted them from their ambition to free the Peninsula from Islam. Castile later succeeded in driving a wedge between Aragón and Granada with the capture of Murcia. Granada then had no land frontier with Aragón. After a period of confrontation with Castile, Portugal turned its attention south and

east, capturing Ceuta in 1415 and Tangier in 1471. These events marked its beginnings as a maritime power. Meanwhile Aragón, with its Catalan mariners, expanded eastwards towards Italy and Sicily. This legacy of almost total confusion amongst the Christian powers enabled Granada to survive as a state far longer than expected. It was not until Castile and Aragón resolved their differences and were united through the marriage of Isabella of Castile and Ferdinand of Aragón in 1469 that the fate of the kingdom of Granada was inevitable. Although a succession of different Nasrid kings ruled here, some, as before, reigning for very short periods, there were many Muslim raids into Castile with less and less coordination from the centre.

Another romantic coloured rendering by de Prangey of a courtyard within the Alhambra. This is the Patio de los Leones with a projecting portico on the left and the celebrated fountain on the right. Again the planting was different in his time when there was considerably more vegetation than at present. (See p. 125.)

CHAPTER 6

The Sala dos Arabes in the Palácio Nacional at Sintra in Portugal is one of the apartments built by King Manuel I in an individual oriental style using azulejos for the dados and framing for the door openings.

Survival of the MUDÉJAR STYLE
against the odds

The perceived threat of the Ottoman Empire, underlined by the capture of Constantinople in 1453, hastened the deterioration of the *convivencia*, the sometimes reluctant acceptance of Muslims and Jews in those parts of the Peninsula that had been reconquered by the Christians. The Inquisition, established by Pope Gregory IX in the thirteenth century, had encouraged intolerance by the institution of the *auto da fe* or public prosecution of heresy which was sometimes followed by the burning of those found guilty. The Moors, whether converted or not, were often presented as potential enemies within the gate. By the fateful year of 1492, when the last Muslim territory in the Peninsula, the emirate of Granada, surrendered to Ferdinand and Isabella, the Catholic monarchs of Spain, it seemed that the situation of non-Christians might become impossible. The terms of the surrender, however, allowed hostages and prisoners to be exchanged and Moors were permitted to retain their property, whereas those who wished could leave and sell up and were guaranteed safe passage. Those who elected to remain could continue their own customs, and religious freedom was maintained. Boabdil (d. *c.* 1493), the defeated emir, was allowed to leave in safety for Morocco and was followed there by many Muslim emigrants.

This pattern of emigration to the countries of the Maghreb had been established in the earlier times of the Reconquest. Many had decided that they preferred to move to an Islamic country where they would be received with friendliness and especially to those countries where Andalusians had already settled. The relatively generous terms of the surrender were maintained for five years, but there was a change of policy when Ximenez de Cisneros became Archbishop of Toledo. In 1499 a programme of forced baptism was instituted in Spain. A quantity of Islamic books was burned and the largest mosque in Albaicín, a district of Granada just below the Alhambra, was converted to a church. This was followed, as might have been expected, by a revolt which in turn provided the justification for Ferdinand's decree that the Muslims should face the choice of conversion or expulsion. This was immediately enforced in Castile but was somewhat delayed in Aragón and no action at all was taken in Valencia until 1525.

The nobility and large landowners had never been in favour of harsh treatment of the Moors, mainly as a matter of self-interest because so many of them worked as skilled tenant-farmers, particularly in the Valencia region and the Ebro valley. Similarly, their unique skills in the construction and ceramic industries could not be readily replaced by Christians. Moorish music and musicians had been appreciated by Christians from the fourteenth century onwards, and Andalusian music and verse forms had spread through North Africa as far as Baghdad. The Andalusian style of music has survived to the present day in both Morocco and Tunisia.

Finally, however, the implacable hostility of the Catholic Church and the middle class prevailed upon Philip III (r. 1598–1621) to sign a series of decrees from 1609 to 1614 ordering the expulsion of the Moors. The final exodus was carried out with extreme inhumanity. A small minority was allowed to stay under strict conditions, which included a ban on the use of the Arabic language and Moorish clothes. But then only total assimilation was considered acceptable by the authorities.

The Jews had already been expelled from Spain in 1492 and from Portugal in 1497 with a consequent loss of skills in finance and the professions. From 1614 onwards the Peninsula had achieved complete *limpieza de sangre* (blood cleansing) but at a great cost to both its economy and culture. It has been estimated that between 275,000 and 470,000 Moors were forced to leave Spain. Their final destinations were countries where Andalusians had previously fled and established themselves. The general direction was from north to south, but towards the south the areas of immigration fanned out, a large number from Aragón going to Tunisia in the east, while many from Extramadura moved to Rabat on the Atlantic coast of Morocco. An important street in the medina of Tunis is still known as the street of the Andalusians. Many immigrants from the Ebro valley in Aragón settled in the towns of Tozeur and Testour in Tunisia. They were farmers searching for land and conditions similar to those in Aragón. The older section of Tozeur provides an urban environment identical to that in parts of Calatayud or Teruel. The minaret is octagonal in plan and, although it appears to have lost its original decoration of ceramic tiles, it could be mistaken for an Aragonese bell-tower. The *mihrab* is richly decorated with star patterns and intricately carved and it includes *artesonado* work. The domestic architecture displays all the devices of Mudéjar builders, with prominent panels of *espina de pez* (fish-bone) patterned brickwork. An extensive use of blind arcades creates a dense inward-looking layout of narrow streets. Some houses are built over the street at first-floor level to provide shade for social events. There are also many hidden paradise gardens reminiscent of Spain.

Testour was created on the ruins of a Roman city. The minaret of the Friday Mosque has a square plan but it is surmounted with an octagonal tower and lantern which lacks large openings as there are, of course, no bells. The plan of the mosque follows the traditional Islamic form, its width greater than the depth in the proportion of nine bays to seven. It is approached through an open arcaded courtyard. The dome above the *mihrab* has squinches in the shape of shells, and the roof of the prayer hall consists of ribbed vaults supported on 48 columns, the capitals of which were recovered from the Roman ruins. The upper section of the unusual *mihrab* is shaped like a shell and flanked by two Classical columns which support a Baroque pediment with inscriptions in Arabic. This is evidence of Spanish influence, but it is unlikely that the builders realised that the shell is considered by many Christians of the Peninsula to be the emblem of Santiago de Compostela.

Salé, across the river from Rabat, contained the sanctuary of Sidi Achmed ben Achir, an Andalusian marabout or holy man. It became the principal port of Morocco in the late Middle Ages and a centre of attraction for Andalusian refugees. The first group came from a small town near

145

Badajoz called Hornachos and were given accommodation and employment as mercenaries by Sultan Zaydan. More followed from other parts of Spain. They eventually proclaimed an independent republic and became pirates. The immigrants who had once appeared Muslim to the Spaniards now appeared Christian to the Moroccans because of their 'Europeanised' customs. The medina of Rabat soon developed the characteristics of an Andalusian town with patio houses accompanied by fountains and gardens. The internal walls were frequently decorated with *azulejos* and intricately carved stucco.

The greatest journey travelled by non-Christian refugees from the Iberian Peninsula appears to have been to Istanbul, the capital of the Ottoman Empire, where many settled in Galata to the north of the Golden Horn. Galata had been founded by the Genoese during the Byzantine period. After 1453 it became the main quarter for foreigners, particularly those of European origin. Both Jewish and Muslim refugees from the Peninsula were welcomed, and they joined a mixed population which included Greeks and Armenians. A building known today as the Arab Mosque is a former church that was built during 1323–37 and converted in the early sixteenth century for use as a mosque and allocated to the growing number of Muslim immigrants from al-Andalus. Most of Galata was destroyed by fire in the nineteenth century, which may explain the lack of any architectural evidence of the presence of Andalusians, but the production of coloured glazed tiles in geometric designs using the *cuerda seca* method appeared in Turkey during the sixteenth century, and this may have been due to their influence and activity.

The district of Balat, farther up the Golden Horn on the south side, became one of the principal quarters of the Jewish community. The original occupants were Greek-speaking Jews from early Byzantine times. They were later outnumbered by Sefardis (Jews of Spanish or Portuguese descent) who had been invited to take up residence by Beyazit II after the 1492 decree of expulsion from Spain. The Sultan doubted the wisdom of this act of King Ferdinand and believed that he was impoverishing Spain and enriching the Ottoman Empire with those who could strengthen its capabilities in finance and administration. The few remaining synagogues date from the nineteenth century but the use of *Ladino*, the Latin-based dialect of their Andalusian ancestors, has survived up to the present day, although it is now spoken only by a minority of Turkish Jews.

The Jews in the Iberian Peninsula had been subject to hostility from the Catholic church for well over a century before their final expulsion. Emigration to Palestine for a select few had started as early as the twelfth century but it was not until 1391, when pogroms took place in many cities, that emigration took on the nature of a mass movement. The Archdeacon of Ecija had initiated the persecution with a series of inflammatory sermons in Seville from 1378 onwards in which he called for the destruction of the 23 synagogues in the city. The Inquisition claimed to have established that

13,000 *conversos* (Jews who had accepted forced baptism) had continued to practise Judaism. Ferdinand and Isabella gave in to this increasing pressure, in spite of the fact that two Jewish financiers had been instrumental in helping them to fund their last campaign against the Muslims of Granada. The expulsion was effected with speed, and all synagogues, cemeteries and community property were confiscated by the royal treasury. The majority, about 100,000, went to Portugal while another 50,000 sailed from Almería to North Africa. In 1497 there followed a royal decree declaring their expulsion from Portugal. A minority left for the Netherlands but most remained, accepting baptism. In 1504 anti-Jewish riots occurred in Lisbon and a pogrom followed two years later. The Inquisition was not introduced to Portugal until 1531.

The departure of the Jews had not been wanted by all Andalusian Christians, and it is on record that the councillors of Teruel tried to persuade the Jewish community to accept baptism and stay, apparently with some success. In 1504 the city council of Zaragoza had ordered the building of the Torre Nueva in a Mudéjar style and appointed two Christians, two Muslims and one Jew to take charge of the construction. This building was a tall handsome octagonal brick tower, which was unfortunately demolished in 1894 but illustrations and photographs of it survive. Richard Ford, the author of *A Handbook for Travellers in Spain and Readers at Home*, made a pencil sketch of it in 1831 when it appears to have been inclined.

The synagogues that were converted to churches in the fifteenth century included those that have survived in Toledo, Córdoba, Segovia and Seville. All have suffered physical alteration to a greater or lesser degree. Only one has survived in Portugal, an example at Tomar, dating from the fourteenth century. The Mudéjar style was applied successfully to the Iberian synagogue, and Hebrew calligraphy was substituted for the Arabic. But after their expulsion from the Peninsula, it seems that the emigrating Jews adapted the current style they found in their new home countries to the traditional plan. In Italy they used the Renaissance style, in the Netherlands the Spanish and Portuguese synagogue of Amsterdam was built in a local neo-Classical style, whereas the synagogue at Bevis Marks in London had much in common with the simple neo-Classical English non-conformist chapel of the time. It was not until the nineteenth century that the designers of synagogues felt the need to express in architectural terms the nostalgia that some Jews in Europe and North America had for their ancestral origins in the Iberian Peninsula or Morocco.

Meanwhile in Spain some aspects of Mudéjar elements had been absorbed into the main trend of development, dominated as it was by Renaissance and Baroque ideas imported from Italy and France. The taste for intricate surface decoration was evident in the Plateresque style, a rich Spanish version of the Early Renaissance. Lope de Vega (1562–1635), the celebrated dramatist, named the craftsmen who created the elaborate filigree work in plaster and stone *plateros de yeso*, silversmiths in plaster, hence the

The inclination of the Torre Nueva, built at Zaragoza in a brick Mudéjar style at the beginning of the sixteenth century, may have accounted for its eventual demolition in 1894.

name Plateresque. The early sixteenth-century façade of the University of Salamanca, which contains a wealth of surface ornament, including Renaissance motifs, arabesques, modillions and other patterns within a Gothic frame, is a typical example. The ornamentation includes the medallion of Ferdinand and Isabella as well as the coat of arms of Charles V.

The cloister inside the Convento de Nossa Senhora de Conceição at Beja in the Alentejo has walls and window openings lined with geometric azulejos *within a simple Gothic structure.*

The chapter house in the same convento *at Beja also has the dados and door and window openings lined with azulejos but with more complex patterning. The simple painted vaulted ceiling is supported on a single Classical marble column.*

The attraction of polychrome tiled decoration was strong in Portugal even in religious buildings and when the Convento de Nossa Senhora da Conceição was founded in Beja in the fifteenth century by Don Fernando and his wife, the parents of King Manuel I, the walls of the four galleries of the cloister were faced with a variety of *azulejos* including some lustre tiles

FAR LEFT
The sixteenth-century stone façade of the University of Salamanca was carved in an elaborate style termed Plateresque which was based on Renaissance proportions but decorated with intricate surface patterns.

attributed to artists of Seville. This building is now the Museu Regional, and it contains an interesting terracotta grille dating from the early fifteenth century which had been part of a passageway to the nearby royal palace.

The most characteristic and easily recognisable Mudéjar feature to survive in the Peninsula after the departure of the Moors was the *artesonado* ceiling. This was produced by an embellished system of carpentry to support a pitched roof above. It was used extensively in religious buildings, other public buildings and palaces. A number of skilled carpenters, some of whom had the abilities to design complete buildings, possessed the comprehensive knowledge of the geometry involved in the setting-out and construction of such a complicated roof and ceiling system. There were available source books and written by-laws administered by master-masons (*alarifes*) on behalf of the appropriate municipality. The geometric principles were explained in the documents and set squares, specially prepared in the workshop, were used to ensure the correct angles of the different slopes. The sizing of the members and the network of geometrical patterns were decided according to accepted mathematical rules. These integrated the functional elements, such as the beams, ties and trusses, with the interlacing decorative motifs. Although the dominant theme was abstract and geometric, many of the coffered spaces between beams and rafters were painted with portraits, heraldic devices, animals and other designs. A celebrated example is the ceiling of Teruel Cathedral.

The setting-out required the use of repeating mathematical grids based on the square, the circle, rectangles of varying proportions including the golden section, the octagon, hexagon, pentagon and star patterns with from five to twelve points. The structural systems included a flat ceiling with parallel beams and rafters (*alfarje*) or the interior expression of a double pitched roof with two inclined planes or three planes including one central

150

horizontal plane. If the span were relatively wide, tie beams were used and exposed, often in pairs. Sometimes hipped ends to the roof would create at least four or more inclined planes to the interior surfaces.

An important document, dating from 1519, written by Diego Lopez de Arenas, who was the official *alarife* of Seville, dealt with the subject of *'la carpinteria de lo blanco'*, which was the name given to this type of carpentry. It includes drawings and, amongst other written matters, some descriptions of the difficulties encountered in the course of his official duties. He incorporated most of the by-laws that had been applied during the previous centuries – the *artesonado* ceiling had been in use since the thirteenth century.

Isabella of Castile and Ferdinand of Aragón were married in 1469, and they inherited their respective thrones in 1474 and 1479. The previously rival kingdoms were thus united to form the powerful kingdom of Spain (Navarre was not absorbed until 1512), but they continued to hold court in Zaragoza, the former capital of Aragón where the Aljafería continued as the royal palace. In 1486 the tribunal of the Holy Inquisition was also accommodated in the large complex. Two years later the royal couple initiated a programme of works to expand and improve the palace and engaged a team of craftsmen under the control of Faraig de Gali, a Mudéjar, to undertake the work. This appointment was made with the agreement of the officials of the Inquisition, and he continued to supervise building in the Aljafería until 1508, when he was succeeded as master of the royal works by his son, Mahoma de Gali, again with royal and religious approval.

Below the gilded and coffered ceiling of the throne room at the Aljafería in Zaragoza there is an arcaded gallery for important guests. Under the gallery in this setting of regal splendour there is a cornice which has a continuous calligraphic inscription commemorating in Latin the liberation of Andalusia from Muslim rule in 1492.

In the fateful year of 1492, a throne room was erected within the palace as a symbolic expression of the power and magnificence of the Catholic monarchs. It is approached via a noble staircase which leads to an upper gallery overlooking the Patio de Santa Isabel. This gallery acts as a reception space for the throne room, which is long and high with the impressive proportions appropriate for important ceremonial occasions. It has a magnificent horizontal *artesonado* ceiling with beams that stretch in both directions forming 30 coffers on a square grid. Each coffer has an octagonal inset with a carved and gilded pine-cone at its centre. The undersides of the beams are decorated with interlacing geometrical patterns which create eight-pointed stars at the intersections. Below the ceiling an arcaded gallery for invited guests runs the full length of all four walls and below the gallery there is a richly embellished cornice which incorporates a calligraphic inscription in Latin which reads:

> Ferdinand, King of the two Spains, Sicily, Corsica, and the Balearics, the best of the princes, prudent, brave, devout, constant, just, happy, and Isabella, Queen, above all women for piety and greatness of spirit, illustrious and most victorious couple, with the help of Christ, after the liberation of Andalusia from the Moors, expelled the ancient and proud enemy, commissioned the construction of this work, in the year of Salvation 1492.

It has been suggested that the gallery was reserved for the use of the ladies of the court so that they could observe the court ceremonial from a position of vantage. The plain stone walls below the cornice were probably hung with sumptuous tapestries and draperies to complement the splendour of the ceiling, gallery and the floor, which was paved with *azulejos* in a variety of coloured geometrical and vegetal patterns. It is not surprising to learn that it was known as the Golden Hall; there is a legend that the gold used in the gilding was brought by Columbus himself, the first to come from the New World. This is not impossible as the work was not completed until 1495, when the palace was visited by a German traveller, Jeronimo Munzer, who wrote a vivid description of the throne room in all its glory. Because of the increasing urbanisation and economic development taking place in Europe, it was believed that the resulting serious shortage of gold was hindering the expansion of international trade. This was the impetus behind the voyages of the explorers of the fifteenth and sixteenth centuries and their promoters. Africa had been the source of gold, imported through North Africa, through many centuries for the Iberian Peninsula and Northern Europe. As Christian power expanded eventually to overwhelm the whole of the Iberian Peninsula, the attraction of the continent of Africa as a source of gold increased. The royal house of Portugal became interested in expanding its influence southwards, although there had been no previous Portuguese naval tradition. The celebrated Prince Henry the Navigator was active in crusading and in looking for profitable overseas trade. Infidels had long been purveyors of gold, spices and slaves, and there appear to have been dual motives in the search for gold and the conversion of souls on the part of Henry and his team of sailors, navigators and astronomers. Whether the initial intention was to invade or bypass Morocco is not clear, but both Ceuta and Tangier were captured by the Portuguese. Madeira and the Azores were discovered and colonised. The Cape Verde Islands and Sierra Leone were reached by 1460, the year of Prince Henry's death. The Crown revenues doubled when the fort of São Jorge da Mina, in Ghana (formerly known as the Gold Coast), was established in 1482 and it became a source of gold and slaves.

Manuel I (r. 1495–1521) came to the throne of Portugal a year after the Treaty of Tordesillas had been signed between Spain and Portugal through papal arbitration in order to put the expansionist rivalries of the two countries on a manageable basis. The line of division was made 370 leagues west of the Cape Verde Islands. Territories west of the line were allocated to Spain while those to the east became the sphere of influence of Portugal, allowing the later Portuguese colonisation of Brazil (originally called Terra de Vera Cruz). In 1496 Manuel decreed the purification of the Great Mosque of the Mouraria in Lisbon and a convent was constructed nearby. Before this, all Moorish gravestones had been removed and all Muslims except the very poor had fled. The influence of the Society of Jesus, a religious order with special loyalty to the Pope and missionary in purpose, became very strong in the sixteenth century and its intolerance towards non-Catholics spread. The Jewish cemetery was also removed. The convent on the site of the mosque later became the first house in Lisbon to be owned by the Jesuits.

Manuel had married Princess Isabella, daughter of the Catholic monarchs, Ferdinand and Isabella, so uniting the two royal houses of the Peninsula. In 1498 Manuel, his queen and their retinue made a round tour of Spain. They crossed the border at Badajoz where they were received by the Duke of Alba. Passing through Mérida, Guadalupe and Talavera they reached Toledo. There, in the cathedral, they were sworn in as the successors of the Catholic monarchs. From Toledo they travelled towards Aragón to Calatayud and then Zaragoza, where they stayed at the Aljafería. They continued their triumphal progress eastwards to Barcelona. Here tragedy overtook them; Isabella died giving birth to her first and only son. Manuel then returned as quickly as possible to Portugal, through León via Coimbra to Lisbon, leaving the child in the care of its maternal grandparents. Sadly the son also died two years later.

During the eastward part of his journey Manuel had become fascinated by the Moorish and Mudéjar buildings of Spain and developed a taste for the elements of the Mudéjar style. He had already become attracted by the exotic, not only Arab, cultures which had become popular in Portugal since the conquest of Ceuta in 1415, but also the art forms which were appearing amongst the trade goods from the new colonial settlements in the Far East. The king particularly enjoyed the music and dances performed by Moorish musicians at court. At bullfights he is reported to have distributed

FAR RIGHT
A view of the central patio of the Palácio Nacional at Sintra showing an ajimez *window opening into the courtyard and the prominent conical chimneys of the royal kitchens beyond.*

A close-up of the unusual circular marble fountain at the centre of the Sala dos Arabes and set in a square of azulejos. *(See also p. 142.)*

A detail of the azulejo wall facing to the Sala dos Arabes which incorporates square green tiles set in alternate blue and white tiles in the shape of a parallelogram which give a three-dimensional effect to the pattern as a whole.

Detail of the azulejo patterns that border the arched door opening in the same room. The most remarkable are those that make the horizontal band of formal flower patterns at the top.

Arab harness and vestments. He then set about the renovation of the summer palace at Sintra, the foundations of which dated from the time of the Muslim occupation.

John I had already made additions to the palace at the beginning of the fifteenth century, and it is believed that he planned the Ceuta expedition here. The Palácio Nacional, or Palácio Real, is situated amongst thick green woodland on the northern slopes of the Serra de Sintra to the west of Lisbon. The site has been much praised in poetry and prose; Byron called it 'a glorious Eden'. The gardens, with their many sub-tropical shrubs and flowers, are especially beautiful, although the climate is predominantly humid and pleasantly cool in summer, very different from the dry heat of Castile, Andalusia and Morocco. The exterior of the palace is relatively restrained with four simple pointed arched openings to the entrance porch. At first-floor level there are a number of *ajimez* windows, some with carved stone decoration in what came to be known as the Manueline style. Its skyline is dominated by two tall conical chimneys to the extensive kitchens, reminiscent of the chimneys of the Topkapi Palace at Istanbul.

Manuel's band of craftsmen created a palace of internal courtyards with a definite Moorish character. Later additions and amendments make it a very complicated arrangement of spaces. *Azulejos* of many colours and geometrical patterns were brought from Seville. The main reception space, known as the Sala dos Arabes (Arab Hall), contains a small marble fountain of Classical design tiled with green, blue and white *azulejos*. There are five

doorways in the form of an *alfiz* with carved arabesque decoration. The walls of the audience chamber, known as the Sala das Pêgas (Hall of Magpies) because of the magpies painted in the seventeenth century on the coffered ceiling, with roses in their beaks (a decoration conceived by John I to mock the gossiping of his lady courtiers) are lined with *azulejos* of the *cuerda seca* type.

The Sala das Pêgas at the Palácio Nacional at Sintra is so called because of its painted ceiling of magpies representing gossiping lady courtiers. The dados, window and door openings and fireplace are also faced with azulejos.

*The Sala dos Cisnes has a similar decor except that the timber ceiling has a
series of octagons containing paintings of swans.*

The Sala dos Cisnes (Hall of Swans) is also lined with *azulejos* but its main feature is the magnificent polychrome ceiling panelled in octagons and embellished with 27 swans with gilded collars. The royal chapel has a rich vaulted *artesonado* polychrome ceiling with geometric grids defined by eight-pointed stars. The geometrical patterning is echoed in the floor, which is paved with *azulejos*. In the bedroom of Don Sebastião the walls are covered with remarkable *azulejos* with moulded patterns of vine leaves. The largest room of the palace, the Sala das Armas (Hall of Coats of Arms), is square; its timber dome rests on squinches, and on the ceiling square panels are painted with the coats of arms of Portuguese nobles of the sixteenth century. The walls are decorated with *azulejo* compositions of hunting scenes in blue and white dating from the eighteenth century. Some of the courtyards' exterior walls are tiled with geometrical *azulejos*, but the strongest external expression of the Mudéjar style lies in the use of the *ajimez* for balcony, door and window openings.

Manuel I built another palace between 1507 and 1520 at Évora in the Alentejo. The Palácio de Dom Manuel is a two-storey building 70 metres

The ceiling to the chapel is in the artesonado *tradition. The geometric pattern to the main ceiling is based on a sixteen-pointed star whereas the narrower section is based on squares and eight-pointed stars.*

Part of the long elevation of the Palácio de Dom Manuel at Évora that has an open ground floor of round arches and piers that support the the upper section with its continuous arcade of windows above.

FAR LEFT
The balcony intended for the use of the ladies at the Casa Cordovil at Évora is accentuated by its more ornate treatment of ajimez windows above and the use of complicated carved multi-lobed horseshoe arches below.

LEFT
The eccentric design of the first-floor balcony of the Casa Cordovil incorporates columns so slender that the structure appears to be top heavy with the solid conical dome above.

long with multi-lobed horseshoe arcades at ground level and double horse-shoe-arched window openings in the upper storey. At the same level a prominent balcony was intended for the use of the ladies of the court. It is on record that two Castilian masters, Alonso de Pallos and Pedro de Trillo, worked on its construction. The Palácio Vimioso was constructed opposite the cathedral of Évora, also in the Mudéjar manner. It was used as the residence of the bishop whose son, Dom Francisco, was a member of Manuel I's retinue on his 1498 Spanish tour, so probably it predates the Palácio Nacional. There are five twin-arched window openings in a ruinous condition which were re-erected in the public gardens near King Manuel's palace some time in the last century. The Casa Cordovil is another example of Manueline architectural detailing in Évora from the same period. It has a balcony at first-floor level where a conical dome on horseshoe arches with crenellations above is supported on slender columns with Moorish capitals. The effect is striking if only for the disturbing visual impression that the columns are too thin to give stability to the structure above.

Probably the most prominent structure of the period in Lisbon that shows Manuel's taste for the Mudéjar is the Torre de Belém (Tower of Bethlehem) built in the river Tejo (Tagus) close to the north bank. This appears like an Arab castle with circular projecting lookout balconies at the four corners of the battlements and a similar set repeated at first-floor level. There are also projecting balconies at the centres of three external walls at the third-floor level with *ajimeces* above. At the same level of the side facing across the river there is a continuous balcony in the same style. An artillery platform juts out over the water to one side of the tower. The entrance gate-way is set in the wall of the platform that faces the land, and there are circular sentry boxes at the corners. The construction period was 1516–21 and the architect was Francisco de Arruda whose brother, Diogo, worked at the Convento de Cristo at Tomar.

A close-up of the upper storeys of the Torre de Belém showing the projecting double-arched balconies and the windows above in a version of the

There is a continuous covered balcony on the side of the tower that faces the river. It has seven arches and an open colonnade. Above the balcony are two single-arched widows either side of a heavily sculptured heraldic shield.

FOLLOWING PAGES
A view of the Torre de Belém at Lisbon looking across the river Tejo. It was built by King Manuel in the first quarter of the sixteenth century.

ABOVE LEFT
The conical almenas *that were added during the time of Manuel I to the eaves of the former mosque after it had been in use for some time as the parish church at Mértola. (See also p. 67.)*

ABOVE RIGHT
The plain exterior of the manor house at Alvito which was built by one of King Manuel's nobles and is now in use as a pousada. *The* ajimez *windows at first-floor level are in a restrained Manueline style.*

The king's liking for the Mudéjar set a fashion amongst the nobles, and other more modest manor houses in this style were built. A typical example at Alvito, which was completed in 1502, is now restored and in use as a *pousada* (government hotel). At about the same time the parish church at Mértola, a former mosque of the Almohad period, received the crowning of a new parapet wall decorated with *almenas* (merlon) similar to those at the palace at Sintra. This work, which was part of a renewal programme, was supervised by the master-builder Fernão Pires.

The enthusiasm of the king for both architecture and the exotic affected the appearance of every major building of his reign. As a result, the term 'Manueline' was applied by nineteenth-century historians to most buildings of that period, including those already mentioned that were conceived by him or his courtiers. It is not easy to define its meaning. It is not equivalent to Mudéjar because it is used to describe some buildings, particularly religious ones, that are predominantly Gothic in style but that nevertheless show a taste for intricate surface decoration of exotic inspiration. The adjective 'Luso-Moorish' has been used by some specifically to describe those buildings with a more direct resemblance to the Mudéjar, such as the Palácio Nacional at Sintra, the Torre de Belém and some work at the Mosteiro de Santa Maria da Vitória, or Batalha Abbey, and the Convento de Cristo at Tomar.

A spectacular example of the Manueline style is the addition to the Dominican Mosteiro de Santa Maria da Vitória Batalha where the main west façade has a magnificent flamboyant window with intricate tracery and two blind arcades of interlaced tracery, one above the window and the other above the elaborate Gothic entrance doorway. An octagonal mausoleum, the

At the Dominican Mosteiro de Santa Maria da Vitória at Batalha there is an unfinished octagonal mausoleum, known as the Capelas Imperfeitas, which has a typical Manueline interlaced cinquefoil archway to the porch which connects it with the main part of the monastery.

Capelas Imperfeitas, at the east end lies unfinished. Seven chapels radiate from the centre, and it is connected to the church by a lofty porch. It was designed in 1434 by Ouguete and abandoned in a partly constructed state. Work was resumed during Manuel's reign but the vaulted roof was never finished. The elaborate stone decorations, which include interlacing vegetal patterns and a medley of maritime motifs in the shape of ropes, knots and anchors, were carved by the mason Mateus Fernandes who spent 25 years

The complex arabesque tracery that decorates the base of one of the piers supporting the archway.

at work there. The archway to the opening from the chapel to the porch is a spectacular display of the stonemason's art with its cinquefoil arch and interlacing tracery. There are some exceptional arabesque medallions in three-dimensional plastic form on the architraves.

The Claustro Real (Royal Cloister) to the north of the main nave also has luxuriant carved stone decoration in interlacing vegetal patterns, including (according to Sacheverell Sitwell) the poppy, cardoon and artichoke. This is contained in perforated stone panels at the upper section of the simple Gothic windows. These panels are believed also to have been carved by Mateus Fernandes for Manuel I. At one corner of the cloister there is a lavabo consisting of a basin surmounted by two smaller basins. From this corner there is a fascinating view of the cloister as a whole and the arresting play of light on the water of the lavabo seen through the tracery.

FAR LEFT
The delicate vertical lines of the piers and the varying curves of the cinquefoil opening, seen from the porch looking into the roofless central octagonal space.

The unique window in the west front of the Convento de Cristo at Tomar which was extended by Diogo de Arruda between 1510 and 1514. The wrought-iron grille is contained within an extravagant mixture of nautical themes and vegetation, including rope and seaweed, sculpted in stone.

A detail of the window sill revealing the head and shoulders of a sea captain who is supporting the roots of a cork oak which is the source of the vegetation.

The church of the Military Order of Christ, at the Convento de Cristo in Tomar, was extended between 1510 and 1514 by Diogo de Arruda with a vaulted nave added to the original sixteen-sided sanctuary which had been built in the twelfth century on the model of the Holy Sepulchre in Jerusalem. The latter is known as the Charola and is linked to the nave by a large archway. The Order was the successor to the disbanded Knights Templar who had driven out the Moors in 1190. Their wealth helped to finance the voyages of discovery, and Prince Henry the Navigator had been their Grand Master. The same master-mason was responsible for the Chapter House below. The west front of the church is an extravagant example of Manueline carving. The design of the central window is unique. A rectangular opening with a wrought-iron grille like a *celosia* is decorated with two flanking masts showing a profusion of marine vegetation, ropework, cables, chains, seaweed and cork. At the centre the window is surmounted by the cross of the Order over the royal arms supported on a tangle of seaweed and cables. Below the sill the head and shoulders of a sea captain appear under the roots of a cork oak which is the source of the vegetation.

Why marine memorabilia should have become three-dimensional symbols on these two religious buildings is not obvious. It seems unlikely that the senior clerics would have been enthusiastic about them, especially as there is no equivalent in contemporary churches or monasteries in Spain, the rival maritime power. The monastery at Guadalupe, Spain, where Columbus received permission to sail to the New World and where many conquistadores spent time in prayer in front of the miraculous image of the Madonna before leaving for America, would have been a more likely site. The most probable explanation therefore is that these symbols were the result of Manuel I's desire to have produced an expression of his keenness for sailing the oceans, the unrivalled expertise of the Portuguese in navigation and its potential for the spread of the Word of God to the infidels across the seas.

Although in theory the Catholic monarchs represented a unified Spain, the mission of Columbus was considered as an agreement between him and the monarch of Castile alone. Because of this, the overseas empire was legally an extension of Castile and the trade with America was monopolised by Seville, where the royal office of trade, the Casa de Contratación, was established. So all Spaniards travelling to the empire would have spent some time there preparing for embarkation. Amongst them was Andrés de San Miguel who was born in Medina Sidonia in Andalusia and sailed as a young man from Seville in 1593. He later became a Carmelite brother in Mexico but did not want to become a priest and decided to study architecture instead. He designed two monasteries but later tended to specialise in civil engineering and became involved in drainage schemes in Mexico City and the design of a bridge over the Rio Grande. He is most remembered for his book *Arte y Uso de Arquitectura*. In this volume there is a very clear description of the principles of *la carpintaria de lo blanco* in a similar manner to that of Diego Lopez de Arenas. Perhaps the most beautiful examples of *artesonado* joinery in Mexico (New Spain as it was then known) are the ceilings in the nave and chapels of the church of San Francisco at Tlaxcala. They demonstrate the influence of Andrés de San Miguel's book.

He and others like him must have been influenced by memories of Seville, the last city of Spain they saw, and his book must have reinforced the use of Mudéjar elements in the colonial architecture of America. This would have been in spite of the instructions of the Spanish Crown, as early as 1501, to the Governor of Hispaniola, Nicolas de Ovando, that Moors, Jews and recent converts were to be strictly excluded from the Indies, as though they were foreigners. Stone was in short supply, so its use for constructing vaulted roofs was discouraged and the skill of carpenters to make timber *artesonado* roof trusses and ceilings became vital. They became the dominant craftsmen and even mastered brickwork and stonecutting when necessary. Timber construction was considered to be suitable for hot climates and also less liable to collapse in earthquakes, from which many parts of Latin America suffered at regular intervals. So the leading carpenters became builders and architects.

The oldest surviving example of *artesonado* work in America is in the Iglesia de la Concepción at Bogotá in Colombia (formerly known as New Granada) and there is another exceptionally beautiful ceiling in Bogotá at the church of San Francisco. *Artesonado* ceilings are also to be found in Quito, the capital of Ecuador, where the cathedral in the Plaza Mayor had a wonderful example, which has since been spoilt after earthquake damage. It was supposed to have been similar to the surviving ceiling at the church of Santo Domingo, also in Quito.

Other Mudéjar features were also adopted by the early Spanish colonials. The *ajimez*, the twin window with slim central column first used in the mosque at Córdoba, occurs in the design of the palace of Admiral Diego Columbus (son of Christopher) at Santo Domingo in the island of Hispaniola, the first Spanish settlement in America. In the southern zone of Colombia, brick was favoured for walls as demonstrated at the church of San Francisco, Cali. The square bell-tower has brickwork geometrically patterned in the Mudéjar manner, and the main entrance is through a single horseshoe archway surmounted with decorative brickwork and flanked with buttresses decorated with *azulejos*. It dates from the eighteenth century and continues an earlier tradition, examples of which survive only in old illustrations. At Puebla in Mexico the manufacture of *azulejos* was established, and they were widely used, often in conjunction with polychrome stucco. The main façade of the Casa de los Alfeñiques in Puebla was covered with large octagonal unglazed red tiles interspersed with smaller blue and white *azulejos*. This geometrical patterning was combined with pictorial panels on mythological and sacred themes. An earlier example in Mexico City, Casa de los Condes de Orizaba, has the wall surfaces divided into rectangular panels of *azulejos* in geometrical patterns while the rest of the external detailing is in a fanciful neo-Renaissance manner. Another outstanding example is the façade of the church of San Francisco at Acatepec where the style is Baroque but every flat surface is decorated with a geometrical polychrome pattern of tiles.

Antigua Guatemala, the original Guatemala City, was the repeated victim of shattering earthquakes. In 1717, a terrible earthquake required the reconstruction of the complete city on better foundations, but yet another in 1751 meant a second reconstruction. The third disaster of 1773 led to the abandonment of the site altogether, and the name has since been shortened to Antigua. The University is the most interesting of the buildings of Antigua to survive. It was built in 1763 to the designs of José Manuel Ramirez, a mestizo (of mixed descent) architect. The heavy structure, so often adopted to resist seismic forces, has been softened by the use of a proliferation of curves in the convoluted arcades of the cloister. They are a delightful reminder of the heritage of al-Andalus.

In North America there are a number of mission buildings from the Spanish period. They are relatively simple compared with the florid exuberance of Mexican Baroque, but some vernacular traces of Mudéjar are to be found in the few that remain in California, Arizona and New Mexico. The simplicity of their structure was due to the scarcity of stone and timber, the lack of skilled craftsmen and the frequent fighting and hostility between the Spaniards and the indigenous Indian people, which resulted in the semi-military character of the missions. The most common material to hand was adobe, and both Indians and Spaniards were familiar with its use. There is a legend that the first foreigner to enter Arizona was a so-called Moorish slave of the Viceroy of Mexico who was a member of the 1539 expedition. Vincent Scully in his study of the 'Pueblo' states 'the first white man that they saw was a black man who they treated as an intruder and killed'. If he really was of Moorish origin it is unlikely that his skin colour was darker than that of the Indians. On the other hand he might have been a slave of African descent. His presence, however, might indicate that the Mudéjar characteristics to be found in the colonial architecture of the period could be explained by the presence of Moors, including building craftsmen, among the Spanish colonists. The Moor's name is said to have been Estevan and there is a fortress-like church from this period at Acoma in New Mexico dedicated by the Franciscans to San Estevan, but this is probably a coincidence.

The taste for exuberant surface decoration was strong, in spite of Philip II of Spain's preference for the austere. This taste for the plain and the impressive was demonstrated at his huge palace complex at El Escorial outside Madrid where the Leyes de los Indios (laws of the Indies) were administered at his 'colonial office'. These laws were applied to all activities, including trade and town planning. The layout of almost every Spanish colonial town was based on a strict rectangular grid. The few exceptions were due to particularly difficult site contours.

Just before the capture of Granada, Christopher Columbus had been personally commissioned by Queen Isabella to undertake his voyage of discovery to the Indies, and Seville, as the sole port permitted to trade with the New World, became the most prosperous city in Spain. The traditional courtyard house, which had originally been developed in Córdoba, was now adapted and expanded for the houses of the new rich. The courts, often interconnected within a single residence, were paved with marble, and the planting was supplemented with tall palm trees. Such an example, called the Palacio de las Dueñas, now belonging to the Duchess of Alba, has a shaded patio with a pool as well as a garden planted with orange trees. The summer dining room on the ground floor has views of both of these spaces, creating an exciting relationship between the inside and outside spaces. Because of the extreme climate these Sevillian houses were used in different ways in summer and winter. In winter the family lived upstairs, in order to obtain the warmth of the sun, while during summer they took advantage of the cooler shaded areas at ground-floor level. The detailing of the arcading was usually in the Mudéjar style. The traditionally compact and relatively informal urban design layout was also retained.

Columbus had met Queen Isabella and her advisors outside Granada, which was still under siege, at a new settlement called Santa Fé de Granada, which had been founded the year before as a walled garrison town on an old Roman site. At the centre was the Plaza Mayor, one side of which was filled by the main church, and the streets were laid out on a rectangular grid of streets in the Roman military tradition. Current ideas of urban planning were then dominated by the Italian Alberti's updating of the Roman Vitruvius. In the Americas the opportunity was taken to employ a comprehensive urban philosophy unfettered by the need to accommodate an existing informal layout, as had been the case in Spanish towns. A lower density was adopted because of the availability of undeveloped land at most of the new urban sites. At the centre of the Plaza Mayor was the so-called 'tree of justice' where sentences and executions were carried out. The church, municipal buildings, shops and merchant houses were built on plots facing the plaza which normally had a continuous portico lining the perimeter.

The Canary Islands had been colonised in stages by the Spanish from 1402 until 1496, when the complete group of islands was incorporated under the Spanish crown. Ships *en route* from Seville, or later extended to Cádiz, to America often called at the ports here to load cargoes of sugar, which became one of the Islands' main crops. Abundant supplies of timber ensured a network of skilled carpenters. They followed building ordinances similar to those of Seville. Complicated *artesonado* ceilings were installed in the many new churches. The most interesting of these is the church of Santo Domingo at La Orotova in Tenerife, where it is possible to see almost the entire repertory of the *artesonado*. There is one extended main roof structure and ceiling, with twelve subsidiary spaces, each of which has a different size and design. Another fine example is the ceiling of the church of Santo Domingo at Santa Cruz de la Palma, where the rich geometrical patterns are based on the octagon with the occasional insertion of hexagons. In the church of El Salvador in the same town the ceiling has geometrically decorated tie beams while the central horizontal plane has bright polychrome patterning which features the merging of the nine-pointed star and the octagon.

Mudéjar methods and architectural elements became part of a vernacular tradition that lasted until the eighteenth century but was later revived towards the end of the nineteenth. The building that shows the most obvious reference to Andalusia outside Spain is the Torre Taglia Palacio at Lima in Peru which was the colonial capital of Spanish South America. This dates from 1730 and is arranged around a courtyard with foliated arches. It is now used as the Ministerio de los Asuntos Exteriores (Foreign Affairs). There are Moorish-type projecting timber balconies at the first-floor level of the street elevation. The windows, framed with top-hung shutters, are protected by panels of timber grilles carved and shaped in geometrical patterns very similar to the Arab *mashrabiyya* (see Glossary). They must have found favour because the Neo-classical façade of a street of two-storey courtyard houses built in Lima during the second half of the nineteenth century is embellished with balconies of a similar design. Mudéjar balconies were also placed on the main façades of two prominent neo-Baroque buildings in Lima, the Ayuntamiento (City Hall) and the Palacio Arzobispal (Archbishop's Palace). The latter was designed by Ricardo de la Malachowski, an architect of Polish origin who was trained in Paris, settled in Peru in 1911 and later became government architect. It was completed in 1944, the same year as the Ayuntimento which designed by Emilio Harth-Terre and José Alvarez Calderón. The former had been trained locally as an engineer and became the first licensed engineer-architect of Peru. The few designers in Peru were considered to be members of an elite, and their work was considered by many Peruvians to be neo-colonial in character.

At the beginning of the nineteenth century disillusion with the dictatorial and distant control of the colonies from Madrid and Seville was common throughout Spanish America. Ideas of freedom and self-determination, encouraged by the Declaration of Independence by the United States of America from British rule, then the French Revolution and finally the opportunity provided by the Napoleonic invasion of Spain and Portugal, led to the struggle by Latin Americans for their own independence. In the event, that independence was to be achieved over a long period, and Latin America fragmented into a large number of separate republics in a variety of sizes, the largest being Portuguese-speaking Brazil. The expression of recognisably colonial characteristics in the new public buildings became, therefore, less acceptable.

Most Latin American countries looked to France for inspiration in an attempt to shed the cultural domination of the colonial powers. In Chile, a school of architecture was established, under the headship of a French architect, at the University of Santiago in the mid-nineteenth century. The principal style then became neo-Classical in the manner of the French

Renaissance. However, it is believed that both craftsmen and *azulejos* were brought to Santiago de Chile from Spain in 1862 when a mining magnate wished to build his residence in a style directly copied from the Alhambra by his architect, Manuel Aldunate. It was sold while still under construction to a government minister who imported Arab-style furniture from Paris. The Palacio de la Alhambra, as it was named, has two storeys planned around two courtyards, one of which is a reproduction of the Patio de los Leones. It is now used as an art gallery and cultural centre.

The street elevation of the residence of a wealthy business man in Santiago, Chile. It was designed in a style modelled on the Alhambra by Manuel Aldunate in 1862 and is now used as a cultural centre.

At the same time, at the end of the nineteenth century, there was a vogue in Mexico for the Spanish oriental tradition. This was encouraged by the Academia de Bellas Artes in Mexico City, which organised several exhibitions with oriental themes: a typical painting by Luis Gash was entitled Canto Arabe (Arab Song). Many members of the higher bourgeoisie constructed Moorish patios and others favoured smoking rooms in an Arab pastiche. The architect Antonio Rivas Mercado designed such a room in the Palacio Nacional as well as the interior of the Teatro Juarez in the city of Guanajuato. As elsewhere, the style was perceived as a natural expression of the architecture of entertainment.

In Puebla, also in Mexico, and after travelling in Europe and the East, Eduardo Tamariz built a maternity hospital in brick courses of two-tone horizontal stripes. This colour treatment, which was repeated in the voussoirs of the arches, together with the use of multi-lobed horseshoe arches, became a popular style that was called 'pseudo-Mudéjarism' by some commentators. Tamariz also designed the house of the 'Sociedad de la Santa Concepción'. It has a two-storey patio in a Nasrid manner with the full polychromatic repertoire of *azulejos*, carved stucco and multi-lobed arches. The building has since been renamed Circolo Católico. The Mexican Pavilion at the International Exhibition held at New Orleans in 1885 was also in a neo-Moorish style, the fine detailing being in cast iron. A contemporary publication described it as 'an artistic octagonal temple of Arab style, whose elevations exactly reproduce the beautiful arches of the Alhambra and the Alcázar of Seville'. The design, by Ramón Ibarrola, reflected the taste of the time because it was re-erected in the Alameda Central of Mexico City where it remained until 1910, when it was moved to the Alameda de Santa María de Valera, in the same city.

The Portuguese colonists had no equivalent of the 'laws of the Indies' with the result that an informal layout was usual in their settlements of the colony of Brazil. This approach was said to be reminiscent of the Alfama district of Lisbon, the original site of the city before the Reconquest. Until the eighteenth century there was only one praça in Brazil and that was in the capital, Salvador. The climate of Brazil is predominantly hot and humid and human comfort is dependent on shade and air movement. Society was to a large extent a mixture of cultures – Portuguese, indigenous and African. Intermarriage had been officially encouraged and even subsidised, while the slave trade had brought some Moors amongst the majority who came from West Africa. Because of the lack of a middle class in the home country, a shortage of personnel was felt in the second half of the sixteenth century. Immigration was encouraged and many Italians, Spanish, Germans, Flemish, Muslims and Jews settled in Brazil.

Both climate and social custom influenced the form of domestic architecture, which was based on a typical two-storey house often built of adobe and arranged around a patio with a continuous projecting timber balcony and windows of *celosias* along the street frontage. The segregation of the sexes was strictly enforced, so the use of shutters and *celosias* allowed the dual function of shade ventilation as well as permitting the occupants to see out without being observed by strangers. These balconies were known as *muxarabi,* obviously derived from the Arabic *mashrabiyya.* The use of this term could have been a result of the close contact between the Portuguese and North Africa, particularly the colonies of Tangier and Ceuta.

After Brazil became an independent monarchy in 1822, there was a natural desire to abandon the retrograde social customs of the past. There was strong pressure from the new elite to adopt a modern and more progressive attitude to domestic architecture. Timber screens, *celosias* and shutters were considered to be backward, and, as a gesture of freedom, they were replaced with cast-iron railings and glazed windows. It was not until the late nineteenth century that designers of the eclectic school occasionally produced structures directly modelled on the Luso-Moorish style. Such an example was the library of the Royal Office of Portuguese Literature at Rio de Janeiro, which was inaugurated in 1888 and was one of the first buildings of its kind in Rio based on a metal structure.

In Spain, however, almost simultaneously with the disappearance of the last traces of Mudéjar architecture, there was a revival of interest in the heritage of the age of *convivencia*. In the same year as a Spanish translation of Claude Perrault's French version of the ten books of Vitruvius was published by the Real Academia de Nobles Artes de San Fernando, 1761, the same organisation commissioned the painter Diego de Sarabia to make a study of the Moorish antiquities of Córdoba and Granada. He produced a series of perspectives from different viewpoints. Two years later, at the instigation of two scholars, Bayer and Casiri, the Academia sent two young architects, Juan de Villanueva and Pedro Arnal, under the direction of a captain of engineers, José Hermosilla, to make measured drawings of the palace of the Alhambra at Granada and of the mosque at Córdoba. The result, *Antiguedades Arabes de España*, was published in Madrid in 1780. It included sixteen plates of Arab designs in the form of plans, elevations and sections. It was to attract the attention of scholars outside Spain. Villanueva later became a prominent exponent of neo-Classical design; his most celebrated building is the Prado Museum in Madrid. But he did not forget his early impressions at the Alhambra, especially the Generalife, as the picturesque quality of his landscape designs in collaboration with Pablo Boutelou in the Jardin del Principe (Prince's Garden) at the royal palace at Aranjuez later demonstrated.

CHAPTER 7

The main entrance to the huge Las Ventas bullring in Madrid with ticket offices on either side of the large horseshoe arch. It was built in 1929 in a full-blooded Mudéjar style to replace the former bullring which had been designed in a similar style. (See also p. 194.)

REDISCOVERY, REVIVAL
and TRANSFORMATION

James Cavana Murphy, an Irishman, who was later to measure the Alhambra at Granada, had been commissioned by William Burton Conyngham to make measured drawings of the church and monastery (Mosteiro de Santa Maria da Vitória) at Batalha. He travelled to Portugal in 1789 and his drawings were subsequently published in 1795, the same year he brought out his *Travels in Portugal*. He believed that they revealed evidence of Moorish influence. William Beckford, an eccentric aesthete whose family wealth was based on sugar plantations in Jamaica, was the author of *Vathek: An Arabian Tale* in French and published in 1786. He was a talented linguist as a result of his education in Geneva and visited Spain and Portugal on several occasions. He built a house for his own use near the mouth of the river Tagus and wrote *Recollections of an Excursion to Alcobaça and Batalha* after his journey to the two monasteries in 1794, but it was not published until 1835. On his return to England he built himself an extravagant residence in the Gothic style at his estate at Fonthill in Wiltshire. James Wyatt's plan for the lofty octagonal central tower was strongly influenced by Murphy's drawings of Batalha, and Beckford referred to the 'Batalha windows' which were probably modelled on those in the Capela do Fundador (Founder's Chapel) at Batalha. Shortly after he had been forced by financial losses to sell Fonthill Abbey, he was summoned to the death-bed of its builder who confessed to have not followed the correct specification for the foundations of the tower and warned him of its likely collapse. The tower fell to its destruction in 1825, but fortunately without any loss of life.

Murphy made a second journey to the Iberian Peninsula, arriving in 1802. He landed at Cádiz and travelled through Andalusia to Granada, where the governor granted him access to the Alhambra whenever he wished. He then moved on to Córdoba, where he measured both the mosque and the bridge. He remained in Spain until 1809, when he left for London to prepare his drawings for publication. He employed a number of artists to produce the engravings, which give an impression of accuracy of detail but they were later criticised by experts for their superficiality. They were not to appear until 1815, a year after his death. Richard Ford, who spent several months with his wife in the Alhambra using it as their personal quarters, maintained in his *Handbook for Travellers in Spain* that they were badly copied from the plates of the previous Spanish volume; whatever their degree of accuracy, the plates are attractive. Murphy was the forerunner of many scholars, writers, architects and artists from northern Europe and the USA who were fascinated by the sumptuous decoration and human scale of the palace. The end of the Peninsular Wars against Napoleon brought better access for travellers, many of whom had heard stories and descriptions from returned officers and soldiers who had been deeply impressed by a society and environment very different from those at home.

In 1832, two travellers, both architects, met in Egypt and decided to travel together to Granada via Constantinople. Owen Jones was British and Jules Goury, French; they had previously accompanied Gottfried Semper on a tour of Greece where they had become interested in the polychromatic aspects of the Classical temples, although most Greek Revival designers of the time believed that the temples had always had a natural stone finish. Both Jones and Goury were attracted to the Alhambra where there was still some evidence of the original colours on a greater scale than on the few remaining fragments from the Greek temples. Many of the applied colours of the stucco panels at the Alhambra had faded but nevertheless the richness of the decoration must have been a revelation because Murphy's plates had not been coloured. The ground of much of the decoration was green but, because it was metallic in composition and had probably changed hue through the process of oxidisation, they assumed that it was originally blue. Although later, in one of his lectures at Marlborough House, Jones gave a different explanation, asserting that:

> When the truly enchanted palaces of the Moors fell into the hands of the Catholic Kings, who despised a civilisation they were unable to appreciate, the true principles which the Moors had learned in their worship and observation of Nature's works were despised and rejected, because, as now, not understood. Their blues and reds were repainted with green and purple, without law or reason.

Jones and Goury continued with their measuring and colour analyses but the latter fell ill with cholera and died in 1834. Jones accompanied his body to France and then returned to London. He was anxious to publish their work in colour, but no English printer had yet been able to master the new process of colour lithography. He was forced to set up his own presses and recruit an independent team of craftsmen. He returned to Granada to revise some of the original drawings and extend the coverage of the survey. Eventually two volumes were finished and published in 1845.

Owen Jones continued to be fascinated by the Islamic use of colour and pattern. He concentrated mostly on interior design schemes for wealthy clients, soon earning a high reputation. As a result he was appointed one of the superintendents of works for the new building in Hyde Park, London, for the Great Exhibition of 1851. His main task was the preparation of details for Joseph Paxton's innovative design in cast iron, timber and glass. Construction had already started so he was able only to prepare a limited number of structural details including some iron railings incorporating Moorish fretwork. His most controversial contribution, however, was the interior colour scheme. He favoured painting the cast-iron columns with stripes of red, yellow and blue, separated by narrow lines of white. The use of primary colours derived from the Alhambra, but the use of white was adopted from the theories of Chevreuil, a French colour theorist, who claimed it helped to emphasise the distinctive qualities of the primary colours. Jones was also influenced by the Islamic use of colour, in particular the *cuerda seca* type of *azulejo*. There was much opposition to his proposal so tests of three different possibilities for the columns were made *in situ*. One was covered with a neutral tint, another was coloured in a plain red and the third was painted according to Jones's proposal. In the event, Prince Albert and the Royal Commissioners made the final choice to support Jones's ideas. In the collection of the Victoria and Albert Museum there is a rendering by William Simpson of the internal colour scheme of the Crystal Palace.

Subsequently at a lecture to the Royal Institute of British Architects, Jones explained his approach to colour: he intended that the coloured strips should accentuate the elegance of the structure. As one of his propositions he maintained: 'Construction should be decorated. Decoration should never

This rendering by William Simpson shows the internal colour scheme by Owen Jones of the main space of the Crystal Palace at the 1851 Great Exhibition in Hyde Park. The use of primary colours was derived from his study of the colour scheme of the Alhambra palace.

be purposely constructed. That which is beautiful is true; that which is true must be beautiful.' He went on to say: 'The ornamentation of the Alhambra illustrates most beautifully the law of decorating construction; there not only does the decoration arise naturally from the construction, but the constructive idea is carried out in every detail of the ornamentation of the surface.' As previously mentioned, the use of *muqarnas* in the ceiling decoration in some of the halls of the Alhambra does not strictly follow this principle. He made another proposition in a second lecture of the same series:

Colour is used to assist in the development of form, and to distinguish objects or parts of objects one from another. . . . In Arabian art, again, we always find the constructive lines of the buildings well defined by colour; and in their ornaments in relief, many new forms growing out of the arrangement of the colour, which would have been altogether lost without it. In thus asserting that colour is used to develop form, we find ourselves at issue with a very remarkable writer, Mr. Ruskin, who asserts just the contrary . . . that colour never follows form but is arranged on a totally different system.

John Ruskin, although he admired the Indian exhibits at the Great Exhibition of 1851, considered the Alhambra to be 'detestable . . . and its ornamentation is fit for nothing but to be transferred to patterns of carpets and bindings of books, together with their marbling and mottling and other mechanical recommendations.' Ruskin was not renowned for consistency in his opinions and may in this case have allowed his hatred of the machine to lead him, without due consideration, to condemn the use of repetitive motifs. Another historian, Sir Banister Fletcher, writing at the end of the century, describes the Alhambra as 'a gorgeous pleasure palace' but adds: 'here a surfeit of surface decoration, easily carried out in plaster and colour, takes the place of a more monumental treatment, and suited the fatalistic nature of people who were content to build for the present rather than for all time.' Both Ruskin and Fletcher appear to have taken a moral attitude in their aesthetic judgments.

After the Great Exhibition, the Crystal Palace was re-erected on an open site at Sydenham in south London. A series of courts was built inside to illustrate historical decorative styles. Jones, who was officially involved, insisted that one should represent Islamic design. It was modelled on the Patio de los Leones at the Alhambra and was completed in 1854 in an authentic manner under his supervision. Thousands of visitors were thus able to enjoy some of the visual splendour of the Alhambra without a journey to Spain. In 1856 Jones published his renowned pattern book, *The Grammar of Ornament*. This was intended for the use of design students and contained one hundred coloured plates, including eight plates in a section entitled 'Moresque ornament from the Alhambra', as well as others on Arabian, Turkish, Persian and Indian ornament.

The largest project to be designed by Jones was St James's Hall, a concert hall in Piccadilly, London, opposite the church of the same name. It contained a large hall with 2,500 seats and two smaller halls. It was the major music venue in London for 40 years but was unfortunately demolished in 1905, to make way for the new Piccadilly Hotel. It was said by Helen Henschel to have had perfect acoustics and a unique atmosphere of intimacy and charm. A contemporary issue of the *Illustrated London News* contains an interior view of the main hall, which is described as 'Alhambran'. The semicircular ceiling had a pattern of lozenge-shaped panels framed by gilded ribs on a red background. Behind the platform there was a coved wall to accommodate the organ. This had a hemispherical ceiling decorated in a manner similar to that of the main hall.

A view across Leicester Square, London, of the Royal Alhambra Palace Music Hall. Opened in 1854 as an exhibition centre, it underwent many transformations but consistently in a lavish Moorish style. It set a fashion for the 'orientalising' of buildings intended for public entertainment but was eventually demolished in 1936 to make way for a cinema.

Many theatrical and musical promoters realised the potential of interior spaces designed in an exotic style derived from the Alhambra to create a 'sense of occasion'. Another contemporary building in London was originally known as the Panopticon. It was sited in Leicester Square and intended for exhibitions, but after four years the owners went bankrupt. It then became a music hall and was renamed the Royal Alhambra Palace Music Hall because of its elaborate Moorish detailing both externally and internally. It was refurbished in this style on several occasions, once after a disastrous fire. It remained in use as a music hall until 1936, when it was rebuilt as a cinema in a 'modernistic' style. What was at first considered as a novelty soon set a fashion for Victorian music halls to be decorated in Moorish and other exotic styles, a process termed 'orientalising'. This desire for an exotic atmosphere was inherited by the early cinema industry. Many cinemas built in the 1920s and 1930s enjoyed the names Alhambra and Granada because of their romantic associations.

Another building type was to become influenced by Moorish precedent as a result of two Spanish publications. The first, *Toledo Pintoresco* by Amador de los Rios, published in Madrid in 1845, contained a detailed description of the former synagogue, Santa María la Blanca in Toledo. Then in 1857, *Historia de los Temples de España* by Gustavo Adolpho Becquer appeared. This publication described both Santa María la Blanca and the Tránsito synagogues in Toledo. An article on the Tránsito had been contributed by Heinrich Graetz to the 'Monatshrift fur Geschichte und Wissenschaft des Judenthums', the year before. These writings initiated a growing awareness of Judaic culture in the Iberian Peninsula during medieval times. Many Jewish scholars and architects believed it to have significance for the Jews and European culture in general. Consequently, they were able to equate Jewish spiritual and aesthetic values with an Iberian-Moorish style in the design of synagogues. The growing confidence of the Jewish communities in Germany and Austria-Hungary led to the construction of many new synagogues. Segregation had been abolished and the 'enlightened' Jewish urban communities were playing significant roles in the cultural and business life of the times. They felt confident enough to adopt a style distinctive from the dominant Gothic style of Christian churches.

At first, an interior in the Moorish style was contained within a Romanesque exterior, as Gottfried Semper had done in his design of 1838 for the synagogue at Dresden, in which some of the columns, capitals and other details were derived from the Alhambra. After Otto Simonson, who had studied architecture under Semper at the Dresden Academy, designed his synagogue at Leipzig in an integrated Moorish Revival manner with horseshoe arcades, it became more popular to follow this example. H. A. Meek has likened the pulpit to a *mimbar* and the niche containing the ark of the covenant to a *mihrab* of a mosque. Then Ludwig von Förster, a professor of Architecture at the Academy of Architecture in Vienna, designed the largest synagogue in Europe in Dohany utca at Budapest in a similar manner. It could accommodate 1,492 men and had a gallery on three sides for 1,472 women, but the most prominent features were the twin onion-domed towers which had the appearance of minarets.

The largest Jewish community was then in Berlin, where a large synagogue was built for the Liberal congregation. After an inconclusive competition, a design by Edward Knoblauch, who had been one of the assessors, was accepted. A prominent lofty street entrance hall was crowned with a tall onion dome over an octagonal drum. This dome was flanked by two lantern towers. The exterior surfaces of the domes were finished with gilded ribs in a flowing curved tracery. The interior was lavishly decorated. The dados and holy shrine were finished with marble, while yellow and gold predominated at the higher levels and blue at the lower. A newspaper report of the time reads: 'the light streams through the coloured glass, magically subdued and transfigured. Ceilings, walls, columns, arches and windows have been extravagantly decorated and form, with their gilding and decoration, a wonderful wreath of arabesques which is wound into a harmonic whole of fairy-like and supernatural effect.' The temple was dedicated in 1866 after Knoblauch had died before the building had been completed. It was later incinerated by the Nazis and damaged by Allied bombing. It remained in ruins until recently, when a programme of restoration was started.

Jewish communities in other European countries also adopted the Moorish Revival style in the design of their synagogues. A magnificent

A prominent feature of Oranienburgerstrasse in Berlin is the oriental dome over the large vestibule to the synagogue, whose spectacular Moorish interior is now being restored to its former glory. It is flanked by two lantern towers with domes in a similar style.

FAR RIGHT
The magnificent prayer hall of the Tempio Maggiore synagogue in the Via Farini in Florence is planned as a Greek cross with a lofty dome at the centre. The ark of the covenant is placed before the eastern apse and the intricate and colourful Moorish decoration includes elaborate metal screens at the front of the ladies' galleries punctuated with menorahs (candelabra).

example at Florence is in the Via Farini; it was erected over an eight-year period, ending in 1882 after the demolition of the ghetto. There were three designers, Mariano Falcini, Vincenzo Micheli and Mauro Treves, who used a range of Moorish features on a Byzantine Greek cross plan with a central dome. The cusped horseshoe arch appears extensively inside and out and in the form of the *ajimez* at first-floor level over the main entrance. An elegant synthesis of the full repertoire of Islamic geometrical patterns with a restrained selection of colours has been realised throughout the interior. There were many Jews amongst the great numbers of emigrants to the USA in the mid-nineteenth century and, as the majority came from Central Europe and Italy, the Moorish Revival soon became the fashionable style for synagogues there also.

A taste for the exotic had also developed amongst European royalty and aristocracy. This had probably been initiated by the example of George IV

184

when he was Prince Regent. He built the Royal Pavilion on the south coast of England at Brighton in a style derived from Islamic precedent, chiefly Indian Moghul. In 1937 the king of Wurttemberg had commissioned Ludwig Zanth to design the Villa Wilhelma in the grounds of his palace on the banks of the river Neckar near Stuttgart. This villa was in an integrated Moorish manner, but it does not appear to have been copied from any particular building. The king's interest in the Moorish style was inspired by oriental literature rather than by architecture, and he wanted a pavilion for peace and relaxation adjoining an open air theatre and casino. Zanth had previously studied Greek and Islamic polychromatic ornament in Sicily and was aware of Owen Jones's publication on the Alhambra. The casino was not ready until 1846, when it was used for the wedding celebrations of the king's son.

Prince Ferdinand II of Portugal, who was a member of the Saxe-Coburg-Gotha dynasty and husband to Queen Maria II, was attracted to the spectacular scenery to be enjoyed at Sintra in Portugal. About 1840 he commissioned a German architect, Baron von Schwege, to design a romantic castle on the highest point of the Parque da Pena, the site of a Hieronymite monastery. The Castelo da Pena is an indiscriminate confection of many architectural styles, Moorish, Gothic, Manueline, Renaissance and Baroque. It also incorporates part of the original monastery which contains some Manueline vaulting and walls decorated with *azulejos* of the seventeenth century. The interiors are in a mixture of styles with the Gothic pre-

BELOW LEFT
The Castelo da Pena near Sintra was built for Prince Ferdinand II of Portugal in the 1840s to the design of Baron von Schwege in a romantic profusion of exotic styles including Moorish and Manueline.

BELOW RIGHT
Some of the oriental details of the Castelo da Pena near Sintra.

dominating. The Sala da Reinha (Queen's Room) is simply decorated with plaster in Moorish geometrical patterns based on a sixteen-pointed star. In the gardens a statue of the architect and a Moorish pavilion, known as the Fonte dos Passarinhos, are to be found.

Another romantic oriental fantasy near Sintra is the mansion in the Parque de Monserrate designed in the 1850s by James Knowles, senior, for a wealthy English eccentric. Gothic arches are decorated with a mass of oriental stone detailing.

West of the Parque da Pena is another beautifully landscaped park laid out with exotic species of trees and shrubs known as the Parque de Monserrate. Here in a prominent position stands another oriental fantasy, a mansion that was acquired and remodelled by a rich eccentric Englishman in 1856. His name was Francis Cook and he wished to play the role of a caliph. He commissioned a London architect, James Knowles, senior, to prepare the designs but another Englishman, Samuel Bennett, spent a decade in Portugal supervising the building and the landscape works. The mansion consists of a central square block two storeys high, which supports a large lanterned dome with smaller turrets at each corner, and is linked by single-storey development to a two-storey circular pavilion at either end also crowned with a lanterned dome, resulting in a symmetrical composition which is accentuated by powerful overhanging eaves. Although the arcading and windows are pointed Gothic, the detailing and character are exotic, a mixture of Moorish and Indian, the treatment of the domes deriving from Indian precedent. A long internal gallery runs along the axis between the circular pavilions with a fountain at the centre. The pointed horseshoe arches contain delicately perforated panels in arabesque patterns. This exotic mansion was selected as the setting for the third part of a recent television production of *Gulliver's Travels* by Jonathan Swift in which a fantastic background was needed for the scenes in the flying island of Laputa and its neighbouring continent.

An internal view from the entrance showing the fountain which is at the centre of a gallery which forms the main axis of the building. Again elaborate oriental fretwork is contained in a Gothic frame.

Farther north in Oporto, an Arab Hall was especially decorated in the Bolsa, the Stock Exchange, in a luxurious style loosely modelled on the Alhambra. It is large in scale, with a first-floor gallery encircling the ovoid plan. The designs of 1862 were the work of Gonçalves e Sousa and comprised the full Moorish repertoire of materials and stained glass but employed with a certain lack of discrimination in the use of colour and pattern on the wall surfaces, which were formed in carved stucco and timber. The floor is inlaid with a variety of exotic tropical timbers in geometrical patterns. The craftsmanship is outstanding and was the work of Zeferin José Pinto of Oporto. It was inaugurated in 1880 and has been considered by some to have the atmosphere of the tales of *A Thousand and One Nights*.

The Castelo da Pena is a forerunner of the Romantic palaces built by King Ludwig II of Bavaria who also enjoyed creating fantastic surroundings. At first he favoured the Gothic style, as at Neuschwanstein, but changed to a preference for the French Rococo, as demonstrated at Linderhof near Garmisch, where he did however, incorporate a Maurisher Kiosk. Inside the so-called 'Kiosk' there is the incredible Peacock Throne. Three magnificent peacocks formed in polychrome enamelled cast bronze and mounted with false precious stones make the setting for the throne proper. One is placed above the throne while the other two are at either side. The entire composition is in front of three horseshoe-arched windows of stained glass in geometrical patterns of bright primary colours, making a dazzlingly theatrical effect worthy of a scene from a music drama by Richard Wagner, whose work the king so much admired.

The peacock motif appealed to an Italian marchese who carried out a series of alterations and additions to the family residence, the Villa di Sanmezzano at Rignano sull'Arno near Florence, during the 1850s. The family name was Ximenes d'Aragona and the Marchese Ferdinando Panciatichi inherited the villa, which had been in family ownership since 1605. His love of the exotic and the Moorish style in particular, perhaps because of his Aragonese ancestry, led him to transform the interior into an extravagant and eccentric display of pyrotechnic decoration. In one of many luxurious rooms, the elaborate rainbow-coloured carving of the fan-vaulted stucco ceiling delineates the shape of a peacock's tail. This motif is echoed in the doorway, which has a horseshoe architrave in stucco with polychromatic arabesques. The dado is finished with contrasting coloured glazed tiles in dynamic geometrical patterns in which the diagonal is stressed. This overwhelming space is not surprisingly known as the Hall of the Peacocks.

There is a more direct reference to the Alhambra in the design of the Hall of Lilies, where there are multi-lobed horseshoe arches and brightly coloured stucco arabesques. Throughout the highly ornate halls, however, the Marchese's enthusiasm for colour and pattern exceeds what, in contrast, seems to be the dignity and restraint of the Nasrids. And, in the circular two-storey White Hall, compensation for the lack of bright colour is provided by the intricacy of the stucco, especially on the domed ceiling and

the cusped arches to the gallery. An inscription on the wall here reads in Italian: 'Proud blood of Aragón runs in my veins'. Another space intended to appeal to the romantic spirit of visitors is called the Hall of Lovers; here are inscribed in gold the names of many famous lovers, including Clorinda, Tancredi, Orlando, Tristan and Isolde. After twenty years spent working on the interior as both client and architect, Panciatichi turned his attention to the exterior. He endeavoured to complete the neo-Moorish effect by building a tower entered through a large central doorway with a pointed horseshoe arch and a huge clock face above. He also added surface detailing to the rectangular window openings as well as a surrounding parapet with merlons. The parkland was planted with exotic species, including palms, giant sequoias and cedars of Lebanon. In spite of all this, the exterior lacks conviction and does not have the vitality of the 'Arabian Nights' interior spaces.

Although there is no recognised aristocracy in the USA, there were a number of extremely wealthy families who wanted to express this distinction in their lifestyle by building in an extravagantly exotic manner. The most powerful influence was literary, and a young American of Protestant

The Hall of the Peacocks in the Villa di Sanmezzano at Rignano sull'Arno near Florence is a unique space with a fan vaulted stucco ceiling expressing the theme of a peacock's tail which is also reflected in the design of the door surrounds. The dado is faced with vivid and dynamic patterns of azulejos.

descent with such ambitions, Washington Irving, travelled to Europe in 1815. Based in London, he toured through Germany, Austria and Italy. He reached Spain and obtained a post at the US Embassy in Madrid. After writing a long history of the life and voyages of Christopher Columbus, he journeyed south to Seville, where he spent a year. Eventually he reached Granada where, like other privileged visitors, he obtained permission from the governor to use three rooms in the Alhambra. He listened to the stories of the local people who lived in the palace and nearby. These provided background material for his later writings, a history of Granada and the now world-renowned *Tales of the Alhambra*. He described his feelings thus:

> I tread haunted ground and am surrounded by romantic associations. From earliest boyhood when on the banks of the Hudson I first pored over the pages of an old Spanish story about the wars of Granada, that city has ever been a subject of my waking dreams, and often have I trod in fancy the romantic halls of the Alhambra. . . . As I loiter through these Oriental chambers and hear the murmur of fountains and the song of the nightingale, as I inhale the odour of the rose and feel the influence of the balmy climate, I am almost tempted to fancy myself in the paradise of Mahomet . . .

Although eclecticism had become the norm in architectural design in the USA, as in Europe, the specific use of the Moorish style was exceptional for building types other than the synagogue and homes for those individuals who had been swayed by Irving's writings, like Barnum the celebrated showman, or those who had travelled in Spain and the Near East. Barnum's house, which he named 'Iranistan', was designed by Leopold Eidlitz who originated from Prague and was later responsible for several synagogues in the Judeo-Moorish tradition. Frederick E. Church, a painter, commissioned Calvert Vaux to incorporate motifs copied directly from the Alhambra in the studio apartments of his house 'Olana' at Greendale in the state of New York. The house was eclectic in character, featuring a picturesque medley of Arab, Persian, Moghul and Hindu themes.

The taste for the picturesque was also to become an important aspect of Spanish literature. *Escenas Andaluzas* by Serafín Estébanez Calderón was published in 1847 and set a trend for regionalism. *La Gaviota* by Cecilia Boehl de Faber followed in 1849, continuing the portrayal of Andalusian life and customs. *Costumbrismo* was the description given to this realistic type of writing based on local colour, especially that found in Andalusian towns and villages. This approach also affected the visual arts. The Mudéjar tradition still existed to a limited degree in vernacular buildings. Simple geometrical pattern-making continued in carpentry, brickwork, ceramics and stucco. Gothic and Renaissance were dominant in the formal sector.

When the first Escuela de Arquitectura (school of architecture) was established in Madrid in 1844, the syllabus combined both technical and artistic subjects, but the study of the history of architecture was stressed and the preparation of drawings copied from the Greek and Roman orders was compulsory. In this, the teachers were following the French Beaux-Arts model. The emphasis on historicism resulted from public realisation that the buildings of the past should be regarded as historic monuments and those in a state of disrepair should be restored for future generations. Then the 'battle of the Styles' developed in all European countries as the Classical was not unanimously accepted as the only style, especially for religious and some public buildings. There was a general preference for the Gothic amongst the Catholic hierarchy. But the new trend for eclecticism meant that the repertoire of styles expanded to include the neo-Arab and the neo-Mudéjar. This coincided with the growth of nationalism and individualism. The historic revival of the medieval styles related to the oriental period of the history of the Peninsula was seen by some as the expression of national characteristics which were unique in Europe.

The popularity of international exhibitions during the second half of the nineteenth century gave an opportunity for such expression in the design of national pavilions. At the Universal Exhibition held at Vienna in 1873 a small pavilion for the display of wines contained a copy of the fountain from the Patio de los Leones at the Alhambra. The two-storey façade of the main Spanish Pavilion, designed by Lorenzo Alvarez Capra for the same exhibition, displayed a repetitive treatment of horseshoe arches in an obviously Hispano-Arab manner. Agustín Ortiz de Villajos used neo-Arab elements to distinguish the Spanish Pavilion on the Street of the Nations at the 1878 Paris International Exhibition. Once again, the Patio de los Leones was the source of the detailing of the entrance portico. The pavilion consisted of five blocks, one central and one at each of the four corners. Other familiar devices such as the *alfiz* and horseshoe arcades were featured on the elevations of this two-storey complex. The success of this design was followed by another pavilion at Barcelona in 1888 and at Chicago in 1893 where Joaquin Pavia reproduced the arcades of the mosque at Córdoba.

José Amador de los Rios had revived interest in the Moorish heritage with his volumes *Pintoresco Sevilla* and *Pintoresco Toledo* in the mid-1840s. The latter had important consequences in the design of synagogues beyond the Peninsula (see p. 182). It has been suggested that the romantic attraction of the neo-Arab style for the bourgeoisie lay in the luxurious and uninhibited pleasures of the flesh promised in the oriental perception of Paradise. This was in contrast to the double standards of their own way of life, which depended on a strictly correct public moral persona that might conceal more relaxed private behaviour. In architecture, a royal example was a powerful indicator of the fashion. The Gabinete Árabe (Arab Hall) in the Royal Palace at Aranjuez was based by Rafael Contreras on the Sala de las Dos Hermanas in the Alhambra. The Marques de Salamanca then transformed one of his rooms at the Palacio de Vista Alegre on the outskirts of Madrid into another Moorish retreat; in this case the model was the Sala de la Barca at the Alhambra.

In Britain brick as a building material had for some time been regarded as inferior to stone but this attitude began to change when John

The similar but beautifully proportioned brick detailing of the Mudéjar entrance façade of the church of Santiago de Arrabal in Toledo. (See also p. 64.)

Ruskin and others stressed the need for an honest expression of the structure and material. The Red House of William Morris in Upton, Kent, was quoted as an example of brickwork used in a pleasing and straightforward manner. In Spain there are many examples of Mudéjar churches in restrained but decorative brickwork that express the structure. These also have a unique national character. Such an example is the church of Santiago de Arrabal in Toledo. Attention was drawn to the neo-Mudéjar style with an emphasis on brick arches and panels of patterned brick. This approach could be combined with the introduction of new technology, the structural use of iron and steel.

The activity of bullfighting has been a unique characteristic of the Iberian Peninsula for centuries and it may date in some form from Roman times. A bullfight is portrayed in one of the miniatures illustrating the Cantigas de Santa María de Alfonso X from the thirteenth century. It was customary to stage bullfights in the main plaza, which was frequently set out in a rectangle or octagon for such public spectacles. The rectangular Plaza Mayor of Madrid was used in this way, whereas the old Plaza de Toros in Tarazona was defined by a series of houses arranged in an octagon. Seating was usually arranged in a temporary manner by the provision of portable timber tiers.

It was not until the eighteenth century that a specialised building type for bullfights was developed. It was normally based on a circular or polygonal plan with covered balconies at the periphery and open tiered seating immediately in front of the arena. The Roman amphitheatre was an obvious predecessor. Because of the large amount of space required, the new bullring would sometimes be sited on the outskirts of the city. The oldest example of a purpose-built bullring, the Plaza de Toros de la Real Maestranza at Seville, was sited in the city centre on the banks of the Guadalquivir river. It has a capacity of 12,500 spectators. Its construction was initiated in the mid-eighteenth century, but it was extended and modified at first in the 1880s and later in the beginning of this century. Most of the exterior elevation is hidden by surrounding development, except for the entrance portal and a part which faces the river. The architectural expression is a simple and pleasing version of the Renaissance style typical of its period. The plan is partly circular and partly irregular, because of the many changes it has undergone.

With increasing urbanisation in the nineteenth century came the demand for larger bullrings, and in the age of eclecticism came the problem of the choice of an appropriate architectural style. This was especially important because of the dominance of the exterior structure, which by necessity was composed of a repetitive treatment of bays interrupted by one or more entrances and staircase towers. Usually a Romanesque treatment was used, incorporating semicircular arches or neo-Mudéjar with horseshoe arches. Both styles embodied colour, expressed in brick and varying numbers of *azulejo* panels.

In 1874 Rodriguez Ayuso designed the Plaza de Toros (Bullring) in Madrid in a neo-Mudéjar manner combining decorative brickwork with the

The former bullring in Madrid, designed by Rodriguez Ayuso in 1874, set the fashion for neo-Mudéjar brickwork combined with iron and steel for such structures. It was replaced by a larger structure in 1929.

use of iron and steel. It also incorporated a triumphal entrance doorway with a large multi-lobed horseshoe arch. This initiated a fashion in the design of bullrings which continued into the next century and extended to Latin America. The Plaza de Toros at Bogotá in Colombia was designed with large areas of patterned brickwork. Unfortunately, Ayuso's bullring was demolished but two neo-Mudéjar bullrings in Barcelona survive. The older, no longer used for bullfighting, is known as Plaça de les Arenes and was built in 1899 to the design of August Font i Carreras in a frank expression of the neoMudéjar style in brickwork. Seven years before, Carreras had designed the Baños Orientales (Oriental Baths) in Barcelona which had *ajimez* windows set in a façade of triangular *azulejos*. The second bullring, in current

use, was completed in 1915. The Plaça de Braus Monumentala has a remarkable external elevation in brick and is decorated extensively with blue and white ceramics. The brick stair towers are surmounted with pointed domes encased in white ceramics inset with blue wing-shaped patterns. The architects, Ignasi Mas and Joaquim Raspall, appear to have been influenced both by the work of the Viennese Secession and the Mudéjar tradition. The vigorous mixture of the two styles nevertheless results in an unmistakably Andalusian character. In 1934 a vast bullring, the largest in Spain, accommodating 23,000 spectators, was completed in Madrid after a construction period of eleven years. It is known as La Plaza de Toros de las Ventas and was designed in a full-blooded neo-Mudéjar style by architect Espelius.

ABOVE LEFT
The entrance to the older of the two bullrings in Barcelona, known as Plaça de les Arenes de Barcelona, which was built in a rich Mudéjar style in 1899 and is now no longer used as a bullring. In the foreground is the former ticket office for the desirable seats in the shade.

ABOVE RIGHT
The higher level of the entrance façade has a vigorous display of azulejos in strong colours combined with brick patterning, and horseshoe arches.

RIGHT
The second bullring to be built in Barcelona is the Plaça de Braus Monumentala which was completed in 1915 in a bold style that derives from both the Mudéjar and the Viennese Secession. The entrance façade is decorated with simple patterns of blue and white azulejos in squares and circles set in a brick framework. The 'sombra' (shady) ticket office is on the left while 'sol' (sunny) tickets are sold on the right.

ABOVE
The square brick staircase towers are topped with pointed domes finished with blue wing motifs against a white background of azulejo mosaics.

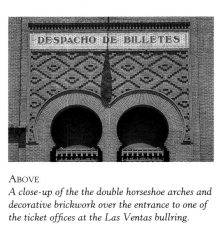

ABOVE
A close-up of the the double horseshoe arches and decorative brickwork over the entrance to one of the ticket offices at the Las Ventas bullring.

ABOVE
Each of the upper three floors of the Las Ventas bullring at Madrid has a different treatment of the brick horseshoe-arched openings but they all have panels of azulejos in arabesque patterns, shown in detail below. (See also p. 176.)

RIGHT
Details of the mosaic decorations at eaves level.

The main entrance to the bullring at Lisbon which is known as the Praça de Touros do Campo Pequeno and was inaugurated in 1892. It is emphasised by the presence of three metal covered onion-shaped domes. The central dome appears over the stepped gable on the axis of the multi-lobed horseshoe entrance arch.

Bullfighting is also practised in Portugal, but since the eighteenth century the bull has never been killed. The display of courage and skill is similarly performed in a purpose-built bullring. The largest and best known is the Praça de Touros do Campo Pequeno in Lisbon. It was designed by Dias de Silva in 1889 and opened in 1892. In 1902 it was visited by Edward VII of Great Britain and Alfonso XIII of Spain. Set at the centre of a large open space, it presents an imposing circular mass of red brick with simple horseshoe arcading in neo-Mudéjar fashion, and is influenced by Ayuso's Madrid structure. The unique features of this building are the four attached square stair towers, one of which has a huge multi-lobed horseshoe-arched gateway. These towers have the unusual addition of tall double onion-shaped domes covered with metal and painted red. The entrance doorway is flanked by two additional smaller towers attached at the corners and surmounted with smaller versions of the main onion domes. The combination of the domes and the neo-Mudéjar brick structure gives the bullring an eccentrically exotic air deriving from both Andalusian ancestry and oriental precedent in the Portuguese colonial experience in India.

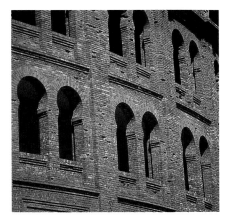

The external structure consists of simple brickwork with double horseshoe-arched openings without any embellishment.

195

Another building type, which was to provide justification for the combination of new technology with a degree of eclecticism, was the railway station. In a terminus, a lofty glazed roof was required to shelter both passengers and trains. Some form of steel structure was the only solution to this problem, but it was felt that bold architectural statements were needed to make a powerful presence in a city centre. Some kind of historical reference was believed to be necessary to achieve this, and the designer was therefore faced with choosing a suitable style. An element of regionalism was introduced by those who financed the railway boom.

The elevation to the Plaza de las Armas in Seville of the former Córdoba railway station. It was designed by Santos Silva in 1899 with a liberal use of Mudéjar elements but in a way that did not disguise the use of steel and wrought iron in the roof of the train shed.

For example in Andalusia, neo-Mudéjar was considered suitable. In Seville, the new station, known as the Estación Córdoba, in the Plaza de Armas, which was designed in 1899 by a Portuguese engineer, Santos Silva, expressed the train shed in glass and steel, with the addition of an arcade of multi-lobed horseshoe arches at ground level. It is flanked by two double-storeyed blocks of brickwork with panels decorated in a wide variety of patterned *azulejos*. There are neo-Mudéjar arched openings to the windows upstairs and the doors below. The structure of the train shed is skilfully integrated with the Mudéjar character of the brickwork surrounding it by the use of *almenas* at the top of the gable end of the curved roof as well as the incorporation of pointed horseshoe arches in the vertical glazing. Over the centre of the entrance arcade is a clock; below this is an *azulejo* panel incorporating a calligraphic monogram which, at first sight, appears to be in Arabic script, but closer inspection reveals it to be the initials of the railway company, MZA, in a flowing script with strokes of varying thickness (MZA refers to Compañía de los Ferrocarriles de Madrid a Zaragoza y Alicante).

The simple and bold composition combined with the beautiful and sensitive detailing makes it one of the most successful neo-Mudéjar buildings. It has not been used as a railway station since the 1992 Expo, when a new station was built at Santa Justa, but the impressive interior is now being used as an exhibition hall.

A decade before, in the 1880s, the same railway company had decided to adopt one style, neo-Mudéjar, for all the buildings on the Seville-Huelva line. The station at Huelva consists of two double-storey blocks linked by a single-storey section. On the side facing the city the central entrance portal is formed by a stepped gable over a large horseshoe arch. The entire building is in brick and divided into bays by vertical buttresses. Each bay has a horseshoe-arched opening at each floor. There is no train shed, but the waiting space to the rear is protected with a simple pitched roof supported by cast-iron columns and capitals decorated with geometrical strap and arabesque patterns.

A close-up of the colourful pediment housing the station clock and the monogram of the railway company in cursive script. The wrought-iron Mudéjar detailing of the roof structure appears behind the clock.

The front elevation of the station at Huelva which was built by the railway company that had adopted the brick Mudéjar style in 1880 for all its buildings on the line to Seville. It is unfortunately disfigured by the positioning of the modern RENFE signs.

When a design for a railway terminus was needed for a site in the Rossio square in Lisbon in 1889, the architect, José Luis Monteiro, was required to embody a hotel in the complex. He was also expected to convey a national character in his design, for patriotic reasons. He therefore decided to present a façade to the square in a form of neo-Manueline style which gives the impression of a hotel rather than a railway station. No attempt was made to integrate the new technology of the train shed with the façade, which would in any case have been difficult because of the difference in levels between the tracks and the square. The stone façade is symmetrical, three storeys divided into three bays by four buttresses expressed as cylinders at the higher levels. The central bay has two large entrance doorways with horseshoe arches curving to the steps at ground level. There is a clock at the centre above the roof line; three windows of varying types but with

Manueline decoration are set in the upper storeys of each bay. At the ground floor of the two outer bays there are three sets of doors with pointed arches, also decorated with Manueline stone carving.

At Toledo in 1916 a magnificent new station was built to replace the previous modest building of 1857. Its asymmetrical composition was

ABOVE
The double entrance doorway has exaggerated horseshoe arches that reach to the ground and are decorated with flowing curved patterns that suggest knots.

ABOVE RIGHT
The main façade to Rossio square in Lisbon of the central railway station. It was designed by José Luis Monteiro in 1889 using a neo-Manueline style that expresses the character of a mansion or luxury hotel.

The asymmetrical façade of the railway station at Toledo expresses the Mudéjar character of many of the city's historic buildings. It replaced a mid-nineteenth-century structure in 1916 and has a remarkable tall clock tower that suggests the form of a minaret.

designed in a vigorous neo-Mudéjar style. The lofty façade of the main passenger concourse incorporates at a high level five multifoil pointed horseshoe arches combined with window tracery above the entry doorways below. The smaller subsidiary two-storey blocks on either side have five window openings in the upper floor. These are more widely spaced and each has a simpler window under a multifoil horseshoe arch. At each end are projecting gable walls with double windows of the same type above a single arched doorway below. But the most spectacular element is a tall clock-tower plus a slim lantern at the summit. It is placed at the corner of the station at one end of the façade and displays the full range of features to be found in the original Mudéjar buildings of Toledo. Inside the concourse the façade of the ticket office incorporates timber latticework in geometrical patterns above a dado of multi-coloured *azulejos*. The latticework shows the characteristics of *mashrabiyya* and the solid panels are derived from the *artesonado* tradition. The architect's name is Narciso Claveria.

The booking hall has a rich selection of Mudéjar features in stone, brick, timber and azulejo. The ticket office is a unique example of joinery and azulejo work in a Moorish manner.

The scale of market trading had increased during the nineteenth century and created a demand for larger covered markets. Although the planning requirements were different, the means of providing a spacious well-lit area free of obstruction were similar to those required for large railway stations. The need for improved hygiene, fresh air and easily cleaned surfaces reinforced the suitability of glass, iron, steel and glazed tiles. Les Halles market in Paris was seen as a prototype, and the French designer Hector Horeau presented an imaginative project to the new municipality of Madrid, but his design was never built. Several new market structures were erected during the 1870s in Madrid and Barcelona, usually planned with a central space, often octagonal, accompanied by subsidiary wings appropriate to the chosen site. Other cities followed suit. Cast iron was used for prefabricated columns and other structural elements. These provided the opportunity for some stylistic expression although the main structure was usually simple and functional in appearance.

In Andalusia, however, there had been urban economic expansion, and the municipal architect of Málaga, Joaquin Rucoba, who originated from Santander and was a graduate of Madrid, designed the market of Las Atarazanas in a vigorous neo-Mudéjar style. This was built on the site of a manor house which had been demolished except for the entrance gateway which Rucoba managed to save and make the centrepiece of the new complex. The large horseshoe arch in white marble became the entrance to the middle of the three naves of the market. The outer walls had verandahs supported on cast-iron columns divided into bays, each having two round arches either side of a larger central arch, a neo-Mudéjar composition in ironwork, while the glass windows were protected by timber latticework. Rucoba was municipal architect for Málaga from 1870 to 1883, when he took up the same post at Bilbao. In 1874 he designed the Plaza de Toros (Bullring) at Málaga, and in Bilbao he was responsible for the Salón de Actos (Arab Hall) in the Ayuntamiento (City Hall). This meeting room is like a theatrical set for the *Arabian Nights* within a sober Classical exterior. All the elements of the Nasrid period were assembled and mirrors were included to increase the impression of spatial depth. Lamps and furnishings were selected to complete the exotic effect.

Regional pride was also evident in Aragón where Felix Navarro, who was born in Teruel, designed a new building for the Mercado Central (Central Market) of Zaragoza at the end of the century. Many of the cast- and wrought-iron elements show an awareness of the Mudéjar tradition. The municipal architect, Ricardo Magdalena, had in 1886 built the Faculdad de Medicina y Ciencias (Faculty of Medicine and Sciences) in brickwork using details that were clearly derived from the Aragonese Mudéjar. In 1908 a Franco-Spanish trade exhibition was held in Zaragoza, and Magdalena was the architect in charge. Eclecticism was the most powerful influence on the design of the exhibition pavilions, in addition to a flavour of *Modernismo* from Barcelona, which later became the dominant mode up to 1915. The latter is demonstrated by the only building surviving from the Exhibition, the Kiosko para la Música, a bandstand whose dome, elliptical in profile, is covered with coloured glazed tiles. This dome rises over a glazed roof supported on a cast-iron structure with flowing curved floral motifs.

A Catalan architect trained at Barcelona during the zenith of *Modernismo*, Pablo Monguia Segura exchanged the post of municipal architect at Tarragona for another official post in Teruel. But he only spent a few years there before he left for Tortosa after a furore following the collapse of a school built under his supervision. After six successful years at Tortosa, where he designed a number of buildings in a manner influenced by *Modernismo*, he was reinstated as provincial architect at Teruel where he remained for many years. The first commission on his return was the sen-

The bandstand at Zaragoza, known as the Kiosko para la Música, is the only structure to survive from the Franco-Spanish trade exhibition of 1908. It is an elegant and colourful fantasy which expresses both oriental and Art Nouveau influences in the design by the brothers José and Manuel de Ubago.

sitive problem of rebuilding an entrance doorway to the cathedral. This he successfully inserted in the Mudéjar monument using a mixture of stone, decorative brick and ceramics in an individual but respectful manner.

However, his most remarkable building in Teruel is the Casa del Torico, a four-storey residential block in a street frontage facing Plaza de Carlos Castel. It is set back at one side, creating a corner containing a small circular tower at the level of the top floor and incorporating a balcony and elaborate iron railings crowned with a lantern and conical roof. This tower gives the impression of a minaret. The ground floor is used for commercial purposes (at present a savings bank) and recessed to create a sheltered arcade. The continuous cantilevered first-floor balcony supports seven columns with elaborate capitals and bases which in turn support the second-floor balcony which has three window openings framed by cusped arches. The top floor also has three openings with separate balconies. There are rounded horseshoe arches framing the two outer windows and above them is a blind arcade with a plaque giving the date of construction, 1912, over the middle window. A rich variety of materials and elegant ironwork has been integrated into a fusion of *Modernismo* and neo-Mudéjar.

The Casa del Torico is a four-storey building in Teruel whose street façade is a mixture of oriental features with influences of Modernismo. It was built in 1912 and was the work of Pablo Monguia Segura, who trained in Barcelona.

The main Post Office in Zaragoza dates from 1917 and its façade contains panels of brick and azulejo that derive from the Mudéjar towers of Teruel.

A more directly historical rendering of the Mudéjar reasserted itself from 1917 onwards. First, the main Casa de Correos (Post Office) of Zaragoza was constructed using decorative brick extensively accompanied by both interlacing and geometrically patterned panels to the designs of architect Rubio. The new Post Office was one of a national building programme in regional capitals, the choice of style depending on the perceived regional expression. This was followed by the Academia General Militar (General Military Academy) in Zaragoza, the main brick façade of which was similarly treated in a neo-Mudéjar manner; but Rationalism was introduced in the 1920s and resulted in the adoption of a more simplified

RIGHT
*A detail from the public flight
of steps known as La
Escalinata showing a vivid
arrangement of flat and
moulded* azulejos *set in brick in
the Mudéjar manner.*

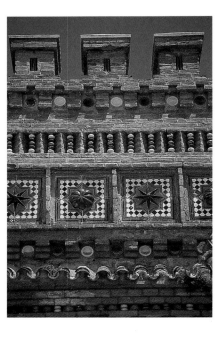

FAR RIGHT
*A close-up of one of the towers,
a smaller and simplified version
of the historic Mudéjar towers
of Teruel which also embodies
the use of green glazed roofing
tiles to match the* azulejos.

*A general view of La
Escalinata seen from the lower
level by the railway station
showing one of the twin towers
at the top of the stairs.*

functional architecture. Elsewhere in Aragón the neo-Mudéjar was employed when considered appropriate. In Teruel a public flight of steps leading up to the town from the railway station, known as the Escalinata, was completed in a fanciful medley of Mudéjar detail. Two small towers at the upper level were built in brick with coloured ceramic inserts, an over-elaborate composition of such details. After the Spanish Civil War (1936–9) the new regime favoured what it considered to be traditional values. Teruel had suffered considerable war damage and a programme of restoration was initiated. The Mudéjar style was the norm for new building, which was expected to match the old. An exhibition building, La Feria de Muestras, was completed in 1950 at Zaragoza to the designs of two brothers, Regino and José Borobio. Its principal feature is a tall square tower in brick with a plain rectangular grid pattern in brickwork. It was conceived as an abstraction of the traditional Mudéjar tower. The main body is windowless except for three vertical arched openings on each square face at the top. Above, instead of a floor to accommodate the bells, there is a square glazed section which is crowned with a pointed lantern, also glazed. The remainder of the complex is in a simplified Romanesque style with a single-storey portico formed with rounded arches.

In Madrid, a French architect who had worked with Viollet-le-Duc in the nineteenth century in the restoration of national monuments, Emile Boeswillwald, designed the Palacio Xifre for a member of the Catalan bourgeoisie whose father had been a property developer in Barcelona. This palace, which is opposite the Prado Museum, has two three-storey wings with horizontal stripes in two-tone brickwork. At the centre of the façade is a two-storey portico with pointed horseshoe arches; the interior, which contains some genuine Islamic works of art, is decorated throughout in the neo-Arab manner. It has been suggested by Revilla that a possible explanation for the presence of neo-Arab buildings in Catalonia, a region that has little or no historical link with al-Andalus, was the popularisation of things Moorish during and after the Moroccan wars of 1859–61 in which Catalan troops, under the Catalan General Prim, played a major part. An outstanding example is a building named La Giralda at L'Arbos near Tarragona built for Roquer Mari in the last quarter of the nineteenth century. It comprises a copy of the Almohad tower of the same name at Seville alongside a square block with a courtyard at the centre which is derived from the Patio de los Leones at the Alhambra. Another section is modelled on the Salón de Ambajadores of the Alcázar at Seville. It is believed that the owners' fascination with the architecture of Andalusia was a consequence of their having spent their honeymoon there.

Another factor in the growing popularity of the colour and vigour of the Moorish and Mudéjar traditions was the exhibition of an extensive collection of photographs of oriental buildings held at the Academia de Arquitectura at Barcelona in 1871. The search for a new vocabulary of visual elements to express the need for a new industrialised society to be perceived as modern and cosmopolitan was encouraged by the statement by Rada Delgado of the Academia Real Royal Academy of San Fernando of Madrid that the architecture of the nineteenth century must be eclectic. Victor Hugo and other Romantics had earlier declared that all cultures are worthy of study and that there should be a freedom of choice in style. The rising tide of Catalan nationalism created a desire for a style that was distinct from the rest of the Peninsula.

A young architect, Antoni Gaudí (1852–1926), received his first commission from a successful industrialist, Eusebi Güell, and while working on the preliminaries Gaudí undertook an extensive tour of Andalusia and Morocco. He eventually designed a residence in Barcelona and three

The Casa Vicens is an early work of 1885 by the celebrated Catalan architect Antoni Gaudí. This staggering assembly of azulejos, brick *and random stonework derives from Moorish precedent but is composed in a new and individual manner.*

pavilions in a country estate for Güell. Although he used recognisable Mudéjar elements, especially decorative panels of brick and ceramics, in these buildings the final result was an individual expression of his creative power. An additional factor was his plastic approach to design, which can be attributed to his descent from a family of potters. A small example is the continuous outside bench in Park Güell. The moulded serpentine shape is finished with a three-dimensional surface of broken *azulejos* in a brilliant mixture of bright colours.

FAR LEFT
A close-up of a corner balcony of the Casa Vicens showing the ingenious use of three types of square azulejos *to decorate the square columns, walls and corbelled supports.*

LEFT
A circular corner turret using the same three types of square tile on curved surfaces.

Perhaps the most memorable of his early buildings, and the one that shows the most direct influence of the Islamic tradition, is the Casa Vicens in Barcelona (1885), a large residence for a brick and ceramics merchant. This must be the most extravagant showcase ever built for a builder's merchant. Outside ceramic tiles in geometrical patterns contrasting with brickwork and random stone, are extensively used. The higher surfaces of the three-storey elevations have the brightest and most exaggerated patterns. The upper storey is provided with protruding corner balconies, and there are several small towers at the roof line. All these have a Moorish character and are decorated in a similarly vigorous treatment. The interior is a dazzling display of decorative effects. The smoking room has many elements that show Islamic precedent: its ceiling consists of stalactites in stucco, while the glass lamps are enamelled with calligraphic motifs derived from Arabic. The joinery is formed in interlocking rectangular patterns and the window screens are derived from the Arabic *mashrabiyya*. The upper part of the wall surface is finished with stucco carved in floral relief. The dado is lined with blue and tan coloured *azulejos* in a checkerboard pattern and are overlaid with repetitive and realistic versions of the rose. The total effect is, nevertheless, original and in no way derivative of any particular Moorish building.

A window opening in the Casa Vicens where to achieve the pointed effect Gaudí has had to introduce tiles cut on the diagonal. In the foreground can be seen the balcony railing in flowing curvilinear forms.

The design of buildings for international exhibitions is always controversial. Public awareness is at a maximum; and the need for a striking effect is often combined with some desire for symbolism. When it was decided early in the century to hold an Iberian-American Exhibition at Seville, the choice of venue was in itself symbolic as it had been the headquarters of the Castilian monopoly on trade with the Americas, as well as the Archivos Generales de los Indios (General Archive of the Indies) which is said to contain some 90 million documents. The organisation that sponsored the exhibition still has its headquarters in Seville. The particular site selected was the Parque de María Luisa, so called because in 1893 Princess María Luisa of Orleans had donated to the city the area that had been the riverside gardens of her home, the Palacio San Telmo.

The original intention had been for the exhibition to open in 1914 and the appointment of architects was made in 1911. The onset of the First World War obviously caused postponement, although Spain was neutral in that conflict. In 1917 there was a disastrous harvest followed by inflation, strikes and general civil unrest. In 1921 a difficult political situation was caused by defeats in the Moroccan Wars. Construction had started, but there was a degree of mismanagement and budgets were exceeded. Further delays were caused by the search for more funds. Eventually construction was completed and the exhibition was opened in 1929 by King Alfonso XIII. The attendance from overseas was less than expected, probably because of the Great Depression, and, like many international exhibitions, a large deficit caused further financial controversy. However, at least four prominent buildings and an outstandingly beautiful park are the heritage of the exhibition, and it was said that exports to Latin America increased as a result of business contacts made while the exhibition was open. A flamboyant mixture of historical styles had been selected for the design of the pavilions, but the city council had insisted that there should be an overriding emphasis on architectural effects that could be seen to be typical of Seville and its history.

This policy had been initiated by the municipality in the holding of a competition for the design of multi-storey façades in the city centre in 'estilo Sevillano'. One building to win an award was the Ciudad de Londres, still

FAR LEFT
The smoking room within the Casa Vicens contains design elements derived from Moorish precedent which have been assembled in an original composition by the architect Antoni Gaudí. Particularly striking are the ceiling of muqarnas *and the glass lamps decorated with calligraphic symbols based on cursive Arabic.*

FAR LEFT
The Ciudad de Londres is a four-storey building on a corner site in the commercial centre of Seville and is now used as a draper's shop. It is a typical example of the 'estilo Sevillano', that was promoted by the city authorities immediately before the First World War. The lettering and ground floor fascia are in lustre azulejo.

LEFT
A close-up of the arcaded balcony at first floor level revealing the fusion of Mudéjar and Baroque in the detailing.

surviving today as a draper's shop. It was built during 1912–14 in a very carefully detailed neo-Mudéjar style. The architect, José Espiau, may have been influenced by the design of the Mudéjar Pavilion of the Exhibition by Anibal Gonzalez which was already under construction. Espiau designed another multi-storey building, the Casa Garcia Alonso, on a prominent site in the Avenida Constitución opposite the City Hall. This was also in an elaborate polychrome version of the Mudéjar style. Another interesting work by him was the interior of the Sala Llorens, one of the first cinemas in Seville. Like many early cinemas, it was decorated in a romantic version of an Andalusian royal palace but it is now unfortunately spoiled by later alterations.

Espiau's most celebrated building, the Alfonso XIII Hotel, is currently prospering after refurbishment as Seville's luxury five-star hotel. He won a competition in 1916 and collaborated with Francisco Urcola in the project. The judges' decision was not unanimous and there was some controversy about the design. The hotel has 149 rooms and is of imposing proportions, with four lofty storeys and a basement. The structure emerged from the ground in 1917, the money ran out twice and the building was finally completed in 1928, ready for the opening of the exhibition. The design is a mixture of restrained but pompous Classical with a measure of Mudéjar in the use of *azulejos* and horseshoe arches. Window openings include rectangles with Classical pediments as well as twin horseshoe arches with a central column. The style is a hybrid of the two architectural traditions of Seville, and the hotel occupies a key site between the park and the University (in the former cigarette factory of *Carmen* fame). It is built around a large patio, which is sometimes described as Moorish but the proportions and dimensions are large and Renaissance in scale rather than Moorish in character.

The contrast between the Renaissance ideal of vast imposing spaces and the more modest and human scale of the Iberian oriental tradition is illustrated by the different approaches made by the same architect, Anibal Gonzalez, to the design of the Plaza de España and the Mudéjar Pavilion in

The upper storeys of the Alfonso XIII Hotel at Seville which was designed by the same architect, José Espiau, as the Ciudad de Londres. It was finished in 1928 to coincide with the opening of the Iberian-American Exhibition. The Classical predominates but there is some use of arabesque and azulejo decoration both externally and internally.

The design of the Palacio Español at the Iberian-American Exhibition is in a pompous Classical style of huge proportions. There is an extensive use of azulejos with floral decorations and panels with realistic pictures of historic events. The benches in the foreground have miniature pavilions in an exotic Classical manner placed at the corners and assembled from multi-coloured azulejo elements.

the Plaza de America (now the Museo de Artes y Costumbres Populares). Both are decorated with a flamboyant mixture of *azulejos* in various historical styles; but the vast paved semicircular space of the Plaza de España – bounded by a canal and the neo-Renaissance Palacio Español, the sweeping arcades of which are decorated with the heads of famous Spaniards – has a magnificent fountain at the centre but no shade whatsoever. The Mudéjar Pavilion, on the other hand, was given a more sensitive treatment in the use of polychrome decoration in the Mudéjar manner. It has a lively symmetrical composition with two square flanking towers and a central entrance of three multi-lobed arches with elaborate fretted decoration. The Mudéjar detailing, which includes some incredibly intricate fretted and moulded *azulejos* framing the archways to the entrance doorways, was clearly modelled on the Alcázar of the same city.

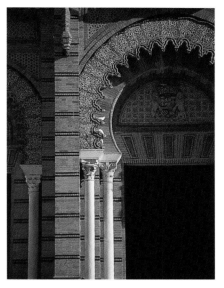

ABOVE
A close-up of the central multi-lobed horseshoe arch over the entrance to the Mudéjar Pavilion. The intricate moulded azulejo *voussoirs are exceptional examples of the potter's artistic skills.*

LEFT
By contrast, the Mudéjar Pavilion at the same exhibition and also by the designer of the Palacio Español, Annibal Gonzalez, uses the full repertoire of the Mudéjar style in a straightforward manner to a more modest scale.

BELOW
The main staircase of the Palace Hotel which was originally built as a royal palace and completed in 1907 at Buçaco in Portugal to the designs of Luigi Manini. Classical elements predominate in this part of the hotel. The blue and white azulejo *panel on the right illustrates a naval battle, one of many realistic historic scenes on the walls of the public areas.*

There is another large luxury hotel in the Peninsula that shows oriental influence. It is sited in the midst of woodland at Buçaco, north of Coimbra in Portugal, where the Duke of Wellington and the Portuguese achieved a military victory over the French in 1810. This victory is illustrated in a panel of *azulejos* inside the great hall of the hotel, which was originally built as a royal palace adjoining a Carmelite monastery, which had been there since 1630. After 1834, when the religious Orders were abolished in Portugal, the woodland was made a national park containing many exotic species of trees and shrubs as well as the entire range of native trees. Wellington had sheltered in the monastery and the cork-lined room where he stayed contains one of the original drawings of an elevation of the palace, which was designed in the neo-Manueline style by Luigi Manini, an Italian theatrical designer who was then working in Lisbon at the São Carlos opera house. The client was Prince Ferdinand of Saxe-Coburg-Gotha who had built the Castelo de Pena at Sintra when he was the Prince Consort of Queen

Maria II. Now he was a lonely and eccentric widower who wished to create another palace next to a poor monastery set in the midst of a wealth of natural beauty.

At first intended as a hunting lodge for royal use, under Prince Ferdinand, who was more interested in building rather than hunting, it became a palace on a huge scale with a tower overlooking the tree tops. Stylistically, it is more consistent in composition than the Castelo de Pena. In spite of the extensive space available, Manini demolished much of the monastery, leaving only the church, a small cloister and a few cells. Construction started in 1888 but it was not completed until 1907. The public rooms are on a large scale and the staircase is grand. It became a luxury hotel, a large part being reserved for the sole use of the royal family. The interior was decorated with a variety of pictures in blue *azulejos*

BELOW LEFT
The arcaded verandah at the Palace Hotel with columns decorated with intricate neo-Manueline motifs. The dados are faced with realistic scenes in blue and white azulejo panels.

BELOW RIGHT
The open loggia used for dining space has views of the luxuriant park surrounding the hotel. The vaulting and the cinquefoil arches and columns are of carved stone in exuberant neo-Manueline style.

The Fonte Mourisca (Moorish Fountain) was originally built for public use in the centre of Sintra in 1922. Azulejos in elaborate geometric patterns are used extensively on the wall surfaces for both decorative and practical reasons.

executed by Portuguese artists in the realistic style of the period. Several illustrate *Os Lusiados* (The Luciads), the national epic by the sixteenth-century poet Camoens. It soon became a fashionable hotel for the wealthy with a taste for the romantic. At the ground-floor level of two sides of the main building there is an arcaded gallery in an elaborate neo-Manueline style with a projecting open arcaded porch at one corner of the dining room. Since 1920 the management of the hotel, which is owned by the state, has been entrusted to a local company which has made a point of using the best local produce, including wines.

At Sintra, the attraction of the neo-Manueline style was still strong in 1922 when the Fonte Mourisca (Moorish Fountain) was built to the designs of José da Fonseca in the important street of the Volta do Duche. It is a striking composition of three multi-lobed horseshoe-arched openings contained within a large single slightly pointed multi-lobed arch springing from ground level. This arch is, in turn, surmounted by an *alfiz* of moulded tiles. All the wall surfaces are lined with *azulejos* in multi-coloured geometrical patterns. In 1960 the fountain was removed to allow for road widening but it was re-erected on another site in the same street in 1982 at the instigation of the Town Council.

The exotic charm of Seville overwhelmed a visitor from the USA, Jesse Clyde Nichols, a developer from Kansas City, Missouri, who was to promote the first out-of-town shopping centre in his home town specifically intended for motorists. After travelling to Spain on several occasions, he came to admire the urban texture of the traditional areas of the Andalusian cities and set about imitating the pattern of courtyards, fountains, ornate towers and balconies, decorative tiles and ornamental ironwork that he found there. He decided to name the shopping area of his new development the Country Club Plaza. The initial buildings were designed by an English architect, Edward Delk, who used a modified Mudéjar style.

The first tenants moved into the Plaza in 1923. The tallest and most striking element in the shopping complex is a copy of La Giralda of Seville. As the enterprise was solely intended to attract customers arriving by car, the parking areas were made as pleasing as possible with paving, landscaping and fountains. The level of the original parking areas was dropped and enclosed within a parapet wall and decorative iron gates so that the cars were hidden from the pedestrian ways and courtyards and the buildings became directly visible. This is an example of fine design that has, unfortunately, rarely been followed since. The Plaza Theatre was constructed in 1928 to the designs of Edward Tanner, Delk's successor. This also has a tower in Mudéjar style but lower than La Giralda. The interior is, in the words of the owners, 'a showplace of Spanish decor', including a carved timber door and iron grille which are said to be genuine seventeenth-century antiques from Seville. Although it was designed before the 'talkies', the first show was a sound film, and the auditorium acoustics proved to be excellent. One of the open pedestrian precincts is called Chandler Court, although it has buildings on only two sides. Here there is a fountain including a statue of Pan in the Italian style, but at first-floor level an *ajimez* with horseshoe arches is set above a single horseshoe-arched opening. *Azulejo* panels and decorative wrought-iron railings maintain a Spanish flavour to the environment, which was intended to create a blend of 'Old Spain, Mexico and Southern California'. Due to the expansion of Kansas City, the district around the Plaza now has many high-rise buildings and has ceased to have a suburban character. Most of the more recent buildings in the Plaza have few or no traces of Mudéjar detailing.

The cinema industry, expanding at a hectic pace in the 1920s and 1930s, was engaged in the manufacture of dreams, often in exotic settings and in some cases derived from the *Arabian Nights*. It became natural to consider the 'palace of dreams' as an anteroom that should create an exotic atmosphere in the same way as designers of theatres, music halls and opera houses had endeavoured to provide similar surroundings for their audiences. It is not surprising, therefore, to find the 'Alhambran' amongst the eclectic styles adopted by early cinema architects. John Eberson trained as an engineer at the University of Vienna and emigrated to the USA in 1901. Based in Chicago, he was responsible for the design of 500 cinemas on what he

The most prominent feature of the shopping centre known as the Country Club Plaza in Kansas City is a rather crude reproduction of the Giralda tower of Seville. It was built in the 1920s by a developer who had been fascinated by the urban landscape of southern Spain.

termed 'atmospheric' principles. He sought inspiration from Mediterranean countries to produce an 'aura of realistic enchantment'. An Italian garden and a Moorish town were his favourite settings. Artificial lighting was vital and skilfully used to create the illusion of being outside under a soft moonlit sky. The Pitkin Cinema in Brooklyn, New York, was decorated in a Spanish oriental style. The Tampa Cinema in Florida had an interior modelled on a Spanish courtyard. The boom in cinema building came slightly later to Britain, where the approach to design was usually more restrained, but there were some luxurious interiors. The Granada chain, as befits the name, built at least two of their cinemas in a style derived from the Alhambra, one at Dover, the other at Walthamstow. These were designed by a Russian theatrical producer, Theodore Komisorjevsky, who had trained as an architect.

There are few examples of buildings designed in the latter half of the

twentieth century in an obvious Iberian oriental style. The motives for such a choice are often to make references to tradition and regional loyalty. When the family firm (as it then was) of Pedro Domecq SA of Jerez in Andalusia, the famous producers of sherry and brandy, needed to extend the storage space for the maturation of brandy in rows of oak butts, a traditional method of the region, their designer, Javier Soto, chose a form of repetitive structure similar to that of the Great Mosque of Córdoba. A square grid of horseshoe arches and columns with a clear space above gives the impression of a lofty continuous space. An unimpeded lateral view was not required, only ready access to the aisles of butts stacked one above the other. The warehouse, or *bodega*, which covers nearly 3 hectares, is both functional and symbolic. It is known locally as 'La Mezquita' (The Mosque) and was finished in 1974, the centenary of the production of the first Spanish brandy.

The vast bodega of Pedro Domecq at Jerez de la Frontera is used for the ageing of brandy in wooden butts. The repetative horseshoe arcades, which give the effect of continuous space, are reminiscent of the interior of the Great Mosque at Córdoba. Consequently the local nickname of the warehouse is 'La Mezquita'.

The sun brings life to the intricate patterns of the stucco panels above the arches of the portico at the north end of the Patio del Cuarto Dorado at the royal palace of the Alhambra at Granada. Beyond the valley of the Rio Darro below and through the mirador of the Cuarto Dorado itself, the houses of Albaicin can be seen. (See also p. 133.)

EPILOGUE

After the First World War the oriental approach to the design of permanent buildings had become extremely rare. The designs of the pavilions of the Spanish-American Exhibition in Seville in 1929 and the Alfonso XIII Hotel also at Seville had been conceived and commissioned before the end of the war. The last major building that makes direct reference to this style is the Domecq *bodega* at Jerez (1974). There are occasional villas in the tourist areas of Andalusia that are designed with arcades, the details of which are copied from the Alhambra with the purpose of giving a 'Moorish' appearance. This is sometimes done to attract the attention of prospective owners from the prosperous countries in the Middle East who appreciate the allusion to oriental culture. Otherwise the Iberian oriental style in architecture has faded away except as a form of temporary theatre.

In Seville every spring the great festival of the Feria is held, an occasion for much rejoicing, colourful parades in traditional costumes and bullfights. It was initiated 150 years ago to promote the local livestock trade but it has since become an annual celebration for all the citizens of Seville and their visitors. Each year a wide ceremonial entrance gateway to the main space for the festival is erected. Although a temporary structure, in recent years of tubular steel, it is always elaborately decorated, gaily coloured and illuminated at night. Traditionally, the ceramicists of Triana, a district on the south bank of the river Guadalquivir renowned for the skill of its potters, have contributed to the decoration of the gateway. Because it is expected to express a local character, it is often designed in a neo-Mudéjar manner; in the 1990s three out of six have incorporated Mudéjar elements in their designs. The Iberian oriental tradition as expressed in three dimensions can therefore be seen to have been ephemeral.

In another mode of expression it remains very strong: in the decoration of interiors, particularly in hotels, restaurants and bars, the display of *azulejos* is widespread throughout the Peninsula, particularly in the southern regions. Not only are they attractive in appearance but they also have the practical advantage of being hard-wearing and easy to clean. Similarly the craft of joinery is practised at a high level of skill within the *artesonado* tradition. The use of geometrical patterning on timber ceilings and doors is often combined with dados of bright polychrome *azulejos* and floors of inlaid marbles of different colours to produce interior surface effects in the oriental tradition, which has been absorbed in local practice. The probable purpose is to give a sense of place which appeals to both visitors and residents. This awareness of the use of colour, pattern and modelling is more evident in the informal sector in the Peninsula than in the rest of Europe, particularly Northern Europe. The choice of the colour and pattern of glazed tiles in bathrooms in homes and hotels is more lively and confident. This is not only typical of interiors, but the use of polychrome patterned *azulejos* to face the external walls of private houses is also very common in some areas, particularly in the Algarve. The ceramics industry is active in maintaining a wide range of patterns, including all those of the Moorish tradition that employ, for example, *cuerda seca, cuenca* and lustre, as well as the later floral and representational designs of the Baroque. Across the Straits in Morocco the traditions of the Islamic approach to colour and pattern in stucco and glazed tiling are flourishing. Moroccan craftsmen and their material skills are in great demand for the restoration of historic monuments and in the construction of new religious buildings throughout the Muslim world.

In appealing to the senses, a perfect balance was often achieved by the designers and builders of such masterpieces of the Iberian oriental tradition as the Alhambra. Here, the splendour of pattern and colour on architectural surfaces is complemented by an awareness of similar effects in the arrangement of flowers, shrubs and trees in gardens and landscape. Beauty perceived through the eyes is then associated with the pleasures of perfume. Delight in sight and aroma is often combined with reassuring sounds. The murmuring of flowing water and fountains, accompanied by the song of birds attracted by the water and flowers, lends enchantment to the entire experience of moving through the architectural space and landscape. This overall sense of well-being depends also on the right temperature; usually taken for granted, only its absence intrudes upon our consciousness. The total pleasure of such achievements is a result of the skilful composition and combination of space, structure, openings, light, shade and planting. The experience of the enclosed and partly enclosed spaces is reassuring because they are always in harmony with the human dimension, in scale with the human frame and its social groupings.

It was these qualities that captured the imaginations of poets and musicians during the golden ages so marvellously demonstrated in the surviving buildings of Córdoba, Granada, Zaragoza, Sintra and elsewhere. The inspiration they created continued with the rediscovery of these wonders by visitors from Northern Europe and America, as well as many writers from the Peninsula. The Romantic poets like Gautier and writers such as Washington Irving and Mérimée were influenced by the literature of *costumbrismo*, which was similarly inspired by the charms of al-Andalus. Such composers as the Italians Boccherini and Scarlatti, who both lived for many years in Spain at the end of the eighteenth century, absorbed the special qualities of the Iberian musical tradition. In the nineteenth century and later, many composers from Northern Europe – Glinka and Rimsky-Korsakov from Russia and Bizet, Chabrier, Debussy and Ravel from France – created works in a conscious Iberian idiom. This choice of style could be seen as a form of musical eclecticism. The Spanish composers Albéniz, Granados, Turina and Falla composed in a deliberately colourful Andalusian style. Falla and the poet and dramatist Garcia Lorca were among the prime movers of a festival and competition dedicated to the study and performance of *El Cante Jondo* (The Deep Song) held at the Alhambra in 1922. This characteristic form of folk music is derived from the traditions of succeeding immigrations of Moor, Jew and Gypsy to Andalusia. Falla maintained that the adoption of the Byzantine liturgical chant by the

217

Church was also an important influence. Oriental cross-cultural effects on the music of the Peninsula gave it that sound and rhythm that distinguishes it from other Western music. This is parallel to the unique forms of Iberian oriental architecture, although the arrival of the Gypsies from India in the fifteenth century has never been said to have had any influence on the built environment. Apart from the fact that Falla and Garcia Lorca were born in Cádiz and Granada respectively, it is not surprising that the Alhambra was chosen as the appropriate backdrop for the performance of *El Cante Jondo* before a large audience. Falla's *Nights in the Gardens of Spain* for piano and orchestra had received its first performance six years earlier. The first movement is set in the Generalife and the last in the gardens of the Sierra de Córdoba. His music conveys the poetic magic of perfumed gardens like the Generalife in the serenity of Andalusian nights.

The design of the Gran Teatro at Cádiz by Morales de los Rios incorporates exotic Andalusian features both inside and outside. It was completed in 1910 after a lengthy construction period. Manuel de Falla, born in Cádiz in 1876, must have been familiar with this theatre in his younger days.

Although Manuel de Falla was a strict Roman Catholic, the oriental flavour of his music was not extended to the liturgy. This echoes the reluctance of the Church to adopt neo-Mudéjar motifs for buildings used for Christian worship, although the original style had been developed for that purpose. The revival of neo-Mudéjar had been confined to public buildings that required a sense of occasion or national or regional symbolism. It was therefore logical to decorate the interiors of theatres and cinemas in this way – at least until the taste for a more restrained and simple style coincided with the need for cost savings during the economic depression of the 1930s. The design of a bullring was an opportunity to express both national and regional symbolism, but the Iberian oriental style was a common but by no means universal choice. The ritual of bullfighting is confined to the Peninsula and thus the bullring as a building type could be regarded as a national symbol, while the choice of style was a regional decision. As the origin of the bullfight was assumed to be pre-Christian, an oriental style was acceptable and associated with the romantic and theatrical trappings of the ritual, even in Catalonia where there is little or no historical precedent.

In domestic architecture, the concentration on the use of oriental allusions in the decorative surfaces of walls, ceilings and floors meant that they normally appeared only in the homes of the wealthy, where an atmosphere of beauty and luxury, worthy of a palace, was demanded. Nostalgia for a past was often one motive, a past that was perceived as relaxed and colourful in contrast to the present and its associated social disturbance and the dreary environment of rapid industrialisation. Both economy and fashion were to influence the design of new houses between the two World Wars. The principles of the so-called Modern School based on the slogan 'Ornament and Crime' became powerful and have remained so. Adolf Loos, the Austrian architect who wrote an article with this title in 1908, nevertheless used a variety of rich marbles and exotic timbers in his interiors in a skilled and sensitive manner. This was a natural reaction to the overwhelming and indiscriminate use of bright colours and elaborate patterning that was the hallmark of some eclectic designers in the Iberian-oriental style. The neo-Arab hall of the Bolsa at Oporto is just such an example.

The introduction of new technology was combined with eclecticism in the design of new building types for the railways. There was not always a successful balance between the relatively simple and light structures needed to span the large space of the train shed and the sometimes elaborate expression of a past style. The composition was sometimes compartmentalised for the sake of impressive urban design in a city centre. Administrative offices and an impressive entrance were attached to a luxury hotel in a single block in front of the train shed, resulting in a dichotomy between the passenger's experience of the two. St Pancras station in London is typical of this approach. Separation of the hotel from the terminal building, as was done at King's Cross station nearby, made it easier to achieve integration of the entrance, train shed and auxiliary buildings in which the nature of the terminus was clearly expressed and a new building type was created. Similarly, the Córdoba station at Seville is an example where the composition is not only pleasing but the plan functioned well (it is no longer used as a station) and the neo-Mudéjar detailing was executed with verve and discipline in both traditional and modern materials like steel and glass. Its new role as an exhibition hall promises to be as successful as the converted Musée d'Orsay in Paris.

The reaction against eclecticism led to a desire for an expression in architecture that did not depend on the direct imitation of past styles. *Modernismo*, as exemplified by the work of Gaudí and others of his time, meant the recycling of traditional features and materials in a new expression that did not regard ornament as crime and did not imply the abandonment of well-established crafts. New techniques, however, were adopted when considered suitable. Increasing industrialisation enabled the economic mass production of some elements used in the building industry, and this led to the choice of plain, unadorned units or the use of machine-made patterning. The latter was often lifeless in effect and condemned by such influential critics as Ruskin and Morris, who had promoted design based on handicraft. The increasing use of machine tools and prefabrication coincided with the spread of the ideas of the so-called Modern Movement. These favoured concentration on a functionalism expressed as simply as possible in modern materials. This philosophy is still very powerful especially in the design of buildings the purpose of which is closely related to technology. Although shape and form have now developed beyond the simple rectangle and cube through the influence of Expressionism and Deconstructivism, the use of bright colour, texture and pattern in permanent finishes is still rare. Even in theatres, decoration is frequently regarded as additive and ephemeral, a matter of paint and hangings.

However, the need for colour and pattern in the physical environment is not dead. There is still wide appreciation of good quality and hard-wearing finishes, especially in public buildings. This is particularly so in the Iberian Peninsula, where many modern buildings show an increasing awareness of the desire for colour, pattern and texture, a desire that is currently demonstrated in the home and in places of social gathering. The Iberian-oriental tradition in architecture has met this need for over a millennium in an environment that has provided deep spiritual satisfaction. Some of this tradition has been absorbed into the Iberian psyche. 'The fires of excellence' are not extinguished, a glow of appreciation lives on, inspiring those who shape the contemporary scene.

RIGHT
*The Patio del
Cuarto Dorado,
royal palace of the
Alhambra, at dusk.*

GLOSSARY

Abbasids — Sunni dynasty which controlled much of the Islamic world from Baghdad. AD 749 to 1258.

Al-Andalus — Islamic Iberia, derived from Arabic.

Alcázar — Fortified house or palace, deriving from the Arabic, al-Qasr. Spanish.

ajimez — A pair of windows, usually with horseshoe arches and divided by a single column.

alfiz — A rectangular moulded frame, often above a horseshoe arch.

almena — A merlon. Spanish and Portuguese.

Almohads — This ascetic group succeeded the Almoravids in North Africa and the Iberian Peninsula. They dominated the area from AD 1130 to 1269.

Almoravids — An ascetic Berber dynasty who created an empire in North Africa and the Iberian Peninsula. AD 1056 to 1147.

arabesque — A stylised and intertwined plant motif developed from the spiralling vine, with leaves and tendrils.

artesonado — A style of Spanish joinery with Islamic precedent, usually applied to coffered ceilings.

azulejo — A glazed tile. Spanish and Portuguese.

Byzantine — Relating to Byzantium (Constantinople) or the Eastern or Greek Empire. AD 395 to 1453.

Caliph — Title of the supreme head of the Muslim community, as successor to Mohammed. From Arabic.

cantiga — Medieval narrative poem set to music. Spanish and Portuguese.

celosia — A perforated stone screen. Spanish.

convivencia — Co-existence of the people of the three religions in the Iberian Peninsula during the medieval period. Spanish and Portuguese.

costumbrismo — Style of literature giving special attention to local manners and customs of a particular region. Important in the literature of nineteenth-century Spain.

cuenca — Meaning hollow, the term applied to ceramic tiles with indented patterns. Spanish.

cuerda seca — A technique for decorating ceramic tiles in which a cord or mixture of manganese burned away during the firing separates the glazes and leaves a slight depression between the colours. Spanish.

dado — The lower part of the walls of a room, expressed horizontally.

Fatimids — A dynasty of the Shi'a sect which established itself in North Africa and expanded into Egypt and Syria. AD 909 to 1171.

Hadith — Tradition recording the words of Mohammed and his Companions. Second only to the Quran.

hammam — Bathhouse. Arabic.

harem — The private family quarters of a Muslim house.

hypocaust — Underfloor space used for the circulation of hot air in order to heat Roman villas and baths.

imam — The prayer leader in a mosque. Also applied to the leader of the entire Islamic community.

Judería — The Jewish quarter of a medieval Spanish town.

Kufic — Early Arabic script; thick, compressed and angular and often discontinuous. Named after Kufa in Mesapotamia.

Luso-Moorish — A style peculiar to Portugal that combines Moorish features with the Gothic style.

madrassa — A Muslim school, particularly a theological college. Arabic.

Maghreb — That part of northwest Africa stretching from Morocco to Libya. Arabic.

Manueline — The style of the reign of King Manuel I of Portugal (r. 1495–1521) characterised by features from marine life and the Moorish tradition.

Marinids — A dynasty that succeeded the Almohads and ruled Morocco from AD 1196 to 1549.

mashrabiyya — Latticework of turned or carved wood used for screens or enclosing balconies where privacy and ventilation are needed. Arabic.

masjid — Literally, a place of prostration. A mosque. Arabic.

merlon — A projection between the embrasures of the battlements of a parapet wall.

mihrab — A niche in the wall of a mosque which indicates the direction of Mecca.

mimbar — A pulpit and flight of steps set to the right of the *mihrab* for the reading of the Friday sermon in a mosque.

minaret — A tower, part of or closely adjoining a mosque, from which the muezzin makes his call to prayer.

Modernismo — A movement in the arts and literature of the Spanish-speaking world at the end of the nineteenth and beginning of the twentieth centuries. It promoted the search for an expression of the modern and encouraged experiment.

Moresque — A term used from the sixteenth to nineteenth centuries (including by Owen Jones) to mean Moorish, probably derived from the French 'Mauresque'.

Morisco	A Muslim converted to Christianity at the time of the Reconquest in Spain.
Mozarab	Relating to the Christians who lived in Islamic-occupied parts of the Iberian Peninsula.
Mudéjar	Relating to the Muslims who remained in Christian parts of the Iberian Peninsula and to the style of architecture that largely derived from their culture. Spanish and Portuguese, derived from Arabic.
muezzin	Mosque official who makes the public call to prayer.
muqarna	A niche unit forming part of a decorative honeycomb, often compared with stalactites and used for internal treatment of curved surfaces and especially in the transitional zones between domes and their supports. Arabic.
Nasrids	A dynasty centred on Granada which ruled Andalusia from AD 1231 to 1492.
Ottoman	Relating to the Turkish dynasty, founded by Othman in the thirteenth century, which conquered the Near East and invaded Europe in the sixteenth century. The Ottoman sultanate was finally abolished in 1922. Can also refer to a long low upholstered sofa.
patio	An open courtyard. Spanish.
qibla	The direction of Mecca which Muslims must face when praying.
Quran	The holy scripture of Islam, containing the revelation of the Prophet Mohammed. Arabic.
rejola	A standard brick, theoretically two hands by one hand in size, used by the Mudéjar builders of Aragón.
sahn	Central courtyard in front of a mosque. Arabic.
Shi'a	Relating to a sect of Islam which believes in a hereditary Caliphate descending from Ali, the son-in-law of Mohammed.
squinch	Section of a vault acting as an intermediary between a square or rectangular room and the circular dome above.
stucco	Gypsum plaster used for coating walls and making decorative casts. Italian.
Sufi	A Muslim mystic.
Sunni	Relating to the major sect of Islam, opposed to Shi'a, which rejects the theory of a hereditary Caliphate.
Sura	Chapter of the Quran. There are 114.

taifa	A petty dynasty. The Islamic section of the Peninsula was ruled by a number of these after the fall of the Umayyads. Arabic.
Talmud	The code of Jewish civil and canon law. Hebrew.
Torah	The book of the Mosaic Law, the first five books of the Old Testament. Hebrew.
Umayyads	A dynasty who ruled the Muslim world from Damascus from AD 661 to 750, when they were overthrown by the Abbasids. A branch of the Umayyads established itself in the Iberian Peninsula from AD 756 to 1031.
Visigoths	The Western Goths who emigrated to southern France and the Iberian Peninsula and established a Christian kingdom there prior to the Muslim invasion in the eighth century.
voussoir	A wedge-like stone that forms part of an arch.
zillij	Glazed ceramic tiles cut in geometric forms. Arabic.

CHRONOLOGY

IBERIAN PENINSULA	DATE	ELSEWHERE
Roman occupation	*362*	Roman Empire at maximum extent. Visigoths in Rumania
	406	Roman Empire divided into two
Suevi kingdom in northwest	*450*	
Visigothic kingdom in Peninsula and France	*476*	
	532	***Building of Haghia Sophia, Istanbul***
	562	Expansion of Eastern Roman Empire
Suevi defeated by Visigoths	*585*	
Visigoths Conversion to Catholicism	*587*	
	622	Hijra; foundation of Islam
	632	Death of Mohammed
	643	***Dome of the Rock, Jerusalem***
Quintinilla de las Viñas church	*650*	
	661	Beginning of Umayyad caliphate, Damascus
	705	Building of Great Mosque, Damascus begins
Invasion by Muslims of Iberian Peninsula	*711*	
	732	Defeat of Muslims at Poitiers
	750	Beginning of Abbasid caliphate
Abdel Rahman founded caliphate of Córdoba	*756*	
	767	Baghdad becomes Abbasid capital
Kingdom of Galicia founded	*770*	

IBERIAN PENINSULA	DATE	ELSEWHERE
	771	Charlemagne, king of the Franks
Building of Great Mosque, Córdoba begins	*786*	
	910	Cluny Abbey founded in Burgundy
Mozarabic church, Lourosa	*950*	
Final phase of Great Mosque at Córdoba	*990*	
Cluniac monks at San Juan de la Peña	*1025*	
Break-up of Umayyad caliphate	*1030*	
Building of Aljafería at Zaragoza	*1047–81*	
Romanesque style at Jaca Cathedral	*1063*	
Alfonso VI captures Toledo	*1085*	
Almoravids cross the Straits	*1086*	
Christians capture Badajoz	*1094*	
	1099	Crusaders take Jerusalem
Portuguese Independence	*1143*	
Portuguese capture Lisbon	*1147*	
Almohad capital at Seville	*1147*	
	1187	Saladin captures Jerusalem
Christian victory at Las Navas de Tolosa	*1212*	
Gothic style at Burgos	*1221*	
Christians capture Córdoba	*1236*	

IBERIAN PENINSULA	DATE	ELSEWHERE
Christians capture Seville	1248	
Portuguese capture Faro	1249	
Alfonso X of Castile	1252–84	
	1269	*Marinids established at Fez*
	1288	Ottoman Empire founded
Building of Alhambra, Granada	1309–91	
Mudéjar towers at Teruel	1315	
Extension of Alcázar at Seville by Pedro I	1364–66	
Tránsito Synagogue, Toledo	1366	
	1378	Great schism – 2 Popes
	1415	Portuguese capture Ceuta
	1419–44	Foundling Hospital, Florence Start of Renaissance
	1453	Ottoman capture of Istanbul
Spanish Inquisition	1483	
Manueline period in Portugal	1490–1520	
Capture of Granada and expulsion of Jews from Spain	1492	Columbus' voyage to the Indies
	1494	Treaty of Tordesillas between Spain and Portugal; division of New World
Plateresque style in Spain	1515–30	
Machuca's additions to the Alhambra for Charles V	1526–50	
	1609	Expulsion of Moors from Spain
Antiguedades Arabes de España published	1780	

226

IBERIAN PENINSULA	DATE	ELSEWHERE
	1789	French Revolution
	1800–30	Romantic Movement in literature
Murphy's visit to Granada and Córdoba	1802–9	
	1810	Mexico and Chile declare Independence
Castelo da Pena, Sintra	1840	
Toledo Pintoresco published	1845	Owen Jones's plans of the Alhambra published
	1851	Great Exhibition, London
	1866	Oranienburger-strasse Synagogue, Berlin
Ayuso's Bullring, Madrid	1874	
Casa Vicens, Barcelona	1888	
Córdoba Estación, Seville	1899	
Palace Hotel, Buçaco	1907	
Casa del Torico, Teruel	1912	
	1920–30	Cinemas in exotic styles
	1923	Country Club Plaza, Kansas City
Spanish-American Exhibition, Seville	1929	
'La Mezquita', Jerez	1974	

BIBLIOGRAPHY

ALI, ABDALLAH YUSUF (trans.), *The Koran*, Cairo, 1938, Dar Al Kitab al Masri.

ARTS COUNCIL OF GREAT BRITAIN, *Homage to Barcelona*, London, 1986, exhibition catalogue.

BARRUCAND, MARIANNE, *Moorish Architecture in Andalusia*, Cologne, 1992, Taschen.

BREFFNY, BRIAN de, *The Synagogue*, London, 1978, Weidenfeld & Nicolson.

BREND, BARBARA, *Islamic Art*, London, 1991, British Museum Press.

BROOKES, JOHN, *Gardens of Paradise*, London, 1987, Weidenfeld & Nicolson.

BURCKHARDT, TITUS, *Moorish Culture in Spain*, London, 1972, Allen & Unwin.

— , *Art of Islam*, London, 1976, World of Islam.

CALVERT, A. F., *Moorish Remains in Spain*, London, 1906, Lane.

CONDE, DOMINGO BUESA, *Teruel en la Edad Media*, Zaragoza, 1980, Guara.

— , *El Monasterio de San Juan de la Peña*, León, 1991, Editorial Everest.

CRESPI, GABRIELE, *Gli Arabi in Europa*, Milan, 1979, Jaca.

CRESTI, CARLO, *Civiltà delle Ville Toscane*, Udine, 1992, Magnus.

CRESWELL, K. A. C., *Early Muslim Architecture*, Harmondsworth, 1958, Penguin.

DANBY, MILES, *Moorish Style*, London, 1995, Phaidon.

DARBY, MICHAEL, *The Islamic Perspective*, London, 1983, World of Islam.

DUNN, R. E., *Adventures of Ibn Battuta*, London, 1986, Croom Helm.

EL-SAID, ISSAM, *Islamic Art and Architecture: The System of Geometric Design*, Reading, 1993, Garnet.

EL-SAID, ISSAM, & PARMAN, AYSE, *Geometric Concepts in Islamic Art*, London, 1976, World of Islam.

ETTINGHAUSEN, R., & GRABAR, O., *The Art & Architecture of Islam 650–1250*, Harmondsworth, 1987, Penguin, Pelican History of Art.

FLETCHER, Sir BANISTER, *A History of Architecture*, London, 1987, Butterworths.

FLETCHER, R., *Moorish Spain*, London, 1992, Weidenfeld & Nicolson.

GALERIA DE PINTURA DO REI D. LUIS, *O Neomanuelino*, Lisboa, 1994, exhibition catalogue.

GHULAM, YOUSIF MAHMOUD, *The Art of Arabic Calligraphy*, Riyadh, 1982, Department of Antiquities.

GIBB, H. A. R. (trans.), *Travels of Ibn Battuta*, Cambridge, 1958–62, Cambridge University Press.

GLASSTONE, VICTOR, *Victorian & Edwardian Theatres*, London, 1975, Thames & Hudson.

GOBIERNO DE ARAGON, *Signos-Arte y Cultura en el Alto Aragón*, Huesca, 1993, exhibition catalogue.

GOITIA, FERNANDO CHUECA, *Historia de la Arquitectura Española-Edad Antigua y Edad Media*, Madrid, 1965.

— , *The Mosque of Córdoba*, Granada, 1971, Albaicín.

GOITEIN, S. D., *A Mediterranean Society*, vol. 1, Economic Foundations, Berkeley, 1967, University of California Press.

GOMEZ, EMILIO GARCIA, & PAREJA, JESUS BERMUDEZ, *L'Alhambra: Le Palais Royal*, Granada, 1969, Albaicín.

GOODWIN, GODFREY, *Islamic Spain*, Harmondsworth, 1991, Penguin.

GRABAR, OLEG, *The Formation of Islamic Art*, New Haven, 1973, Yale University Press.

GUALIS, GONZALO M. BORRAS, GUATAS, MANUEL GARCIA, & LASAOSA, JOSE GARCIA, *Zaragoza a Pricipios del S. XX: El Modernismo*, Zaragoza, 1977, General.

GUALIS, GONZALO M. BORRAS, *Arte Mudéjar Aragonés*, Zaragoza, 1978, Guara.

— , *El Arte Mudéjar*, Teruel, 1990, Instituto de Estudios Turolenses.

GUTIERREZ, RAMON, *Arquitectura y Urbanismo en Iberoamerica*, Madrid, 1983, Ediciones Cátedra.

HARVEY, L. P., *Islamic Spain 1250 to 1500*, Chicago, 1992, Chicago University Press.

HEDGECOE, JOHN, & DAMLUJI, SALMA SAMAR, *Zillij: The Art of Moroccan Ceramics*, Reading, 1992, Garnet.

HERNANDO, JAVIER, *Arquitectura en España, 1770–1900*, Madrid, 1989, Ediciones Cátedra.

HILLENBRAND, ROBERT, *Islamic Architecture*, Edinburgh, 1994, Edinburgh University Press.

HOAG, JOHN D., *Islamic Architecture*, London, 1987, Faber & Faber.

IBN AL-KARDABUS, *Historia de Al Andalus*, Madrid, 1986, Akal.

IBN KHALDOUN, *The Muqaddimah*, New York, 1958, Pantheon.

JAYYUSI, SALMA KHADRA (ed.), *The Legacy of Muslim Spain*, Leiden, 1994, E. J. Brill.

JONES, OWEN, *On The True and The False in The Decorative Arts*, London, 1863.

— , *The Grammar of Ornament*, London, 1986, Studio Editions.

JONES, OWEN & GOURY, J., *Plans, Elevations, Sections & Details of the Alhambra*, 2 vols., London, 1845.

JULLIAN, PHILIPPE, *The Orientalists*, Oxford, 1977, Phaidon.

LAFORA, CARLOS R., *Andanzas En Torno Al Legado Mozarabe*, Madrid, 1991, Encuentro Ediciones.

LAFUENTE, J. L. C., & GONZALVO, F. J. P. (eds), *La Cultura Islámica en Aragón*, Zaragoza, 1986, Diputación Provincial.

LEES-MILNE, JAMES, *William Beckford*, Tisbury, 1976, Compton Russell.

LIVERMORE, HAROLD, *The Origins of Spain & Portugal*, London, 1971, Allen & Unwin.

MACKAY, ANGUS, *Spain in the Middle Ages*, London, 1977, Macmillan.

MARÇAIS, GEORGES, *L'Architecture Musulmane d'Occident*, Paris, 1955.

MARQUES, A. H. DE OLIVEIRA, *History of Portugal, Vol. 1, from Lusitania to Empire*, New York, 1972, Columbia University Press.

MCEVEDY, COLIN, *The Penguin Atlas of Medieval History*, Harmondsworth, 1984, Penguin.

MEEK, H. A., *The Synagogue*, London, 1995, Phaidon.

MONEO, RAFAEL, *The Life of Buildings: The Córdoba Mosque Extensions*, Lausanne, 1983, Ecole Polytechnique.

MOVELLAN, ALBERTO VILLAR, *Arquitecto Espiau (1879–1938)*, Sevilla, 1985, Excma. Diputación Provincial de Sevilla.

MURPHY, JAMES CAVANA, *The Arabian Antiquities of Spain*, Granada, 1987, Procyta.

ORDAX, S. A., & ALVAREZ, J. A., *La Ermita de Santa María, Quintinilla de las Viñas*, Burgos, 1982, C. D. Ahorros Municipal.

PALACIO EPISCOPAL, MALAGA, *El Mudéjar Iberoamericano*, Málaga, 1995, exhibition catalogue.

PALOL, PEDRO DE, *Arte Hispanica de la Epoca Visigoda*, Barcelona, 1968, Poligrafa.

PAUL, ANA ISABEL LAPEÑA, *San Juan de la Peña*, Zaragoza, 1994, Gobierno de Aragón.

PRANGEY, PHILIBERT JOSEPH GIRAULT DE, *Impressions of Granada and the Alhambra*, Reading, 1996, Garnet.

READ, J., *The Moors in Spain & Portugal*, London, 1974, Faber & Faber.

RECASENS, GONZALO DIAZ-Y, & CONSUEGRA, GUILLERMO VAZQUEZ, *Plaza de Toros*, 3rd edition, Sevilla, 1995, Consejería de Obras Públicas y Transportes.

ROGERS, MICHAEL, *The Spread of Islam*, Oxford, 1976, Phaidon.

SAID, EDWARD W., *Orientalism*, Harmondsworth, 1985, Penguin.

SCULLY, VINCENT, *Pueblo: Mountain Village Dance*, Chicago, 1989, University of Chicago Press.

— , *Pueblo Architecture of the South West: A Photographic Essay*, Texas, 1971, University of Texas Press.

SEBASTIAN, M. E., GRACIA, J. L. P., & SAURAS, M. J. S., *La Aljafería de Zaragoza*, Zaragoza, 1986, Cortes de Aragón.

STEVENS, MARY ANNE (ed.), *The Orientalists: Delacroix to Matisse*, London, 1984, Royal Academy, exhibition catalogue.

STEWART, DESMOND, *The Alhambra*, London, 1974, Reader's Digest.

SWEETMAN, JOHN, *The Oriental Obsession*, Cambridge, 1988, Cambridge University Press.

TALBOT RICE, DAVID, *Islamic Art*, London, 1965, Thames & Hudson.

TERRASSE, H., *L'Islam D'Espagne*, Paris, 1958.

TREVELYAN, RALEIGH, *Shades of the Alhambra*, London, 1985, Secker & Warburg.

VERON, JESUS MARTINEZ, *Arquitectura Aragonesa: 1885–1920*, Zaragoza, 1993, C.O. de Arquitectos de Aragón.

VIGUERA, MARIA JESUS, *Aragón Musulman*, Zaragoza, 1981, General.

VIVES, J. VICENS, *Atlas de Historia de España*, Barcelona, 1977, Editorial Teide.

ZAMORA, MARIA ISABEL ALVARO, *Ceramica Aragonesa*, Zaragoza, 1982, General.

ZERBST, RAINER, *Antonio Gaudí*, Cologne, 1988, Taschen.

ACKNOWLEDGEMENTS

I am particularly indebted to my editor Anna Watson who conceived the overall framework of this volume and continued to give enthusiastic support throughout the production process.

Matthew Weinreb the photographer has greatly increased the scope and value of the text through his imaginative and sensitive response to the visual heritage of Spain and Portugal.

Many people have assisted in the assembly of background material and amongst them I owe special thanks to Sundus Omer Ali, John and Vivien Boucher, Carlos Buil, Filipa Fernandes, Edwin Haramoto, Manuel Herz, José Granádos, Fernando Malo, Hernan Montecinos, Issam El Said and Fernando Varanda.

My grateful thanks are due to my wife Ilse for her constant help and companionship during research trips and the preparation of the text. I would also like to express my appreciation of the interest and encouragement of our daughters Josephine and Claudia.

This azulejo decoration over a doorhead in the Sala dos Cisnes has a rendering in perspective of an exotic three storey tower.

All the photographs in this book are by Matthew Weinreb except for the following photographs or illustrations.

PAGES 7, 108 maps drawn by GeoProjects (UK) Ltd., © 1996.
PAGE 22 © 1992 Saïd Nuseibeh Photography.
PAGE 24 courtesy of the Creswell Archive, Ashmolean Museum, Oxford, neg. C. 386.
PAGES 55 (top and bottom), 56, 67 (top), 70 (top), 82 (left), 98 (left), 200, 201 (top), 211 © Miles Danby.
PAGE 98 (right) © Salma Samar Damluji.
PAGES 104, 122, 131 (bottom), 147, 193 (top) courtesy of Badr El-Hage.
PAGES 114, 140 courtesy of Garnet Publishing, from *Impressions of Granada and the Alhambra* by Girault de Prangey, Reading, 1996.
PAGE 131 (top), courtesy of Phaidon Press Ltd, London, from *Moorish Style* by Miles Danby, London, 1995.

PAGE 145 courtesy of the Office National du Tourisme Tunisien.
PAGE 151 courtesy of Cortes de Aragon, Palacio de la Aljafería, Zaragoza, Spain.
PAGE 172 courtesy of Ediciones Cátedra S.A. from *Arquitectura y Urbanismo en Iberoamérica* by Ramón Gutiérrez, Madrid, 1992.
PAGE 180 courtesy of the Board of Trustees of the Victoria & Albert Museum.
PAGE 182 © R. Dennis.
PAGE 184 courtesy of Stiftung "Neue Synagoge Berlin – Centrum Judaicum", © Margit Billeb, 1995.
PAGE 189 courtesy of Magnus Edizioni S.p.A. from *Civiltà delle Ville Toscane* by Carlo Cresti, Fagagna, 1992.
PAGE 206 © Peter Aprahamian.
PAGE 212 courtesy of Pedro Domecq, S. A..

The Publishers would like to thank the many people whose assistance and co-operation made this book possible. In particular, Carmen Brieva from the Cultural Office of the Spanish Embassy who helped with our picture research well beyond the call of duty, and the cultural attachés of Spain and Portugal in London who also lent their support. In addition, we would like to thank all those who allowed us to photograph the architectural monuments of Spain and Portugal.

INDEX